Penguin Handbooks
The Rock Primer

The Rock Primer

edited by
John Collis

Penguin Books

Penguin Books Ltd, Harmondsworth,
Middlesex, England
Penguin Books, 625 Madison Avenue,
New York, New York 10022, U.S.A.
Penguin Books Australia Ltd,
Ringwood, Victoria, Australia
Penguin Books Canada Ltd, 2801 John Street,
Markham, Ontario, Canada L3R 1B4
Penguin Books (N.Z.) Ltd,
182–190 Wairau Road, Auckland 10, New Zealand

Published in Penguin Books 1980

Made and printed in Great Britain by
Hazell Watson & Viney Ltd,
Aylesbury, Bucks
Set in Monotype Times

Contents

Introduction		7
Rock & Roll	John Collis	9
Folk & Blues	Dave Laing	39
Rhythm & Blues	Ian Hoare and John Collis	63
Soul	Ian Hoare	93
Country	John Collis	121
British Beat	Mick Houghton	149
California Sun	Mick Houghton	179
Dylan and After	Dave Laing	209
Reggae	Nick Kimberley	235
Punk	Ian Birch	261
The Seventies	Steve Taylor	291
Index		325

Introduction

The Rock Primer offers a guide to the history of post-war pop music (and its roots in earlier folk and blues styles) as reflected on record. 220 albums are dealt with in detail, many more are referred to in the text, and ten of the sections also include an appendix of essential singles, usually by artists too important to be overlooked who nevertheless did not warrant an album selection, or by otherwise obscure performers who had one great moment of glory. Seven writers were involved, and there was no editorial attempt to force a 'common line' on the music (the editor, for example, would find it impossible to name three soul artists, let alone twenty, without including Percy Sledge, but in the Soul chapter Ian Hoare has relegated him to the appendix. Mick Houghton passed over the claims of *Sergeant Pepper* to be the quintessential Beatles album in favour of the transitional *Revolver*. And so on . . .). Thus the book attempts to preserve the idiosyncrasies of its contributors while still fulfilling the 'definitive' promise of its title. As an expert, you will have something to test your prejudices against; as a newcomer, you will find every important artist somewhere in these pages. The ideal of recommending only albums currently in catalogue is, of course, unattainable: record companies often shamefully neglect their illustrious past in favour of the latest sensation (at the time of writing, for example, you cannot go out and buy a Ray Charles album on Atlantic); furthermore, in the time lapse between the completion of the book and its publication, there will inevitably be both deletions and additions to the racks. However, deleted albums have been kept to a minimum, and it should be possible to unearth them at a shop specializing in the relevant genre. Similarly with American imports: a suitable British equivalent has been chosen wherever possible.

John Collis

JOHN COLLIS

Rock & Roll

There was no specific point in time, in the continuing history of popular music, when something characterized as 'rock & roll' suddenly appeared. Even more easily identifiable movements, such as psychedelia or the British punk rock of the mid seventies, will be seen to have antecedents, to have evolved into a recognizable form from what had gone before. The term 'rock & roll' was in common use in the rhythm & blues music of the forties as an obvious euphemism for the sex act, often cloaked as a reference to dancing. Just as female blues singers had long been looking for a 'chauffeur' to 'drive their car', so urban blues singers of the immediate post-war years were in the habit of suggesting that 'we rock & roll all night', without having only the dance-floor in mind. The credit for lifting this phrase from blues parlance, and applying it to the black music of the day, is usually given to Cleveland disc jockey Alan Freed. In 1951, noticing that white youngsters were demanding black records at the local record store, he inaugurated a radio programme which he called 'Moondog's Rock & Roll Party': he presumably felt that a new title was necessary since existing descriptions of the developing black music – from 'race records' to 'rhythm & blues' itself – had pejorative racial overtones, and would doubtless have been vetoed by his sponsors.

Freed was captivated by this music, working against the segregationalist mood of the time, and communicated his enthusiasm to his audience. It is of course inconceivable that the racial attitudes towards music categories would have persisted long if Freed hadn't existed, but it is fair to identify his pioneering radio programme as the early catalyst of change. Everything that has happened since is based, however tentatively, on the gradual emergence of black music from its ghetto, a fact which *should* make the concept of a white racist pop musician an untenable one. There was inevitable resistance; it was a slow process. Elvis *had* to be white, though it was the 'blackness' of his sound that made him a unique 'hillbilly' singer.

Within the scope of this book we could not devote a whole section to the blues (its roots are covered in 'Folk & Blues'), but it must be considered as the basis of rock & roll, and of rhythm & blues, as well as being a significant and identifiable strand in folk music. Over the years one form of the blues came to be the most usual – a twelve-bar structure in 4/4 time consisting of the tonic, sub-dominant and dominant chords. For example, it starts in E for four bars, goes to A for two and back to E for two; it then climbs to B for a bar, drops to A for a bar, drops right back to E for a bar, and then resolves itself in B for a further four beats. This, often with slight modifications (for example, with only the *two* final beats in the dominant chord, or with a 3/4 rhythm) became the commonest form of rhythm & blues, which can be crudely defined as the blues transposed to an urban setting and amplified electrically. Hence the twelve-bar blues passed into rock & roll.

Since hillbilly ('poor white' or 'white trash') musicians were often raised with their black equivalents, it is not surprising that early white country music also consists in part of the blues, translated into a different context and coloured by other influences. It is pointless to wish, therefore, that early post-war pop music would fall neatly into two categories, 'black' and 'white', which subsequently merge; sociological and cultural cross-currents often transcended the contemporary racial divisions. The impetus of rock & roll came from the red meat of black music, but the situation at the time required white musicians, and above all white entrepreneurs, to spread the word (and usually make the money).

Inevitably, then, part of rock & roll's story is that of black musicians being 'ripped off' by white businessmen – it wasn't until 1960 that the first major black-owned record company, Tamla Motown, was formed.

The urbanization of black music from its rural southern origins is dealt with elsewhere; suffice it to say that, in the early fifties, it was being gradually exposed to a wider audience than hitherto. Bill Haley, a disc jockey and leader of the Pennsylvania band the Four Aces of Western Swing, was one of the first to recognize this development (though Johnny Otis had been working *with* black musicians for some years), and from 1951 onwards Haley's records were based on, or more usually were cover versions of, black r&b tunes.

Together with the selling of black music in white versions came the gradual infiltration of black musicians into the national pop charts, breaking out of the 'race' category. But for a black singer to achieve this degree of commercial success in the early fifties, he had to be comparatively pallid: acceptable to white taste. From Sonny Til and the Orioles ('Crying In The Chapel', 1953), through the Crows ('Gee', 1954) to Johnny Ace ('Pledging My Love', recorded late in 1954) the sound was more and more 'black', but still comparatively safe. The real change came in 1955, with Fats Domino's 'Ain't That A Shame' and, in particular, Little Richard's 'Tutti Frutti'. There was no trace of Uncle Tom left in Richard's music, but it must be noted that at the time the bland white singer Pat Boone outsold both Domino and Richard with his cover versions, more precisely orchestrated and clearly enunciated. The process continued, black records finding it progressively easier to gain national exposure, until by the late fifties a record was allowed to be judged, by all but racists, on its merits alone. One should remember, though, that the men making the money were still usually white.

Since the black music of the time has a section of this book ('Rhythm & Blues') devoted to it, and has a further section for its development into soul, the emphasis of this chapter is on those *white* artists who overcame this accident of birth and produced music to stand beside that of the best of the black performers. Racism is a social, not a musical, problem, and for the commercial explosion of music in the fifties to take place, it had to involve whites.

Before the mid fifties, which brought with it the post-war technological developments that allowed for an expansion in the music industry, the 'teenager' hadn't been invented. These developments included cheaper record-playing equipment and the less fragile, more easily distributed 45 rpm record, which, very quickly, superseded the '78'; its advent coincided with the expansion of local radio, which made the music more accessible. The stars of the early fifties, even Johnny Ray, did not appeal specifically to adolescents. Rock & roll, from the simple espousing of black music by white youth to the dangerous sexuality of Elvis, marked the arrival of the 'generation gap', of adolescent rebellion, on a scale formerly inconceivable. It was fuelled by the increased spending power of the teenager as America, and more slowly Britain, recovered from the war; the music industry soon became geared to relieving young people of their pocket money.

When Elvis Presley was sold by his small label (Sun) to a major record company (RCA) with the capacity to peddle him world-wide rather than locally, the revolution arrived. In this brief essay, complex developments must be reduced to their key moments. The arrival of Bill Haley was one, of Little Richard another. Elvis's 'Heartbreak Hotel' was the biggest yet. Those early-fifties American teenagers who picked up on black music were an élite; to the rest of us, Elvis was a revelation.

The great white rockers who followed were galvanized by the success of Elvis: Carl Perkins (referring to Elvis on Sun) – 'I suddenly heard on the radio what I'd been doing all along'; Buddy Holly – 'Without Elvis, none of us would have made it.' Gene Vincent got his chance because the Capitol label was deliberately searching for their own Presley-styled artist to compete with RCA, who had bought out Elvis's contract from Sun, and had succeeded immediately with 'Heartbreak Hotel'. These were all *country* musicians who now knew that the injection of black influence into their music, together with 'teen-appeal', gave it the missing ingredient.

It is now possible to chant, with conviction, the slogan 'Rock & roll will never die'. Not so in the fifties, in spite of Danny and the Juniors' optimistic 1958 song title 'Rock & Roll Is Here To Stay'. It was seen by the older generation, because they wanted it to be so, as a temporary aberration. The businessmen were happy to milk it for a while, but in the end it was they who signed the death certificate (prematurely, as it turned out). Convinced it was a craze, they looked for anything – even calypso – to keep them in the style to which they'd become accustomed when the fad passed away. It seems strange now to consider that such a mistake could be made – a failure to recognize that rock & roll grew from strong 'folk music' roots embedded in American culture. The most noticeable change was the creation of the instant 'teen idol', who didn't have to qualify, as did the first generation of rockers, by a brief lifetime's devotion to music. Satirist Stan Freberg, whose hatred of rock & roll didn't prevent him parodying it to perfection, was hardly exaggerating in 'Old Payola Roll Blues', where a kid is pulled in off the street and turned into an instant star.

As the record producer grew in power, he brought in elements that were anathema to 'pure' rock & roll, above all the huge violin section sawing away at something intended to represent rock music. With the exception of the talented Rick Nelson, the late-fifties teen idols need not detain us. If you haven't heard Fabian, for example, you would get an inaccurate impression of his power from the titles of his hits – 'I'm A Man', 'Tiger', 'Hound Dog Man', and so on.

Though rock & roll could never return to the improvised and inspired simplicity of its heyday, there were as consolation a number of talented newcomers. Del Shannon had a rough, urgent voice and came up with some of the best pop of the early sixties – 'Runaway', 'Hats Off To Larry', 'Little Town Flirt'. Neil Sedaka, a production-line songwriter turned performer, had a remarkable talent for writing 'hooks' (the catchy elements of a pop song that glue it to the brain): 'Calendar Girl', 'Happy Birthday Sweet Sixteen', 'Breaking Up Is Hard To Do'. Dion, in the late fifties a white doo-wop singer with the Belmonts, survived into the sixties as a solo artist, and was clearly no cissy: 'Runaround Sue', 'The Wanderer', 'Ruby Baby'. Freddy Cannon displayed a vulgar, frantic energy on such hits as 'Tallahassee Lassie' and 'Way Down Yonder In New Orleans'. Bobby Darin soon discovered an ambition to be a jazz-tinged Buddy Greco-styled vocalist, but at least in 1958 he had left behind 'Splish Splash' and 'Queen of The Hop'. Even Bobby Vee, a mere Holly imitator, double-tracked his voice to great effect on such hits as 'Take Good Care Of My Baby' and 'Run To Him'. Above all, of course, the black rhythm & blues artists, particularly from New Orleans and Chicago, continued to come up with welcome hit records, and black girl groups such as the Angels and the Shirelles, around 1960, pointed the way towards the later Phil Spector masterpieces.

Rock & roll in the fifties retained its regional characteristics. So vast is America that, until the major record companies, in alliance with local radio, gradually increased their hold on the national market to the point where a hit record could be disseminated instantly throughout the continent, little pockets could develop independent of each other. New Orleans music managed to retain its characteristics from the Fats Domino records of the late forties, which were heard only locally, to the early sixties hits of singers such as Lee Dorsey and Ernie K. Doe, which spread even to Britain. Buddy Holly was distinctively a Texan, not just in accent but in the range of music he was exposed to, and so had a different sound to that of Carl Perkins in Tennessee. It is this parochial nature of rock & roll that gives it much of its charm, and it is noticeable that, in spite of the growth of the record business into multinational corporations, the best music still manages to retain the flavour of the area in which it was born.

Rock & roll forms the basis for all subsequent pop music, and such is the cyclical nature of pop that it keeps returning to the surface. The 'British invasion' of the 1960s that, for the first time, wrested musical domination from America, was based on all the American rock & roll records that arrived in the port of Liverpool. The psychedelic band Quicksilver Messenger Service recorded Bo Diddley's 'Who Do You Love', using it as the basis for a lengthy improvisation, though they can hardly have pleased rock & roll fans with their musical doodling. Creedence Clearwater Revival provided a welcome antidote to the pretentiousness of the late sixties, at the same time that Canned Heat were reminding young Americans of their rhythm & blues heritage. Chuck Berry re-emerged in the early seventies with his best album for years, and 'Rock & Roll Revival Shows' were big business. There are dozens of rockabilly bands currently playing in London and, most encouraging of all, when the American r&r legends visit Britain, a large proportion of their audience is under twenty.

Rock & Roll: Albums

Buddy Holly

Legend (MCA CORAL CDMSP 802)

It's So Easy/Tell Me How/Not Fade Away/I'm Looking For Someone To Love/That'll Be The Day/Think It Over/Maybe Baby/Oh Boy/Everyday/ Listen To Me/Well . . . All Right/I'm Gonna Love You Too/Early In The Morning/Words Of Love/Peggy Sue/Heartbeat/Rave On/Bo Diddley/ Midnight Shift/Brown Eyed Handsome Man/Rock Around With Ollie Vee/Love's Made A Fool Of You/Baby I Don't Care/Reminiscing/ Wishing/Moondreams/True Love Ways/Raining In My Heart/It Doesn't Matter Anymore/Peggy Sue Got Married/Learning The Game/Love Is Strange/What To Do

Holly heads the rock & roll list because, it could be argued, he 'invented' modern pop music more than any other individual. Presley had more impact, Berry wrote more classic songs, but Holly, dead in '59 at the age of twenty-two, not only performed everything from raunchy rockers to lush ballads, but was often involved at every stage (at a time when a singer usually just sang and did what he was told). He wrote in a variety of styles, played guitar (though he was not often the lead guitarist on record), helped establish the standard group line-up, experimented in production techniques (though at the time the concept of 'record producer' barely existed) and had one of the most versatile but distinctive voices in rock. Coming from Texas, and therefore being surrounded by all the 'folk' forms of music that were being commercially exploited in the fifties, he took the various strands and moved them a step further away from their ethnic roots, towards an international pop music.

Legend is a double album of his best-known titles, but his importance demands that you consider the complete boxed set of his work.

Elvis Presley

40 Greatest (RCA PL 42691)

My Baby Left Me/Heartbreak Hotel/Blue Suede Shoes/Hound Dog/Love Me Tender/Got A Lot Of Livin' To Do/Teddy Bear/Party/All Shook Up/Old Shep/Don't/Hard Headed Woman/King Creole/Jailhouse Rock/A Big Hunk O' Love/I Got Stung/One Night/A Fool Such As I/I Need Your Love Tonight/Stuck On You/Fever/It's Now Or Never/Are You Lonesome Tonight?/Wooden Heart/Surrender/His Latest Flame/Wild In The Country/There's Always Me/Rock-A-Hula Baby/Can't Help Falling In Love/Good Luck Charm/She's Not You/Return To Sender/You're The Devil In Disguise/Crying In The Chapel/Guitar Man/In The Ghetto/Suspicious Minds/There Goes My Everything/Don't Cry Daddy

Presley was a white hillbilly singer whose voice was nevertheless imbued with a unique feeling for the blues; when added to his good looks and 'moody' image the result was a performer that no mid-fifties entrepreneur could have dreamed up more perfectly. It may be a little hard today to imagine the impact that the uncanny voice and abandoned style had on the racially segregated, conservative America of the time. For his earliest, most revolutionary, recordings see *The Sun Collection* (RCA HY 1001); for an anthology of his early hits get *Golden Records*, Volume 1 (RCA SF 8129). Presley's manager, Colonel Tom Parker, clearly saw a limited life for the early 'antisocial' Presley image: army call-up provided the ideal chance for a character change. The sixties saw Presley making an endless series of pap movies; he returned to the stage via a TV special in 1968, and finished his life as the greatest, most charismatic of the Las Vegas entertainers. The recommended album recognizes his entire career, but for Presley the rocker stick to the early material. In the last stage of his life, for every brilliant 'Way Down' there was a handful of 'Don't Cry Daddy's: in the fifties he didn't make a bad record.

Chuck Berry

Motorvatin' (CHESS 9286 690)

Johnny B. Goode/Roll Over Beethoven/School Days/Maybellene/Rock & Roll Music/Oh Baby Doll/Too Much Monkey Business/Carol/Let It Rock/Sweet Little Rock & Roller/Bye Bye Johnny/Reelin' and Rockin'/ No Particular Place To Go/Thirty Days/Sweet Little Sixteen/Little Queenie/Memphis/You Never Can Tell/Brown Eyed Handsome Man/ Nadine/The Promised Land/Back In The USA

Berry has the most imitated of rock & roll guitar styles, and no one else wrote nearly as many songs that have subsequently become standards. Perhaps only Dylan, who clearly learnt a lot from Berry, has so expertly welded the rhythm and imagery of a lyric line to rock melody: Berry was the most consistently witty of rockers, and his music provided the soundtrack of an age. His greatest songs, like 'Johnny B. Goode', mark the end of a line which starts with his blues background, develops under the influence of the Chicago r&b of such mentors as Muddy Waters, and finishes as pure rock & roll. Many of his lyrics were much more than 'we're gonna rock tonite': they were narrative observations of America, condensed into r&r form. Lately Berry, particularly after his biggest hit with the uncharacteristic 'Ding-A-Ling', has tended to become a parody of himself. He seems too mean to employ and rehearse the best back-up musicians; his temperament makes him a promoters' headache; his gigs usually run the contracted time to the second, implying a calculated approach unresponsive to atmosphere. His last great 'new' album was *San Francisco Dues* (1972), and there is a series of three double albums called *Golden Decade*. The recommended record, however, contains twenty-two undiluted Berry classics.

Carl Perkins

The Original (CHARLY CR 30110)

Movie Magg/Turn Around/Let The Jukebox Keep On Playing/Gone Gone Gone/Blue Suede Shoes/Honey Don't/Boppin' The Blues/All Mama's Children/I'm Sorry I'm Not Sorry/Dixie Fried/Matchbox/Your True Love/Forever Yours/That's Right/Glad All Over/Lend Me Your Comb

Rockabilly, though it was not identified by this name at the time, was one of the chief strands of rock & roll: white hillbilly given a beat and updated by the influence of black r&b. Perkins wrote the classic rockabilly song, 'Blue Suede Shoes', recorded in late 1955; his experience when the song was released the following year is one of rock's biggest hard-luck stories. With the record beginning to 'take off', he was involved in a car crash while on a promotional trip. His brother was killed and Perkins put into hospital: when he came out, Presley had had a hit with the song and Perkins was forgotten. In the UK rockabilly is the most popular form of r&r among the fanatics, and Perkins is the king: a new album and tour in 1978 put his career in better shape than it had been for years, since for a decade he had been happy to play as back-up guitarist to his friend Johnny Cash, and before that had struggled with alcoholism. Being a collection of his earliest recordings, the recommended album shows his hillbilly background as well as his own handful of r&r classics, but there are many other records available for investigation.

Fats Domino

20 Greatest Hits (UNITED ARTISTS UAS 29967)

Blueberry Hill/Be My Guest/My Girl Josephine/I Hear You Knocking/The Fat Man/Blue Monday/Walking To New Orleans/Ain't It A Shame/My Blue Heaven/I Want To Walk You Home/Whole Lotta Loving/Country Boy/Let The Four Winds Blow/It Keeps Raining/Jambalaya/

I'm Ready/Going To The River/I'm Walkin'/Goin' Home/I'm Gonna Be A Wheel Someday

New Orleans has been central to the history of American music since the earliest days of jazz, and it maintained this position during the rock & roll era. Of the many artists who broke out of the city for at least a brief moment of national fame, Fats Domino is supreme: without any stylistic compromise beyond the occasional individual interpretation of pop standards, he became one of the biggest-selling artists in recording history. The irresistible rolling rhythm of his music, his rich creole accent and sly, relaxed delivery typify the city's contribution to rock & roll. He had his first hit in 1949, was one of the first black artists to make the national charts, and continued to sell millions of each title until the early sixties. Much of his success depended on Dave Bartholomew, his musical arranger from the earliest days to the present time, and on New Orleans' fertile pool of ace r&b musicians. In 1978 United Artists in the UK issued a definitive chronological six-volume set of Domino's work, *The Fats Domino Story*, from which the featured album selects twenty hits.

Jerry Lee Lewis

The Essential Jerry Lee Lewis (CHARLY CRM 2001)

Whole Lotta Shakin'/Don't Be Cruel/Down The Line/Let The Good Times Roll/Jambalaya/High School Confidential/Jailhouse Rock/Lewis Boogie/Hound Dog/What'd I Say/Lovin' Up A Storm/Wild One/Great Balls Of Fire/Singing The Blues/Little Queenie/Mean Woman Blues/Sixty Minute Man/Lovesick Blues/Breathless/It'll Be Me

The 'pumping piano' of Jerry Lee has played such a central and influential part in rock & roll, and he has recorded in such apparently effortless profusion, that it is sometimes easy to take his extraordinary rhythmic style for granted. It had its roots in the country boogie playing of such forerunners as Merrill Moore, but, when Lewis established himself as the house pianist at Sun Records in 1956, he was on the way to carving himself out a unique place in the history of rock & roll with such loose-limbed but relentless hits as 'Whole Lotta Shakin' Going On' and 'Great Balls of Fire'. Like Presley, Lewis was not a writer, but he makes even a Hank Williams song sound his own, characterized by his echo-laden tenor voice, by the distinctive Sun sound of such session-men as drummer James Van Eaton, and above all by that fluent, contemptuously easy piano style, with an insistent, metronomic left hand decorated by the wild flights of the right. Lewis is not, to say the least, a modest man, and this has led him to record endlessly, on the assumption that his name on the label is 'all you need to know'. Remarkably, his genius almost always shines through. After the rock & roll era, Lewis went back to his roots and became a leading country performer. Nowadays he mixes both roles, but the featured album highlights his career at Sun, 1956–61, and includes his most important r&r hits.

Little Richard

Good Golly Miss Molly and Eleven Other All-time Hits (SONET SNTF 5000)

Tutti Frutti/True Fine Mama/Can't Believe You Wanna Leave/Ready Teddy/Baby/Slippin' And Slidin'/Good Golly Miss Molly/Baby Face/Hey Hey Hey Hey/Ooh My Soul/The Girl Can't Help It/Lucille

Little Richard recorded blues for two labels (RCA, 1951–2, and Peacock, 1952–5) with little success or, indeed, indication of his unique talent, before moving to Specialty in 1955. The first session produced the hit that was to mark one of the important stages in rock: the frantic, anarchic and uncompromisingly black 'Tutti Frutti'. The hits that followed throughout the fifties, such as 'Long Tall Sally', 'The Girl Can't Help It', 'Lucille' and 'Good Golly Miss Molly', were in the same style; pounding twelve-bar rockers with a solid, persistent riff, wild piano decorations (usually by Huey Smith, not Richard himself) and Richard's arrogant, uninhibited vocals. In 1959 he left rock for religion, returning undimmed in 1964 with 'Bama Lama Bama Loo', and the rock revival shows of the late sixties gave him another lease of life. Lately, however, he has fallen more and more under the control of his vast ego, thinking that his mere presence on stage is enough. Instead of standing at the piano and knocking out the hits, he prefers to swan around throwing fragments of his gaudy costume to the audience.

Of the hits mentioned, 'Long Tall Sally' and 'Bama Lama' are on a companion record, *The Original Little Richard* (SONET SNTF 5011).

Eddie Cochran

Legendary Masters (UNITED ARTISTS UAD 60017/8)

Skinny Jim/Let's Get Together/Eddie's Blues/Little Lou/Pink Pegged Slacks/Jeanie Jeanie Jeanie/Something Else/Pretty Little Devil/Who Can I Count On/Thinkin' About You/Opportunity/Latch On/I'm Ready/ Three Stars/Cotton Picker/Summertime Blues/Cut Across Shorty/Milk Cow Blues/My Way/Blue Suede Shoes/Nervous Breakdown/C'Mon Everybody/Sittin' In The Balcony/Twenty Flight Rock/Teenage Cutie/ Hallelujah I Love Her So/Fourth Man Theme/Weekend/Bo Weevil/Long Tall Sally

Cochran inherited Presley's moody teenage appeal, and was the best chronicler of adolescent concerns in the late '50s. Like Holly he was a writer, guitarist (potentially one of the best) and producer, and was also a prolific session player. His best songs, usually co-written by himself – 'My Way', 'Nervous Breakdown', 'Weekend', 'C'Mon Everybody', 'Something Else', 'Twenty Flight Rock' and, above all, 'Summertime Blues' – are a coherent catalogue of teenage rebellion, frustration and excitement, but he performed everything from straight blues to big-band standards, and unfortunately the times demanded that his repertoire also included some rather wimpy ballads. By some oversight, the recommended album omits the hit at the time of his death in 1960, 'Three Steps To Heaven', but this is on the alternative sixteen-track *The Very Best Of* (UAG 29760). Cochran was more revered in the UK than in America, and fan-club pressure has ensured a stream of (largely re-permutated) releases: a couple of 'unofficial' records fill in the picture by including his hillbilly youth and session work. After that of Holly, Cochran's premature death was rock & roll's greatest loss.

Bo Diddley

Bo Diddley's Golden Decade (CHESS 6310 123)

Bo Diddley/Bring It To Jerome/Hey! Bo Diddley/Dearest Darling/I'm A Man/Diddley Daddy/Pretty Thing/She's Alright/You Can't Judge A Book By The Cover/Road Runner/Say Man/Bo Diddley's A Gunslinger/ I'm Looking For A Woman/Who Do You Love/Hush Your Mouth

Bo looks like a lawyer, and is unique among rock musicians in keeping his amplifier turned down too low, and yet in 1955 he appeared with the most 'African' sound in rock & roll; an insistent, repetitive and hypnotic rhythm which often forgets to progress to a second chord. In its most famous form, this rhythm is that which forms the basis of the eponymous hit 'Bo Diddley', a primitive beat sometimes described as 'shave-and-a-haircut, six bits'. In contrast to the earthy basis of his music, Bo predated Link Wray in exploring the possibilities of distorted electric sound: he built bizarre guitars to his own design (square, fur-covered, etc), and fuzzed and reverberated the sound to suit his requirements. Although his most successful numbers were rarely in the twelve-bar blues format, he is clearly only one step away from the blues, and indeed can play it straight as well as anyone; this link with his roots is most clearly seen in his impassioned, urgent vocal style and in the frequent use of call-and-response, either with back-up vocals or guitar echoing the vocal phrase. By the early sixties Bo had written his classics, but he remains a powerful, uncompromising and charismatic performer.

The Everly Brothers

Walk Right Back with the Everlys

(WARNER BROS. K 56168)

Walk Right Back/Crying In The Rain/Wake Up Little Susie/Love Hurts/ (Till) I Kissed You/ Love Is Strange/How Can I Meet Her?/Temptation/ Don't Blame Me/Cathy's Clown/All I Have To Do Is Dream/Lucille/

So Sad/Bird Dog/No One Can Make My Sunshine Smile/The Ferris Wheel/The Price Of Love/Muskrat/Ebony Eyes/Bye Bye Love

The greatest vocal harmony duo in rock, the Kentucky brothers Everly were born into a country-music family; their parents had a hillbilly radio show which Don and Phil joined while still very young. Unlike the other white c&w artists who were successful in the rock & roll era, the Everlys owed little to black music; their hillbilly sound was simply allied to a rock beat, the best Nashville musicians, and to a series of 'teen-appeal' songs usually provided by Tennessee songwriter Boudleaux Bryant, often writing in collaboration with his wife Felice. Their first run of hits was on the Cadence label, starting in 1957 with 'Bye Bye Love'; in 1960 they switched to Warner Brothers for the second stage, and immediately had international success with 'Cathy's Clown'. They continued to have sporadic hits until the later sixties, surviving the impact of British rock on America, but their personal relationship was breaking down, and they went their separate ways in 1973. The recommended album is from their Warners period, but includes five immaculate re-makes of earlier hits. To help complete the picture, you should also consider a collection of their Cadence hits, *Don and Phil's Fabulous Fifties Treasury* (JANUS 6310 300).

Bill Haley and His Comets

Golden Hits (MCA MCF 2555)

Rock Around The Clock/Burn That Candle/Forty Cups Of Coffee/Two Hound Dogs/Rudy's Rock/Shake Rattle And Roll/Rip It Up/Rock-A-Beatin' Boogie/Thirteen Women/Saints Rock And Roll/See You Later Alligator/Don't Knock The Rock/Mambo Rock/Corrine, Corrina/Calling All Comets/Skinny Minnie/Rockin' Thru The Rye/ABC Boogie/Razzle-Dazzle/R-O-C-K

No survey of rock & roll would be complete without Bill Haley, its first figurehead, even if he was soon to be superseded by other artists, in particular Elvis, who had more musical raunchiness and sex appeal. In the early fifties it was by no means an obvious move for a hillbilly bandleader to start fooling around with black r&b songs, and it is to

Haley's credit that he saw the change coming, and moved in the right direction. His first r&b cover version, 'Rocket 88', was recorded in 1951, and by 1953 he had renamed his band the Comets, and enjoyed his first national hit with his own song, 'Crazy Man Crazy', an obvious example of capitalizing on a current catch-phrase. In 1954 he recorded 'Rock Around The Clock', an international hit the following year when re-released to tie in with the classroom-rebellion movie 'The Blackboard Jungle', which featured the song. In Britain, every record from then until 1957 reached the Top Twenty, and 'Clock' has been a hit half-a-dozen times over the years. He still performs, locked in a time-warp maybe, but nevertheless a slick, professional and entertaining father-figure.

Gene Vincent

Greatest (CAPITOL CAPS 1001)

Be-Bop-A-Lula/Race With The Devil/Gonna Back Up Baby/Who Slapped John/Bluejean Bop/Bop Street/Jump Back Honey/B-I-Bickey-Bi-Bo-Bo-Boo/Lotta Lovin'/Dance To The Bop/Dance In The Street/Rocky Road Blues/Say Mama/Anna Annabelle/She-She Little Sheila/Wild Cat

It must be admitted that Vincent makes the rocker's top twenty more because of the fanatical devotion accorded to him in Britain than for the number of his classic singles. Nonetheless several of them, in particular his debut hit 'Be-Bop-A-Lula', are among the greatest of the r&r era. Invalided out of the navy with a permanent disability to his left leg, he began in the mid fifties as a country singer in Virginia (though Link Wray claims to have used him as a rhythm guitarist in the late forties). After Presley's success at RCA, other companies began looking for their own rocker, and Vincent was signed to Capitol. His band, the Blue Caps, included guitarist Cliff Gallup, as important to Vincent's sound as was Scotty Moore to Elvis's. His career faded in the late fifties, his wildness being out of keeping with the blander image of such forgettable stars as Bobby Rydell and the talent-free Fabian. Impresario Jack Good brought him to Britain, dressed him in black leather and capitalized on Vincent's disability (he recalls standing in the wings shouting, 'Limp, you bugger, limp'). Vincent was further injured in the crash which killed his close friend Eddie Cochran, enjoyed more reverence than commercial success in the sixties, and became more and more dependent on the alcohol that finally killed him in 1972. At his best Vincent was the most frantic of rockabilly singers, at his worst a portly drunk unable to survive the tragic pattern of his life.

The Coasters

20 Great Originals (ATLANTIC K 30057)

Riot In Cell Block Number 9/Smokey Joe's Café/Framed/Turtle Dovin'/Down In Mexico/Young Blood/Searchin'/Idol With The Golden Head/Yakety Yak/Zing Went The Strings Of My Heart/The Shadow Knows/Charlie Brown/Along Came Jones/Poison Ivy/What About Us/I'm A Hog For You Baby/Run Red Run/Shoppin' For Clothes/Little Egypt/Bad Blood

Black vocal groups proliferated in the fifties, and the 'doo-wop' style in which they usually sang (multi-part harmonizing behind the lead vocal) is one of the basic sounds of the era. The Coasters, however, were more concerned with comedy than with straight doo-wop; most groups in this field faded after one or two successes, but the Coasters had many fruitful years. The group grew out of the Robins, whose hits like 'Riot In Cell Block Number 9', 'Framed' and 'Smokey Joe's Café' are for the purposes of this album regarded as Coasters records. What brought the Coasters to the fore, apart from the succession of remarkable singers who passed through the ranks, was the song-writing talent of the white duo Leiber and Stoller. Each song was a comic cameo, perfectly served by the group's rich, sly sound, and the participation of such session players as saxophonist King Curtis and guitarist Mickey Baker. Often their finest moments were not without a degree of 'social comment', as in the mournful fade-out line to 'Shoppin' For Clothes', when the frustrated purchaser mumbles, 'I got a good job, sweeping up every day.' Most comedy in rock is limited to 'novelty' one-offs displaying a restricted feel for the music, but the funniest of them all, the Coasters, made great rock & roll as well.

Ricky Nelson

Legendary Masters (UNITED ARTISTS UAD 60019/20)

Be Bop Baby/If You Can't Rock Me/Stood Up/Tryin' To Get To You/My Babe/Milk Cow Blues/Poor Little Fool/Waitin' In School/Believe What You Say/Shirley Lee/Down The Line/I Can't Help It/I'm In Love Again/It's Late/Old Enough To Love/Restless Kid/Just A Little Too Much/A Long Vacation/Lonesome Town/Travellin' Man/Teenage Idol/Young Emotions/Never Be Anyone Else But You/My One Desire/Hello Mary Lou/That's All

All the reservations about Nelson have some validity, but if a sense of historical completeness requires one of the late-fifties, parentally acceptable, teenage idols to be included in this section, then it just has to be him. In one sense his voice is perfect: it has a pleasant, seductive timbre, and his diction is clear: but he never seemed to break into a sweat during a recording session, and rock & roll is all about sweat. And yet, just listen to 'Lonesome Town', and if you've any feeling for pop music, those reservations have to be suspended for a while. He was born into show business, groomed on his parents' TV show as the carefully rebellious youth singing clean rock & roll. Fate decreed that his record company should ally him with the very best musicians, notably the fluid guitarist James Burton, whose presence alone demands that Nelson's records be listened to. OK, Nelson was bland when put beside the meat of most black r&b, for instance, but if that leads you to overlook 'Stood Up', 'Poor Little Fool', 'Believe What You Say', 'It's Late', 'Just A Little Too Much', 'Hello Mary Lou' and 'Teenage Idol', then you're the loser. In his own commercially successful area of rock, he was the best.

Johnny Burnette

Johnny Burnette and the Rock & Roll Trio

(MCA CORAL CDLM 8054)

Honey Hush/Lonesome Train/Sweet Love On My Mind/Rock Billy Boogie/Lonesome Tears In My Eyes/All By Myself/The Train Kept A Rollin'/I Just Found Out/Your Baby Blue Eyes/Chains Of Love/I Love You So/Drinkin' Wine Spo-Dee-O-Dee, Drinkin' Wine

Burnette made no impact on the pop charts until 1960, four years before his accidental death, when he commenced a series of great pop hits including 'Dreamin'', 'Little Boy Sad' and 'You're Sixteen'; these are collected on *Tenth Anniversary Album* (SUNSET SLS 50413). The Rock & Roll Trio recorded in 1956 and 1957, and their crisp, frantic rockabilly style is chosen here as representative of the hundreds of white groups trying to emulate the success of Elvis, of which Gene Vincent and the Blue Caps were briefly the most successful. Burnette played with his brother Dorsey, who went on to success as a country singer/songwriter, and guitarist Paul Burlisson. The spluttering, urgent guitar style is central to the appeal of early Burnette, and lives on in the playing of the Pirates' Mick Green. However, it was Nashville session-man Grady Martin, rather than Burlisson, who was usually responsible for this unique sound. MCA recorded many rockabilly artists in an attempt to capitalize on the music; these are now collected on the series *Rare Rockabilly*. Of all the collections of rockabilly obscurities released in Britain in recent years, however, perhaps the finest is *Imperial Rockabillies* (UNITED ARTISTS UAS 30101).

Roy Orbison

The All-time Greatest Hits (MONUMENT MNT 67290)

Only The Lonely/In Dreams/Uptown/Candy Man/Working For The Man/Dream Baby/Crying/Mean Woman Blues/Running Scared/Love Hurts/

Shahadararoba/Blue Angel/Falling/Leah/I'm Hurtin'/It's Over/Blue Bayou/Pretty Paper/Oh Pretty Woman/The Crowd

Orbison is included here as a link between the r&r era and the early sixties, when he enjoyed phenomenal success with a series of melodramatic ballads. He had started as a Sun rocker, having a modest hit with 'Ooby Dooby' and writing 'Claudette' for the Everlys, for example. He never sounded comfortable on uptempo r&r, however, straining unsuccessfully to sound sufficiently raunchy. After a barren time at RCA he then moved to the new Monument label, and soon came up with a world-wide hit perfectly tailored to his strengths – his mournful sense of drama and his incredible vocal range. 'Only The Lonely' set a pattern for his greatest ballads, which always ended on a throat-stretching crescendo; among the finest are 'Running Scared' and 'It's Over'. Ironically, one of his biggest hits was with the faster 'Oh Pretty Woman', but it's the ballads that carved out Orbison's unique place in pop music. The recommended album contains the classics, unfortunately leavened with a sprinkling of second-division material (don't judge him on 'Pretty Paper'!).

Jack Scott

Jack Scott (PONIE 563NI)

Baby She's Gone/The Way I Walk/Geraldine/My True Love/Baby Baby/Midgie/You Can Bet Your Bottom Dollar/Leroy/Goodbye Baby/Apple Blossom Time/Bo's Goin' To Jail/What In The World's Come Over You/It Only Happened Yesterday/Burning Bridges/Cool Water/Save My Soul

Scott is a Canadian, who started recording for ABC while living in Detroit in 1957. It was on moving to the new Carlton label, however, that he had his greatest success. He had two styles, rockabilly and ballad: for both, the ingredients of the music were pared down to their essentials, allied to some of the crispest production of the period, and glossed with Scott's deep, sensual voice. The simplicity of his lyrics undoubtedly contained an element of humour (listen to the number of times the word 'Geraldine' is repeated in the song of that name, and it is clear that it wasn't done entirely straight-faced). The ballads are to me the most exciting in white rock, their tempo slowed down to the very edge of disintegration, the beat stressed melodramatically, the acoustic guitar recorded with rich, reverberating clarity. Listen to two of the biggest hits, 'My True Love' and 'What In The World's Come Over You'. The album unfortunately omits some classic Scott (watch out for 'With Your Love' or 'Found A Woman' in oldies shops), and it is to the specialist shops that you'll have to go for the album itself – the rights to the Scott catalogue seem in some disarray, and he has no representative outlet on a major label.

Creedence Clearwater Revival

Chronicle: The 20 Greatest Hits (FANTASY FT 528)

Susie Q/I Put A Spell On You/Proud Mary/Bad Moon Rising/Lodi/Green River/Commotion/Down On The Corner/Fortunate Son/Travelin' Band/Who'll Stop The Rain/Up Around The Bend/Run Through The Jungle/Lookin' Out My Back Door/Long As I Can See The Light/I Heard It Through The Grapevine/Have You Ever Seen The Rain?/Hey Tonight/Sweet Hitchhiker/Someday Never Comes

If rock & roll only existed in the fifties then Creedence has no place in this section, but they are included as an example of the artists who have subsequently kept the old spirit alive. For rockers, CCR were particularly welcome, since they flourished in the late sixties. At this time everyone else was indulging in endless psychedelic guitar solos, or sitting on cushions singing about pixies, pot and spaceships. A grim time. The mastermind behind CCR was John Fogerty, their writer, singer, guitarist, arranger and producer: it is difficult to avoid the assumption that the other three musicians were his puppets, particularly as, after the demise of CCR, Fogerty went on to make two superlative albums (*Blue Ridge Rangers* and *John Fogerty*) on which he did everything himself. The British equivalent of Fogerty is Dave Edmunds: see in particular his essential 1977 album *Get It* (SWAN SONG SSK 59404). Both lovingly re-create the whole range of music from hillbilly to r&b, and its projection into the sixties, in a way that is not the slightest bit anachronistic; the music emerges as solid, contemporary pop.

Various Artists

Rockabilly Rules OK? (CHARLY CR 30138)

Come On Little Mama (Ray Harris)/Put Your Cat Clothes On (Carl Perkins)/Vibrate (Mack Self)/Flying Saucers Rock & Roll (Billy Lee Riley)/Lovin' Up A Storm (Jerry Lee Lewis)/Ubangi Stomp (Warren Smith)/Teddy Jive (Crazy Cavan and the Rhythm Rockers)/Redheaded Woman (Sonny Burgess)/Caldonia (Carl Perkins)/Hillbilly Music (Jerry Lee Lewis)/Tongue-Tied Jill (Charlie Feathers)/Redhot (Billy Lee Riley)/Lonely Wolf (Ray Harris)/Jungle Rock (Hank Mizell)/Sadie's Back In Town (Sonny Burgess)/Saturday Nite (Crazy Cavan and the Rhythm Rockers)

This compilation is one of many put out by Charly to capitalize on the British interest in rockabilly: Charly's catalogue is based heavily on their rights to the Memphis label Sun, perhaps the most important of the fifties rock & roll companies. Among those who started their career there were Presley, Perkins, Cash, Orbison and Jerry Lee, a phenomenal roster for a label that started in the early fifties as a local blues imprint. The featured album includes a Carl Perkins classic, 'Put Your Cat Clothes On', which was mysteriously unreleased in the fifties, together with some of the best of rockabilly: Billy Lee Riley's 'Flying Saucers' and 'Red Hot', Charlie Feathers' 'Tongue-Tied Jill' (not from Sun), Warren Smith's 'Ubangi Stomp' and Jerry Lee's 'Lovin' Up A Storm'. It completes the picture by including two sample tracks by Crazy Cavan and the Rhythm Rockers, one of the many British bands who are keeping alive the spirit of rockabilly.

Various Artists

The Many Sides of Rock & Roll

(UNITED ARTISTS 60025/6)

Summertime Blues (Eddie Cochran)/Cincinnati Fireball (Johnny Burnette)/Great Balls Of Fire (Jerry Lee Lewis)/Blue Monday (Fats

Domino)/Over And Over (Thurston Harris)/Bonie Moronie (Larry Williams)/Chicken Shack Boogie (Amos Milburn)/Raunchy (Bill Justis)/Beatnik Fly (Johnny and the Hurricanes)/Let There Be Drums (Sandy Nelson)/Walk – Don't Run (The Ventures)/Bust Out (The Busters)/Wham! (Lonnie Mack)/Walkin' With Mr Lee (Lee Allen)/ Endless Sleep (Jody Reynolds)/Venus (Frankie Avalon)/Oh Julie (The Crescendos)/Mister Blue (The Fleetwoods)/I Love How You Love Me (The Paris Sisters)/Please Don't Ask About Barbara (Bobby Vee)/ Whenever A Teenager Cries (Reparata and the Delrons)/Papa-Oom-Mow-Mow (The Rivingtons)/Love Potion Number 9 (The Clovers)/ Tonight, Tonight (The Mello-Kings)/In The Still Of The Night (The Five Satins)/When You Dance (The Turbans)/Western Movies (The Olympics)/Stranded In The Jungle (The Cadets)

So far this category has covered the major artists, together with an example of the 'inheritors' of rock & roll and an album largely drawn from the major r&r label, Sun. The revival of interest in fifties music, as new generations of listeners grow up too young to remember where it all began, has seen a flood of compilation albums devoted to the archives. The recommended double is in four sections: Stars, Instrumentals (though it omits Duane Eddy, whose simplistic 'twangy guitar' was the most successful of non-vocal instruments), Teen Ballads and Groups. All the tracks are of interest, and the record was followed by Volumes 2 and 3. Other worth-while anthologies include *American Hot Wax* (A&M AMLM 66500), titled after an excellent, if fictionalized, 'bio-pic' of Alan Freed, which captures the youthful excitement of the era; *Rock & Roll Classics '56–'63* (ROULETTE 2940 201); *Alan Freed's Top 15* (PYE PKL 5573); *The London American Legend,* Volumes 1 and 2 (LONDON DREAM R 1/2 AND DREAM R 5/6); and *The Cameo-Parkway Story '57–'62* (LONDON DREAM U 3/4).

Rock & Roll: Singles

Roy Brown: *Good Rocking Tonight* (1948)

With many r&b hits, Brown was an influential forerunner of r&r with an impassioned up-tempo blues style: this song was revived by Presley.

The Platters: *Only You* (1955)

Their brand of sentimental melodramatic ballads, featuring Tony Williams, proved more commercial than the earthier offerings of other vocal groups; they were chart fixtures throughout the r&r era.

Screamin' Jay Hawkins: *I Put A Spell On You* (1956)

Rock & roll's greatest eccentric, Hawkins improvised wild, often hilarious lyrics over tight r&b backing. This manic waltz, not a huge hit though selling over the years, is a marvellous oddity.

Frankie Lymon and the Teenagers: *Why Do Fools Fall in Love* (1956)

Label owner George Goldner was responsible for recording some of the finest black vocal group pop of the fifties: Lymon's gimmick (his voice hadn't broken) made him the most successful.

Danny and the Juniors: *At The Hop* (1957)

By this time the frantic qualities of early r&r could sound formularized, removed from their roots, but this Philadelphia group produced the most engaging of synthetic rock.

The Diamonds: *Little Darlin'* (1957)

A white Canadian group who had a hit with this beautiful, humorous song by covering the Gladiolas' original. The Gladiolas hit back, renamed Maurice Williams and the Zodiacs, with the even-better 'Stay'.

Dale Hawkins: *Susie Q* (1957)

A white Louisiana rockabilly singer who produced this one classic, made unforgettable by the biting, hypnotic guitar riff. His guitarist James Burton, one of the greatest of the era, went on to join Ricky Nelson's band.

Buddy Knox: *Party Doll* (1957)

It was the success of this, and its original B-side (Jimmy Bowen's 'I'm Sticking With You') that attracted Buddy Holly to Norman Petty's studio. A good example of a regional (Texas) hit taken up nationally by a major label.

Larry Williams: *Bonie Moronie* (1957)

A label-mate of Little Richard's, and in the same frantic, heavy-riffing mould, Williams gave the world three classics: this one plus 'Short Fat Fanny' and 'Dizzy Miss Lizzie'.

Link Wray and His Wraymen: *Rumble* (1958)

Instrumental rock & roll, particularly by Duane Eddy and Johnny and the Hurricanes, persistently made the charts. 'Rumble' is the most curious example; a distorted, threatening noise of moronic but intriguing simplicity.

Ritchie Valens: *Donna* (1958)

Teen-ballads were also staple chart fodder in the r&r era: this West Coast example, together with his more typical 'C'Mon Let's Go' and 'La Bamba', suggest that Valens would have become a substantial talent had he not died with Holly and the Big Bopper.

Jody Reynolds: *Endless Sleep* (1958)

A third fruitful sub-category: the 'death disc'. They may often require tongue-in-cheek listening, particularly when they go as far over the top as the hilarious 'I Want My Baby Back' (Jimmy Cross), but the imagery of 'Sleep' is nonetheless effective.

Floyd Cramer: *Last Date* (1958)

Cramer established the 'crushed-note' style of country piano playing, and this haunting, moody instrumental came out of Nashville during its temporary recession, caused by the impact of rock & roll.

Jerry Byrne: *Lights Out* (1959)

A wild, staccato rocker from New Orleans, master-minded by Dr John; the exception that proves the rule that the best rock & roll was usually commercially successful.

Brenda Lee: *Sweet Nothin's* (1959)

Starting as a twelve-year-old country singer, Lee became a teenage rockabilly phenomenon, the most successful of the few female rockers.

Wanda Jackson: *Let's Have A Party* (1960)

Before turning to God and country music, Jackson had some rock & roll hits, notably 'Mean Mean Man' and 'Party', one of the most exciting records of the era and the best female r&r achievement.

Troy Shondell: *This Time* (1961)

Reviving a '58 B-side, Shondell had his moment of greatness with this perfectly ponderous ballad; the fact that the piano solo seems to be in a different key may add to its appeal, and certainly doesn't detract.

Bruce Channel: *Hey Baby* (1962)

This came from nowhere (in fact Texas, where 200 copies were originally pressed) with a unique sound that turned it into an international hit, a sound owing much to the eerie harmonica of the great white r&b musician Delbert McClinton; the Beatles stole the sound for 'Love Me Do'.

Ronnie Hawkins: *Who Do You Love* (1963)

A menacing blast of white r&r, long after the genre was meant to have died, by a larger-than-life Arkansaw rockabilly singer backed by the musicians who were later to be the Band; the song came from Bo Diddley.

Billy Swan: *I Can Help* (1974)

The 'spirit of rock & roll' may be indefinable, but this perfect pop record clearly had it; a breath of fresh air in an era when most hits came off a conveyor belt.

DAVE LAING

Folk & Blues

Before the 1950s, folk music in Britain was generally associated with a small band of people anxious to preserve what they saw as the remains of a dying tradition of rural music. Most agreed with the greatest of the early folk song collectors, Cecil Sharp, in wishing to see the music transplanted from the country pub to the school classroom. Sharp himself believed that exposure to folk songs would make a child a 'better citizen and a truer patriot'.

By the early 1960s, folk music had taken on quite a different meaning. There were now hundreds of folk clubs, held in pub rooms, where a bewildering variety of sounds could be heard. On any one evening there might be a group singing sea shanties with acoustic guitars, a jug band, a blues guitarist, a girl singing ballads after the style of Joan Baez and a nervous songwriter trying out his or her compositions in public.

Not much of this found favour with the modern counterparts of Cecil Sharp. To them songs had to be unquestionably 'traditional' and not composed by an urban teenager. What they had in common with the easy-going attitudes of the folk clubs was an antipathy to the pop music of the time and what it stood for. The difference between folk and pop, wrote one champion of folk music, was 'between something made for love, fun or pleasure and something made for money'.

The folk ideal was anti-commercial, and in the United States it took on political connotations as folk-singers identified themselves with first the union movement of the 1930s and then the civil rights agitation of the 1960s. The term 'folk', then, has come to mean both certain kinds of music that developed before or apart from the mainstream of popular music, and a medium for expressing radical views. These two meanings are combined in the work of many folk-singers, especially in America, where Woody Guthrie and Joan Baez are well-known examples. There is also a third aspect of 'folk', which came to light in the 1960s in particular, and which arose from the freedom to experiment that the folk scene allowed to musicians, a freedom not available in the competitive, commercial world of pop. This was probably the most important reason why figures as diverse as Bob Dylan and David Bowie started out in folk before taking their new ideas into rock music.

In the record list which follows, the main emphasis is on the musicians and kinds of music which have had some contact with, and influence on, rock music itself. By far the greatest influence has been that of the blues, both in its folk form, the country blues, and in the modern city rhythm & blues, which is covered in Chapter 3.

The country blues took shape among black people in the southern states of America in the years after the abolition of slavery. Although he wasn't much better off, the black field hand was now free to sit on his back porch and pick his guitar, composing songs about his life and hard times.

The classic form of the blues is the twelve-bar, divided into three-line verses, the first line of which is repeated while the third is different but rhyming. The blues guitarist will also fill in each line with a little phrase in response to the words. The twelve-bar system may seem restrictive and repetitive, but in the hands of a master musician it is simply a frame inside which any kind of picture can be painted.

Blues styles varied from state to state, but the one which attracted the most white and black guitarists of later generations was the urgent, compelling sound of the Mississippi Delta blues. The essence of blues guitar playing is to make the instrument sound like a second voice, and the voice of the Delta blues is one of extremes, mostly pain, sadness or loneliness, sometimes joy or pleasure. This effect was achieved mainly through the use of a bottleneck on the left hand, which gave a sharper, more piercing quality to the sound.

During the Second World War, when many blacks left the land for the cities, very little country blues was recorded. The revival of interest in the 1960s was due to white folk enthusiasts who sought out heroes they knew only from poorly recorded sides of the 1930s. In this way, men like Skip James and Fred McDowell were able to record again.

Although the blues is undoubtedly the most artistically distinguished of American folk musics, the folk revival in America concentrated more on its white heritage, which it found most of all in the songs of the Carter Family and Woody Guthrie. The blues – however much it had been developed by generations of black slaves in the southern states – had its roots in Africa, whereas the white tradition (which developed into modern 'country' music) was Celtic in origin.

The Carters came from the isolated Appalachian mountain region, where Cecil Sharp had found people singing the same songs their ancestors had brought with them from Britain two centuries earlier. Woody Guthrie was steeped in that tradition too, but his main contribution lay in his own compositions about contemporary events. Through these songs he put his stamp on the folk song revival of the 1960s, though he could not take an active part in it because of an incurable wasting disease, Huntington's Chorea, which condemned him to hospital for the last part of his life and from which he died in 1967. Bob Dylan, Tom Paxton, Phil Ochs and, in Britain, Donovan: a generation of songwriters began their careers in music by following his blueprint for simple, hard-hitting songs.

In England, there were no great figures like Woody or Leadbelly to embody the tradition of folk music. For a long time, the presentation of English folk songs was unnecessarily solemn, more suited to a museum than a club. But as soon as pioneers like Martin Carthy and Davey Graham began to put guitar accompaniments to the old songs, things began to change, especially when the influence of Pete Seeger and Joan Baez began to reach across the Atlantic.

The next stage was the growth of the experimental mood in the folk clubs, and the realization that, through the Beatles and the 'underground' bands, something worth-while was at last happening in rock music. The attraction of a more open-minded rock scene was that it provided a larger audience and therefore more money.

Two sorts of musicians made the move away from the folk clubs at this point: the more individual songwriters like the Incredible String Band and Roy Harper, and the 'electric folk' groups. The electric folk idea was based on the notion that while traditional songs themselves had a timeless quality about them, they could be served today through a presentation that made use of modern musical techniques, with amplified instruments.

The history of electric folk in England has been chaotic and controversial, with groups plagued either by lack of funds or by accusations of 'selling out'. But the idea has survived and along the way has given birth to some very fine records, by Hedgehog Pie, Jack the Lad and most recently the Albion Band, as well as the examples listed below.

The one area in which English folk musicians have undoubtedly excelled in the last fifteen years has been acoustic guitar playing. As well as the more specialized areas like ragtime and blues, two new styles have grown up in that period, associated most of all with Martin Carthy and Davey Graham. Carthy, from whom both Bob Dylan and Paul Simon learnt English tunes that they later used in their own work, developed an accompaniment whose 'English' tone fitted traditional words and melodies. Davey Graham was the great mixer of guitar music, creating the 'folk baroque' style as well as introducing all kinds of exotic sounds to younger players.

The heyday of the English and American folk revivals was in the 1960s. The 1970s have belonged to the Celts, and especially to the Irish. Traditional music never died out in Ireland, but for a long time it was polarized between the respectable 'part of the national heritage' notion, involving competitions and formal concerts, and the rather debased boisterous boozy image of groups like the Dubliners. But recently, a new generation has arrived with the intention of making traditional music which has the impact and excitement of the rock it heard on the radio as it grew up. The number and variety of the new bands shows that the new folk music of Ireland will have a lot more to offer in the 1980s. Apart from the immaculate Planxty, there are the rock-orientated Horslips, the instrumental verve of the Bothy Band and the softer Clannad. They are all proof of the fact that, despite the many gloomy predictions of the imminent death of folk music during this century, it is alive and well. As Bob

Dylan once said: 'There's nobody that's gonna kill traditional music. All those songs about roses growing out of people's brains and lovers who are really geese and swans that turn into angels – they're not going to die.'

Robert Johnson

King of the Delta Blues Singers (CBS 62456)

Crossroads Blues/Terraplane Blues/Come On In My Kitchen/Walking Blues/Last Fair Deal Gone Down/32–20 Blues/Kindhearted Woman Blues/If I Had Possession Over Judgement Day/Preaching Blues/When You Got A Good Friend/Rambling On My Mind/Stones In My Passway/Travelling Riverside Blues/Milkcow's Calf Blues/Me And The Devil Blues/Hellbound On My Trail

'Crossroads', 'Rambling On My Mind' and 'Walking Blues' were part of the standard repertoire of the white r&b groups of the 1960s. Their composer was Robert Johnson, the greatest of country blues artists in the Delta style. In his songs the themes and obsessions of the blues – desire, jealousy, guilt – were brought to a new level of intensity. He recorded only twice, in 1936 and 1937, and a year later he was dead, apparently poisoned by a jealous husband.

Johnson recorded only twenty-nine songs, of which sixteen are on this album, but he was probably the crucial formative influence on the city blues style of Muddy Waters and others that grew up in Chicago after the Second World War. His loud, stinging slide guitar playing is closer to electric than to the traditional acoustic style. The uncompromising sound of bottleneck guitar was matched by Johnson's voice, high pitched, taut and intense. The overall atmosphere of his recordings is ominous, with a feeling of claustrophobia in his relationships with women or of impending retribution from less tangible agents. One of the most enthralling moments in the whole of blues music is the opening of 'Hellhound On My Trail': 'Got to keep moving, blues falling down like hail/The day keeps on reminding me, hellhound on my trail.'

Skip James

Devil Got My Woman (VANGUARD VSD 79273)

Good Road Camp Blues/Little Cow, Little Calf Blues/Devil Got My Woman/Look At The People Standing At The Judgment/Worried Blues/ 22–30 Blues/Mistreating Child Blues/Sickbed Blues/Catfish Blues/ Lorenzo Blues/Careless Love/Illinois Blues

The music of Skip James has been described as having 'the looseness and the lonely introspection of a man singing softly to his mule, as he plodded behind it in the mud furrow of a spring field'. Slightly older than Robert Johnson, Skip James sings and plays with a similar intensity but less of the tension. His timing and his phrasing are squarely in the rural tradition of the cotton plantations of the Delta.

Unlike Johnson, James survived to be 'rediscovered' by young white blues enthusiasts who had heard his 1931 records like 'Hard Time Killing Floor Blues' and 'Devil Got My Woman'. In the intervening years, Skip had 'got religion' and, when he appeared at the Newport Folk Festival in 1964, he sang an unusual mixture of blues and gospel songs. This album was made a couple of years later and includes a joyous gospel piece, 'Look At The People Standing At The Judgment', among a selection of his classic blues. The original features of Skip James's music are the extensive use of falsetto vocal (which often has an eerie effect) and his complex guitar style, which combines a steady bass pattern with ornate finger-picking on the higher strings. He died in 1969, aged sixty-seven.

The Carter Family

Famous Country Music-makers (RCA DPM 2046)

River Of Jordan/I Have No One To Love Me/Lover's Farewell/When The Springtime Comes Again/I Have An Aged Mother/No More The Moon Shines On Lorena/On My Way To Canaan's Land/Where Shall I Be/My Old Cottage Home/Sunshine In The Shadows/Let The Church Roll On/Amber Tresses/Sun Of The Soul/If One Won't Another One Will/On The Sea Of Galilee/Poor Little Orphaned Boy/On A Hill Lone And Grey/Away Out On The Old Saint Sabbath/Darling Daisies/East Virginia Blues/Lover's Return/Hello Central, Give Me Heaven/I'm Working On A Building/There'll Be Joy, Joy, Joy/There's No Hiding Place Down Here/In The Valley Of The Shenendoah/Something Got Hold Of Me/Waves On The Sea/Rambling Boy

August 1927 was the most important date in the early history of white American rural music. It was then, in Bristol, Tennessee, that the first recordings of Jimmie Rodgers (see 'Country') and the Carter Family were made. The best in modern c&w music can trace its ancestry to Rodgers, while the enormous success of the Carter Family's discs was the main influence on the development of 'old-timey' and bluegrass music, as well as the white folk revival singing of people like Joan Baez and Carolyn Hester.

The group's repertoire, collected by A. P. Carter, was large and varied, including sacred songs, love ballads and the occasional topical piece. Many had been sung in the remote mountain areas for generations, but the Carters revolutionized the way they were sung and played. Against a steady guitar rhythm from A. P. and the autoharp of his wife Sara, Maybelle Carter played melody lines on her guitar. Above this group sound soared three-part harmonies. This double-album concentrates on the early and last parts of the Carter Family's career, since they recorded for other companies in the mid 1930s. They split up in 1943 but Maybelle, who died in 1978, later performed with Johnny Cash, to whom her daughter June is married.

Woody Guthrie

A Legendary Performer (RCA PL 12099)

The Great Dust Storm/Talking Dust Bowl Blues/Vigilante Man/Dust Can't Kill Me/Dust Pneumonia Blues/Pretty Boy Floyd/Blowin' Down The Road/Tom Joad – Parts I and II/Dust Bowl Refugee/Do Re Mi/Dust Bowl Blues/Dusty Old Dust (So Long It's Been Good To Know Yuh)

This album contains the famous 'Dust Bowl Ballads' which describe the forced migration of thousands of families from their parched and eroded land in Oklahoma to the low wages and poor housing of California. Woody Guthrie was one of those Okies himself and a folk poet whose words were set to music in the 'old-timey' style popularized by the Carter Family.

The ballads are stark and unadorned descriptions, sombre in tone, with the exception of 'Talking Dust Bowl Blues', which demonstrates Woody's mastery of this humorous form, with its freewheeling shape and space for throwaway comments in each verse. These ballads, apparently rough-hewn, also display the skill that went into Woody's writing in remarkable single lines like 'Some rob you with a sixgun and some with a fountain-pen.' (His special way with words is also what makes his book *Bound For Glory*, published by Picador, a great autobiography.)

The 'Dust Bowl Ballads' were recorded in 1940 and led to Woody's later fame as the best known member of the group of radical folk singers who aimed their work at the trade union and leftist political movements. His influence endures in the singing of Bob Dylan and that of his son Arlo.

Leadbelly

The Library of Congress Recordings

(ELEKTRA EKS 301/2)

Mr Tom Hughes' Town/De Kalb Blues/Take A Whiff On Me/Medicine Man/I'm Sorry Mama/Po' Howard/Gwine Dig A Hole/Tight Like That/ Green Corn/Becky Dean/Work Song/Midnight Special/Rock Island Line/ Governor Pat Neff/Goodnight Irene/Governor OK Allen/Git On Board/ Hallelujah/Backslider, Fare You Well/Amazing Grace/Down In The Valley To Pray/Let It Shine On Me/Run Sinners/Thirty Days In The Workhouse/'Fo Day Worry Blues/Match Box Blues/You Don't Know My Mind/Got A Gal In Town/Alberta/Take Me Back/Henry Ford Blues/ Ella Speed/Billy The Weaver/Frankie And Albert/If It Wasn't For Dicky/ Mama Did You Bring Me Any Silver?/Bourgeois Blues/Howard Hughes/ Scottsboro' Boys/Hindenburg Disaster/Turn Yo' Radio On/Roosevelt Song

If Woody Guthrie was a voice and an example to the young folk-singers of the revival, Leadbelly provided them with a vast reservoir of songs. 'House Of The Rising Sun', 'Goodnight Irene', 'Rock Island Line', 'Boll Weevil Song', 'Midnight Special' and 'Black Betty' (a Top Ten hit for Ram Jam as recently as 1977) are just a few that have become standards of folk, skiffle and rock.

Leadbelly didn't record until he was over forty, when folk song collectors Alan and John Lomax visited a southern penitentiary, where he was serving a sentence for murder. Before his imprisonment, Huddie Leadbetter had been a travelling musician, picking up songs of all kinds, from blues to cowboy ballads, wherever he went. He was also an exceptionally powerful performer. The hard-driving sound of his twelve-string guitar, with its distinctive walking bass line, has the energy of a small group. Born in Louisiana in 1885, his voice was fuller and deeper than those of the Mississippi bluesmen. Leadbelly's importance in the history of American music is considerable, and it is deplorable that his records are so difficult to find in Britain. This double album has now been deleted, but may be available through the specialist shops.

Pete Seeger

The Best of Pete Seeger (CBS 68201)

We Shall Overcome/Where Have All The Flowers Gone/Turn! Turn! Turn!/Little Boxes/Who Killed Davey Moore?/A Hard Rain's A-Gonna Fall/This Land Is Your Land/The Bells Of Rhymney/Masters Of War/If I Had A Hammer/Coal Creek March/Barbara Allen/Guantanamera/Both Sides Now/Last Train To Nuremberg/The Sinking Of The Reuben James/Last Night I Had The Strangest Dream/East Virginia/Hobo's Lullaby/My Rainbow Race.

Although he has written or co-written some well-known songs (among them, 'Where Have All The Flowers Gone', 'We Shall Overcome' and 'If I Had A Hammer'), Pete Seeger's main achievement has been as a popularizer of folk music, especially in the 1960s. A college drop-out in the 1930s, he was a friend and follower of Woody Guthrie and has managed to project the radical idealism of the folk revival over four decades without becoming archaic or narrow-minded. An expert banjo player, Seeger has done much to encourage the use of that instrument, while his singing voice is clear and unadorned, concerned mainly to get the words across.

This double album contains twenty tracks which in themselves are a document of an important era of artistic and political ferment in America. The beliefs of the civil rights and anti-nuclear movements are reflected in the simple, direct metaphors of 'Flowers' and Bob Dylan's 'A Hard Rain's A-Gonna Fall'. There are also Seeger's settings of non-musical texts, the biblical 'Turn! Turn! Turn!' and poems by a Cuban and a Welshman – Marti's 'Guantanamera' and Idris Davies's 'The Bells of Rhymney'.

Joan Baez

Joan Baez (VANGUARD VSD 2077)

Silver Dagger/East Virginia/Ten Thousand Miles/House Of The Rising Sun/All My Trials/Wildwood Flower/Donna Donna/John Riley/Rake And The Rambling Boy/Little Moses/Mary Hamilton/Henry Martin/El Preso Numero Nuevo

Released in 1960, this was the album which summed up the spirit of the new generation of folk enthusiasts, as Pete Seeger had done for the previous decade. Unlike the 'pop folk' of the Kingston Trio, Joan Baez personified the anti-show business attitude in her casual dress, her long hair and the simplicity of her playing and singing. Twenty years later, her voice is more mature and has more contrast of light and shade. But the enduring quality of this first record lies in the almost naïve purity and directness of the voice of a nineteen-year-old.

The choice of songs reflected the diverse sources upon which the new folk movement on campuses and in coffee-houses drew. The Carter Family's 'Wildwood Flower' is there, with Leadbelly's 'House Of The Rising Sun', the Negro spiritual 'All My Trials' and a Spanish song through which Joan Baez acknowledged her Mexican heritage. But the most riveting and remarkable performance remains her version of the Scottish ballad 'Mary Hamilton', which tells the story of a lady-in-waiting at court, hanged for the murder of her child: 'Last night there were four Marys, tonight there'll be just three/There's Mary Beaton and Mary Seaton and Mary Carmichael and me.'

Various Artists

The Iron Muse (TOPIC 12T86)

Miners' Dance Tunes (Celebrated Working Men's Band)/The Collier's Rant (Bob Davenport)/The Recruited Collier (Anne Briggs)/Pit Boots (A. L. Lloyd)/The Banks Of The Dee (Louis Killen)/The Donibristle Moss Moran Disaster (Matt McGinn)/The Durham Lockout

(Davenport)/The Blackleg Miners (Killen)/The Celebrated Working Man (Lloyd)/The Row Between The Cages (Davenport)/The Collier's Daughter/The Weavers' March (Celebrated Working Men's Band)/The Weaver And The Factory Maid (Lloyd)/The Spinner's Wedding (Ray Fisher)/The Poor Cotton Wayver (Lloyd)/The Doffing Mistress (Briggs)/The Swan Necked Valve (McGinn)/The Dundee Lassie (Fisher)/The Foreman O'Rourke (McGinn)/Farewell To The Monty (Killen)/Miners' Dance Tunes (Celebrated Working Mens' Band)

The folklorist A. L. Lloyd and the singers Ewan MacColl and Peggy Seeger presided over the traditional side of the folk revival in England. The dominance of the unaccompanied, nasal singing style (often with one hand over the ear) was due largely to their influence. But their most important achievement was to help to redress the balance of repertoire, which had formerly been heavily weighted in favour of the rural and archaic songs favoured by the Edwardian collectors. As committed socialists, they were keen to emphasize the songs of industrial workers.

The Iron Muse was a concept album of such material compiled by A. L. Lloyd. The songs and tunes are nearly all from the coal-mining and textile industries, apart from 'The Celebrated Working Man', Lloyd's own version of a humorous piece about a man who's prepared to work hard – so long as it's in the pub! Others featured on the record include Louis Killen, who was later to become a neighbour of Bob Dylan's in Woodstock. Here he sings the colliers' songs of his native Durham, while two fine women singers, Anne Briggs and Ray Fisher, present the songs of the mill girls of the cotton towns.

The Copper Family

A Song for Every Season (LEADER LED 2067)

Pleasant Month Of May/Sheap Shearing Song/When Adam Was First Created/Adieu Sweet Lovely Nancy/Wop She 'Ad It-io/The Wind Across The Moor/Claudy Banks/Shepherds Arise/You Gentlemen Of High Renown/My Love Has Gone/Come Write Me Down/Spencer The Rover/Thousands Or More

In 1922, 'Brasser' Copper, a farm-worker of Rottingdean in Sussex, wrote out all the songs he knew. Next to one of them he put, 'My grandfather used to sing this song.' This album is by Brasser's grandsons Bob and Ron and their children. The Coppers therefore are the outstanding English example of the folk process in action, singing songs that have been handed down over six generations.

Their work is also far less daunting to the general listener than the somewhat austere sound of many authentic traditional singers recorded over the last twenty years. Singing unaccompanied, the four Coppers make use of varied harmonies on a well-judged selection of English country songs. An outstanding track is the intriguing 'Spencer The Rover', which compares interestingly with John Martyn's electric version on his 'Saturday's Child' album. Despite the very different arrangements, the spirit of the song itself remains constant. Bob Copper has also written two books describing the way of life in his home village, out of which came this rich musical culture. The first of them, *A Song for Every Season*, is available in paperback from Paladin.

Various Artists

The Electric Muse (ISLAND FOLK 1001)

Introductory Medley (Steeleye Span, Ian Campbell Group, Fairport Convention)/The Gallows Pole (Leadbelly)/Pretty Boy Floyd (Jack Elliott)/She Moves Through The Fair (Margaret Barry)/Hard Case (Alan Lomax and the Ramblers)/The Banks Of Sweet Primroses (Copper Family)/The Twa Corbies (Ray and Archie Fisher)/The Shoals Of Herring (A. L. Lloyd)/Rocky Road To Dublin (Ian Campbell Group)/ Mason's Apron (The Dubliners)/Carolan's Concerto (The Chieftains)/ Kemp's Jig (Gryphon)/Medley (Fairport Convention)/Greensleeves (Morris On Band)/Drops Of Brandy (Hedgehog Pie)/Eibhli Gheal Chiun Ni Chearbhaill (John Martyn)/Angi/She Moves Through The Fair/Better Git It In Your Soul (Davey Graham)/Waltz (John Renbourn)/Veronica (Bert Jansch)/Willoughby's Farm (Ralph McTell)/ Dragonfly (Marc Brierley)/Blues Run The Game (Jackson C. Frank)/ Forever (Roy Harper)/Waltz (Pentangle)/Scarborough Fair (Martin Carthy)/Soho, Needless To Say (Al Stewart)/John The Baptist (John and Beverly Martyn)/Please Sing A Song For Us (Humblebums)/ Chelsea Morning (Fairport Convention)/Pretty Saro (Shirley Collins,

Davey Graham)/Blackwaterside (Bert Jansch)/Lyke-Wake Dirge (Young Tradition)/Bransle Gay (John Renbourn)/Our Captain Cried All Hands (Martin Carthy, Dave Swarbrick)/Let No Man Steal Your Thyme (Pentangle)/The Wedding Song (Shirley Collins)/Nottamun Town (Fairport Convention)/Tam Lin (Fairport Convention)/John Barleycorn (Traffic)/Lord Marlborough (Fairport Convention)/The Weaver And The Factory Maid (Steeleye Span)/Rise Up Jock (Bob and Carole Pegg)/The Gay Goshawk (Mr Fox)/Poor Will And The Jolly Hangman (Fairport Convention)/Turn A Deaf Ear (Lindisfarne)/The Third Millenium (Jack the Lad)/Nobody's Wedding (Richard Thompson)/Albion Sunrise (Albion Country Band)/Upton Stick Dance (Albion Morris)/Furs And Feathers (Fairport Convention)/Spirit Of Christmas (Steve Ashley)/The Magical Man (Mike and Lal Waterson)/Stranger To Himself (Fairport Convention)/The New St George (Albion Country Band)

This is a four-record set whose aim is to show the variety of styles and approaches to the music within the British (mainly English) folk scene of the 1960s, and its continuation in the 1970s through folk-rock and electric folk. One record looks at the new styles which grew under the folk umbrella, the delicate and electric guitar style pioneered by Davey Graham and the new breed of song-writers, accompanying themselves on acoustic guitars. Songs by Al Stewart, Roy Harper and Jackson C. Frank are included. The latter's 'Blues Run The Game' was a particular club favourite of the time.

Another record shows the variety of arrangements given to traditional songs, from the light, jazzy feel of Pentangle to Traffic's soft-rock version of 'John Barleycorn', one of the greatest of English songs. 'A New Tradition' is the title of a further section of the set. It deals with new songs written with a traditional flavour by Bob Pegg, Richard Thompson and members of Lindisfarne. It may be difficult to find *The Electric Muse* (and the Methuen book of the same name) in the shops now, but any reasonable record library should have one.

Shirley Collins

A Favourite Garland (DERAM SML-R 1117)

Prologue/A Beginning/Staines Morris/Lady Margaret And Sweet William/One Night As I Lay On My Bed/The Little Gypsy Girl/Plains Of Waterloo/Nottamun Town/God Dog/Just As The Tide Was A'Flowing/Tunes/Over The Hills And Far Away/Maria Marten/Higher Germanie

A compilation album spanning a decade of work (1964–74) by a singer who's been involved in many important innovations and experiments. From Hastings in Sussex, Shirley Collins sings in the soft, open-voiced style of the southern counties, sounding (in the words of one critic) 'vulnerable, like the maidens who often feature in the songs'. In 1964 she combined with guitarist Davey Graham to record *Folk Roots, New Routes*, an adventurous mingling of traditional songs with an original instrumental approach. Next, Shirley worked with her sister Dolly, who arranged medieval instruments in settings of folk songs like 'Plains Of Waterloo' as well as the highly praised suite, *Anthems in Eden*.

During the 1970s her recordings generally involved collaboration on projects initiated by Ashley Hutchings, bass player with the early electric folk groups and then leader of the Albion Band. Shirley's *No Roses*, made in 1971, is considered by many to be the best electric folk album of all. *A Favourite Garland* includes three of that record's best tracks, notably the dramatic 'Maria Marten'.

Davey Graham

The Complete Guitarist (SONET SNKF 138)

Lord Mayo, Lord Inchiquin/Lashtal's Room/Ein Feste Burg/The Road To Lisdoonvana/Renaissance Piece/Hardiman The Fiddler/Sarah/Frieze Britches/Blues For Gino/The Hunter's Purse/Prelude From The Suite In E Minor/Fairies' Hornpipe/Forty Ton Parachute/The Gold Ring/Down Ampney/Banish Misfortune

A 1978 album by the man who fifteen years earlier led a revolution in acoustic guitar playing in England. Before Davey arrived in the coffee bars of Soho and Fulham, the norm was strumming, skiffle style. But Davey Graham had listened to jazz and Indian music as well as to traditional English tunes, and saw no reason why he shouldn't play the lot. So into the melting-pot went all these styles, plus ragtime, blues and more.

The result was a sound that came to be known as 'folk baroque', where intricate patterns were interwoven with even the simplest chord sequences. His two early albums consolidated Davey Graham's influence and his two main 'disciples' – Bert Jansch and John Renbourn – went on to refine the style. Davey's public appearances became less frequent, but he continued to experiment and to refine his already masterly guitar technique. *The Complete Guitarist* lives up to its title, and adds to Davey Graham's repertoire of blues, folk, ragtime and Renaissance music a new emphasis on Irish jigs and reels.

Bert Jansch

Bert Jansch (TRANSATLANTIC TRA 125)

Strolling Down The Highway/Smokey River/Oh How Your Love Is Strong/I Have No Time/Finches/Veronica/Needle Of Death/Do You Hear Me Now?/Rambling's Gonna Be The Death Of Me/Alice's Wonderland/Running From Home/Courting Blues/Casbah/Dreams Of Love/Angie

'This is a story set in a strange young man's world, where musical truths weave a blue maze.' So began the sleeve note to Bert Jansch's debut album, made in 1965. Although his later work may be more technically proficient, this record more than any other captures the mood of the new folk scene of that time. The songs were well described by one reviewer as 'introspective and quietly melancholy', with the guitar accompaniment buzzing busily underneath. The best known of them is 'Needle Of Death', a low-key but very moving comment on drug addiction. Bert's singing is quiet, almost confidential, with more than a suggestion of his Scottish accent.

It was, however, as an instrumentalist that Bert Jansch was to go on to make an impact, and this first album contains his influential version of the Davey Graham tune 'Angie'. This percussive, jazz-tinged piece has over the years become something of a challenge for aspiring acoustic guitarists. After this album, Bert went on to make *Bert and John* with John Renbourn, an album regarded by many as the high point of the folk baroque style.

Incredible String Band

5000 Spirits or the Layers of the Onion

(ELEKTRA EKS 7257)

Chinese White/No Sleep Blues/Painting Box/The Mad Hatter's Song/ Little Cloud/The Eyes Of Fate/Blues For The Muse/The Hedgehog's Song/First Girl I Loved/You Know What You Could Be/My Name Is Death/Gently Tender/Way Back In The 1960s

The spirit of the folk clubs met the new ethos of the 'underground' in this 1967 album. The Incredible String Band were from Edinburgh and took their musical ideas from almost everywhere, although Davey Graham's introduction of the Indian raga into the British scene was probably particularly influential.

As well as guitars, Robin Williamson and Mike Heron played mandolin, tin whistle, fiddle, harpsichord and the African gimbri. The result was a rich and unusual mixture of sound, with other musicians adding sitar, tamboura and finger cymbals. The songs covered an equally wide range, from Robin's long, reflective 'First Girl I Loved' to lighter, almost fey pieces such as 'Painting Box'. The overall feeling of the record, though, was in keeping with the title: a kaleidoscopic reflection of the chaos of new sounds and thoughts to be found at the Middle Earth Club or in the pages of the *International Times*.

This album and its successor, *The Hangman's Beautiful Daughter*, were the band's best. Later records tended towards the merely eccentric.

Fairport Convention

Liege and Lief

(ISLAND ILPS 9115)

Come All Ye/Reynardine/Matty Groves/Farewell, Farewell/The Deserter/Medley (Lark In The Morning, Rakish Paddy, Foxhunter's Jig, Toss The Feathers)/Tam Lin/Crazy Man Michael

This was the first electric folk album and it remains one of the very best. Previously, Fairport Convention had been most influenced by American folk-rock and San Francisco music. Now, with two former folk-club stalwarts in the band, they decided to do a whole album of traditional songs with a rock band line-up.

The choice of material was faultless, focussing as it did on the grand classic ballads. 'Matty Groves', in particular, allowed full scope to Sandy Denny's voice and the dramatic accompaniment of Dave Swarbrick's fiddle-playing, which built the dramatic tension with phrases added to each verse and the long climactic solo. Equally important was the rhythm section, where Ashley Hutchings and drummer Dave Mattacks avoided the simple importation of rock rhythms, but built on the innate pulse of the old songs.

Released in the last months of the 1960s, *Liege and Lief* set a pattern and a standard for the development of electric folk music as a whole. In particular, it clinched the argument that amplification could release the emotional energies of the old songs, rather than smothering them.

Steeleye Span

Please to See The King

(MOONCREST CREST 8)

The Blacksmith/Cold, Haily, Windy Night/Jigs: Bryan O'Lynn, The Hag With The Money/Prince Charlie Stuart/Boys Of Bedlam/False Knight On The Road/The Lark In The Morning/Female Drummer/The King/Lovely On The Water

Steeleye were undoubtedly the most popular of electric folk groups, though not until after this 1971 album was made. The best-selling albums of the later Steeleye Span followed the established formula of adding a fairly orthodox rock rhythm section plus lead guitar to fiddle and voices. On this, their second album, there is no drummer and the electric guitar of Martin Carthy uses an imaginative 'drone' effect which is more in character with the traditional songs.

Carthy, who stayed with the group for only a year at this point, was the man most responsible for working out an acoustic guitar style to accompany traditional songs. Here he adopts a similar approach, notably on 'Prince Charlie Stuart', where the ability of the electric guitar to sustain a note allows him to set up a constant background of sound (as the pipes might have done) behind Maddy Prior's singing and Peter Knight's fiddle. In contrast is 'Lovely On The Water', with its echoing ripple of guitar behind Maddy's voice, which has a starker quality than the rounder timbre of Fairport's Sandy Denny.

John Martyn

Solid Air (ISLAND ILPS 9226)

Solid Air/Over The Hill/Don't Want To Know/I'd Rather Be The Devil/Go Down Easy/Dreams By The Sea/May You Never/The Man In The Station/Easy Blues

Among the great individualists of the British folk world, John Martyn has remained the most consistent and listenable. He had the distinction of becoming the first white musician on the Island label in 1968; until then it had been devoted entirely to Jamaican music. At that time, Martyn was one among many folk-club guitarist-singers. A spell in America produced two albums, of which *Stormbringer*, made with his wife Beverley and including the Band's Garth Hudson, was elusive and brooding.

Solid Air, made in 1973, was the record on which the special Martyn style began to take shape. It is based on his continuing fascination with technology and the capabilities of the amplified guitar, and with a variety of different musics, notably jazz and Eastern modes. These all come together in the cross-rhythms, the variety of percussive sounds and the mobile singing of Martyn's electronic version of the Skip

James blues 'I'd Rather Be The Devil'. The album also contains the original version of what has become his best-known song, 'May You Never'.

The Chieftains

The Chieftains 2 (CBS 82988)

Banish Misfortune; Gillian's Apples/Planxty George Brabazon/Bean An Fhir Rua/Pis Fhliuch/Jigs And Reels/The Foxhunt/An Mhaighdean Mhara; Tie The Bonnet; O'Rourke's/Callaghan's; Byrne's/Pigtown; Tie The Ribbons; Bag Of Potatoes/Humours Of Whiskey; Hardiman The Fiddler/Donall Og/Brian Boru's March/Sweeney's; Denis Murphy's; Scartaglen Polka

The Chieftains are the nearest thing in Britain to the national folk ensembles of eastern Europe, who perform their folk music in a manner combining formality with spontaneity. The Chieftains arrange Irish traditional material carefully, leaving space for individual solos. Ignoring guitars, drums and voices, they take the rhythm from the ancient Irish hand-drum, the *bodhran.*

But their formality does not dilute the power and excitement of the music. On slow tunes the high-pitched harmonies of flute, whistles and pipes swirl around the evocative melodies like 'Donall Og'. When jigs and reels are played, the instrumentalists, led by Paddy Moloney on *uillean* (elbow) pipes, urge each other on like the front line of a jazz group.

This album accompanied the Chieftains in their rise to international recognition in the mid 1970s. Since then they have recorded many more times and undergone various personnel changes, the most important being the addition of harpist Derek Bell.

Alan Stivell

E Langonned (FONTANA 9101 500)

E Parrez Langonned/Gavotten Pourled/Ne Bado Ket Atao/Bwythyn Fy Nain/Ffarwel I Aberystwyth/Briste Leathair Pheadair/Mairseal A'-Chearc/Dans Fisel/Gavotten Ar Menez/An Sagart Cheolnhar/Bal Fisel/ Deus Ganin Me D'Am Bro/Jenofeva/Sagart O Donaill/Diougan Gwenc'hlan/Ar Vorearion/Faili Faili Oro/Oye Vie

The revival in Celtic music in recent years has involved not only the British Isles, but also Brittany. Alan Stivell is the leading contemporary Breton musician and he has recorded tunes from every Celtic area, including Wales. Unlike Ireland, Brittany had only a small living musical tradition in the 1960s when the young Stivell decided to play his native music using modern instrumentation. With his guitarist Dan ar Bras, Stivell was almost solely responsible for the renewed interest in Breton music that now exists alongside the nationalist political movement in Brittany.

He plays the harp, bagpipes and flute on this 1975 album, as well as singing a variety of songs. In contrast to other records, like the *Live Album* (1974), this is an acoustic album. The band also includes Dan ar Bras's guitar, fiddle, and a rhythm section of Irish *bodhran* and Scottish drums. Stivell's harp-playing is well to the fore, complementing his light, tenor voice.

Planxty

The Planxty Collection (POLYDOR 2383 397)

The Jolly Beggar – Reel/Merrily Kissed The Quaker/The Lakes Of Pontchartrain/The Blacksmith/Hare In The Corn; The Frost Is All Over; Gander In The Pratie Hole/Cliffs Of Dooneen/Cunla/Pat Reilly/Bean Phaidin/Raggle Taggle Gypsy/Denis Murphy's Polka; The £42 Cheque; John Ryan's Polka/As I Roved Out

By common consent, the best all-round band of the new Irish folk scene was the original Planxty during its three-year life in the mid 1970s. The proof lies not only in the music but in the later exploits of Planxty members, both as members of the Bothy Band and as solo performers. According to one critic, the band's genius lay in creating 'a bridge between the informal gatherings common in Irish folk circles and the boozy mass-appeal chorus-style songs'. The singing was bright, and faithful to the traditional material without becoming earnest, but the greatest achievement was in the playing.

To the melodic interplay of *uillean* pipes, fiddle and tin whistle, Planxty added a rhythm section of acoustic guitar and bouzouki. This last was the inspiration of Andy Irvine, an enthusiast for Balkan music, which has many affinities with the Irish tradition. This album contains the highlights from the group's three releases; 'As I Roved Out', featuring Liam O'Flynn's pipes, sums up best what Planxty was all about.

IAN HOARE AND
JOHN COLLIS

Rhythm & Blues

The history of modern pop and rock music consists essentially of the eruption of black styles into the white-dominated entertainment industry. It is not a question of black forms 'influencing the mainstream', as some accounts would have it. In an aesthetic if not a commercial sense, the black popular tradition is itself better described as the mainstream.

Blacks in America have, of course, been heavily influenced by the majority musical culture for three centuries. But because they have generally had to absorb and re-create those influences in the context of exclusion from or repression by white society, mixing the 'European' elements with what had been retained from Africa, their music developed a separate identity; and as particular styles were adopted by – and adapted for – the mass entertainment market, the black audience continued to demand that its own distinctive tastes were satisfied.

This was clearly the case in the 1950s. Records from the 'rhythm & blues' field were promoted to a young white audience as 'rock & roll'; and white *performers* began to make use of the black styles. For a short time, an interaction took place which led to the r&b charts becoming unprecedentedly similar to the national pop charts. But as older show-business values reasserted themselves, rock & roll lost much of its appeal for blacks, and the r&b category had regained its importance by the end of the decade.

The concern of this section of the book is to look briefly at the main kinds of black music which gave birth to the rock & roll phenomenon, at music which survived with black audiences during the rock & roll era but made little impression on the pop market at the time, and at the new kinds of r&b which came to prominence after rock & roll had lost its momentum, and which paved the way for the rise of soul music.

Between the two world wars, black music had at first tended to develop according to the distinction, which evolved around New Orleans, between self-accompanying singers and dance or march bands. To put it crudely – on the one hand there was the multitude of styles known as the blues, and on the other hand there was jazz. But there were also band blues of various kinds, which gradually drifted further from jazz as amplification arrived, taking over its dance function. Furthermore, solo country blues performers who moved to the bigger towns and the cities were often forming their own instrumental groups.

The development of this heritage in the rhythm & blues era was profoundly affected by new social and economic conditions. The migration to the cities accelerated rapidly during the forties: as many blacks left the South then as in the previous thirty years. This shift was accompanied by the establishment of dozens of small, independent record labels specializing in music for the Negro community, and a similar mushrooming of black radio stations. National – as against regional – distribution of black records began to get under way in 1945, and the following year the trade magazine *Billboard* introduced its 'race music' chart, changing the title to 'rhythm & blues' three years later. By 1950 the latest black music was available to an extent not imagined previously – and its commercial exploitation was primarily in the hands of people outside the major record companies.

The music itself was in ferment, although a number of basic styles and regional characteristics can be distinguished. Performers moving up from the Mississippi Delta via Memphis to Chicago – such as Muddy Waters, Howlin' Wolf and Elmore James – played what became known as 'bar blues', using amplification to transform the patterns of soloists like Robert Johnson and Son House into a raucous, aggressive combo sound. In sharp contrast was the predominantly restrained, melancholy approach of the club bluesmen and balladeers – including Percy Mayfield, Cecil Gant, Charles Brown, Ivory Joe Hunter and the early Ray Charles – who were particularly prominent on the West Coast.

Other blues performers played in the country's dance-halls in a wide variety of overlapping styles. In the immediate post-war years, several big blues-based touring bands, such as Buddy Johnson's, were popular, one of the last to emerge being the Johnny Otis Show. Most of these bands died out in the early fifties, although their singers and saxophonists frequently carried on as attractions with smaller groups. It was against this background that many of the city blues 'criers' and 'shouters' came to the fore – Joe Turner, Ruth Brown, Faye Adams, Roy Brown, B. B. King, Bobby Bland, Junior Parker and others, few of whom achieved commercial success among whites.

The handful of established r&b artists who did cross over into rock & roll were mainly from the so-called jump combos. These groups took their cue chiefly from Louis Jordan, whose novelty and boogie material secured him considerable success in the forties. Elsewhere, Ike Turner, Jimmy McCracklin, Jimmy Reed, Wilbert Harrison and Chuck Willis all made their contributions. But the most important source of inspiration, innovation and popular success in this field was the dance blues of New Orleans. Bandleader Dave Bartholomew was the key figure here. The musicians who gathered round him – men like drummer Earl Palmer and tenor saxist Lee Allen – laid the foundations for the careers of Fats Domino, Little Richard, Larry Williams, Lloyd Price and Shirley and Lee, among others. New Orleans r&b continued to develop on its own terms after rock & roll hysteria had subsided, notably from 1960 under the influence of composer-arranger Allen Toussaint on the Minit label.

The term 'rhythm & blues' was not inappropriate for most of these styles, but it was a rather misleading label for two other vital strands in the popular black music of the time – the vocal groups and gospel.

A large number of black vocal harmony groups were successful in the r&b market in the late forties and the fifties. Usually taking the Inkspots as their basic model, their trend was towards sweet ballads of innocence and vulnerability, sung with delicacy. It was hardly the 'jungle music' which the white music establishment saw to its horror in rock & roll; yet the groups appealed almost exclusively to blacks until the Orioles broke into the pop charts in 1953 with the country song 'Crying In The Chapel'. The Orioles never repeated that success, but other black group records – The Chords' 'Sh-Boom', for example – were hits soon afterwards, though the performances remained relatively unobtrusive. The group sound went on to become a vital current in rock & roll in its own right, but its initial significance lay in preparing the mass audience for the more decidedly alien music that was to come.

It was primarily through vocal groups that church singing became an important source of popular styles. Although there were traces of gospel in the work of several city blues performers, particularly Roy Brown, it seems that the first conscious attempt to make hits with a religious feel came from Billy Ward's Dominoes, formed in 1950. Their lead singer, Clyde McPhatter, went on to get together his own group, the Drifters, in 1953, and recorded a series of brilliant r&b hits for Atlantic which straddled the gap between sacred and secular.

The demand among blacks for the powerful emotional expressiveness of the gospel-tinged performers grew steadily during the second half of the fifties. But it wasn't until 1959 that the record companies began to market the church-based styles to whites with any notable conviction or success. This was done through the development of 'uptown rhythm & blues', in which the new r&b vocal sounds were packaged in a manner apparently intended to be acceptable to both black and white radio stations. Producers – Leiber and Stoller, Phil Spector, Bert Berns – took control, sometimes working with the new 'factory' song-writers, such as Goffin and King, Burt Bacharach or Mann and Weil. And Bob Crewe demonstrated that the desired effect could even be achieved using a white act, the Four Seasons. The genre was dominated by groups, but the same period saw gospel-based solo singers – including Ray Charles, Sam Cooke and Jackie Wilson – presented in a variety of orchestral settings, usually to their detriment. The writing was on the wall, however. The early-sixties r&b hits of James Brown and Motown pointed to a far more integrated approach to accompaniment and production. Soul was in the making.

The spirit of fifties rhythm & blues has survived, nevertheless. The funk-jazz of the seventies arguably has more in common with the black dance combos of that time than with the classic soul of the sixties. And the recent comeback by veteran city blues artist Johnny 'Guitar' Watson as a disco star provided exceptionally startling evidence of the continuity of black pop.

Rhythm & Blues : Albums

Louis Jordan

The Best of Louis Jordan (MCA MCFM 2715)

Choo Choo Ch'Boogie/Let The Good Times Roll/Ain't Nobody Here But Us Chickens/Saturday Night Fish Fry/Beware Brother Beware/Caldonia/Knock Me A Kiss/Run Joe/School Days/Blue Light Boogie/Five Guys Named Moe/What's The Use Of Getting Sober (When You Gonna Get Drunk Again)/Buzz Me/Beans And Corn Bread/Don't Let The Sun Catch You Cryin'/Somebody Done Changed The Lock On My Door/Barnyard Boogie/Early In The Mornin'/I Want You To Be My Baby/Nobody Knows You When You're Down And Out

Jordan has received somewhat belated recognition as one of the key forerunners of rock & roll. Born in Arkansas in 1908, he set up his Tympany Five at the age of thirty after working with big bands, and had a string of exuberant blues and novelty hits over a period of more than ten years, defining the 'jump combo' style and providing an important part of the musical atmosphere in which many fifties r&b stars grew up. 'Choo Choo Ch'Boogie' (1942) was one of the first white hits by a popular black band; 'Caldonia' and 'Let The Good Times Roll' were equally influential; and 'Saturday Night Fish Fry' summed up the 'fun-versus-authority' mood of later rock & roll. Jordan himself played alto sax, and sang with exceptionally clear diction – which, along with his non-regional style, helped make him particularly accessible to a mass audience. Chuck Berry has acknowledged his debt to Jordan: he seems to have taken note of the clarity of the words, the cool wit, and the sly portrayal of social pressures, as well as the style of Jordan's guitarist, Carl Hoagan.

Various Artists

Doowop, Doowop (DJM DJSLM 2026)

Sunday Kind Of Love (The Harptones)/Mary Lee (The Rainbows)/In The Still Of The Nite (The Five Satins)/The Closer You Are (The Channels)/Could This Be Magic (The Dubs)/Deserie (The Charts)/ Long Lonely Nights (Lee Andrews and the Hearts)/Sixteen Candles (The Crests)/Florence (The Paragons)/The Gleam In Your Eye (The Channels)/To The Aisle (The Five Satins)/Don't Ask Me To Be Lonely (The Dubs)/One Summer Night (The Danleers)/Try The Impossible (Lee Andrews and the Hearts)/The Plea (The Jesters)/Step By Step (The Crests)/Once In A While (The Chimes)/Once Upon A Time (Rochell and the Candles)

It has been estimated that some fifteen thousand black vocal groups were first recorded in the fifties (see Bill Millar, *The Drifters*, STUDIO VISTA, 1971). Most of them were influenced by the late-thirties music of the Inkspots and by the 'jubilee' and 'quartet' gospel styles, the former featuring harmony lead and the latter a solo singer with harmony back-up. The style filtered through to white audiences with the rise of rock & roll, and this record, covering 1953–61, includes some of the outstanding hits of the genre in that period – particularly 'In The Still Of The Nite' and 'Could This Be Magic'. The tracks by the Crests and the Chimes illustrate another thread to the pattern: the vast number of non-black groups – typically from other minorities, such as the Italians and Puerto Ricans – who sprang up in the wake of the breakthrough. Predominantly from the north-eastern cities, they flourished until the onset of the British invasion in 1963. 'Doowop' or 'street-corner' music, as it became known, was in important respects a folk idiom. Its formal simplicity, and the fact that the basic vocal arrangements could be worked out without instruments ('acappella'), meant that it was possible for anyone familiar with the conventions to make a recognizable attempt at a performance. One result was that many rough-and-ready doowop records were released; another was that groups often made just one or two hits before disbanding or fading into obscurity. Memorable singles were made by the Moonglows, the Silhouettes, the Spaniels, the Flamingos, the Monotones, the Chantels, Rosie and the Originals, the Jive Five, the Jaynetts, the Rays and countless others who helped connect the rock & roll industry to its popular roots for several years. Vocal groups have continued to provide a major current of black music, although the emphasis on instrumentation and studio techniques brought by the soul and rock of the mid sixties pushed the doowop sound itself from the centre of the picture.

Various Artists

The Gospel Sound (CBS M 67234)

Motherless Child (Blind Willie Johnson)/Down Here, Lord, Waiting On You (Rev. J. M. Gates)/My Soul Is A Witness (Arizona Dranes)/ Anyhow (The Golden Gate Jubilee Quartet)/Who Was John (Mitchell's Christian Singers)/Let Your Light Shine On Me (Blind Willie Johnson)/ The Sun Didn't Shine (The Golden Gate Jubilee Quartet)/Jezebel (The Golden Gate Jubilee Quartet)/Nobody's Fault But Mine (Blind Willie Johnson)/When The Saints Go Marching In (Mitchell's Christian Singers)/The Need Of Prayer (Rev. J. M. Gates)/Travelling Shoes (Mitchell's Christian Singers)/If I Had My Way (Blind Willie Johnson)/ Stalin Wasn't Stallin' (The Golden Gate Jubilee Quartet)/One Day (The Angelic Gospel Singers and the Dixie Hummingbirds)/I Will Move On Up A Little Higher (Mahalia Jackson)/I'll Never Forget (Ira Tucker and the Dixie Hummingbirds)/When I Wake Up In Glory (Mahalia Jackson)/Why? (Am I Treated So Bad) (The Staple Singers)/Even Me (Marion Williams)/Said I Wasn't Gonna Tell Nobody (The Abyssinian Baptist Gospel Choir)/He Stays In My Room (The Abyssinian Baptist Gospel Choir)/Just A Little While To Stay Here (Mahalia Jackson)/ I'll Live Again (Ira Tucker and the Dixie Hummingbirds)/Don't Knock (The Staple Singers)/Strange Man (Dorothy Love Coates)/Today (The Angelic Gospel Singers and the Dixie Hummingbirds)/The Day Is Past And Gone (Marion Williams)

This excellent album covers the development of black American religious music over a period of forty years, from 1927 to 1966, and it vividly illustrates the wide variety of styles and moods commonly thrown together under the heading 'gospel'. It encompasses the harsh, primitive spiritual blues of guitarist Blind Willie Johnson; the magnificent tenor of Ira Tucker fronting the polished harmonies of the Dixie Hummingbirds; the rousing ragtime piano of Arizona Dranes; the massed voices of the Abyssinian Baptist Gospel Choir; and even the wartime political humour of 'Stalin Wasn't Stallin'', in which the heroic Russian bear halts the progress of 'the beast of Berlin'. The time-span is sufficient to give a fair indication of the extensive changes which the music has undergone in this century. These have included the replacement of traditional spirituals by original compositions after the work of Thomas A. Dorsey in the thirties; the rise of the female solo singers and the male acappella quartets; the 'golden age' which came in the forties, as the new independent labels and radio stations flourished; and the evolution of full instrumental accompaniments. But the basic message of good news in bad times has remained constant, and the gradual entry of gospel's uniquely intense forms of expression into commercial entertainment is perhaps the most profound aspect of the transformation of popular music that has taken place since rock & roll.

Various Artists

Heavy Heads (CHESS LPS 1522: IMPORT)

Hoochie Coochie Man (Muddy Waters)/Don't Start Me To Talkin' (Sonny Boy Williamson)/Moanin' For My Baby (Howlin' Wolf)/Juke (Little Walter)/Diggin' My Potatoes (Washboard Sam)/Walkin' The Boogie (John Lee Hooker)/I'm A Man (Bo Diddley)/Blues With Feeling (Little Walter)/Sad To Be Alone (Sonny Boy Williamson)/Let's Go Out Tonight (John Lee Hooker)/The Red Rooster (Howlin' Wolf)/I Feel So Bad (Little Milton)

In the fifties the northern industrial city of Chicago was the most important centre of urban blues and r&b: its musicians were often southerners who had left home in search of work. Chess was the leading label reflecting the city's blues activity. Its riches have been permutated endlessly over the years, and the chosen album is therefore only an example: apart from Muddy Waters, Bo Diddley and John Lee Hooker, who are represented in their own right elsewhere, it offers samples of four other Chicago giants, plus the cruder charm of Washboard Sam. Howlin' Wolf was one of the most powerful of all r&b performers: the angry anguish of his style is well indicated by his stage name. Two harmonica players are included: the irresistible shuffling, mumbling style of Sonny Boy Williamson (the second artist to use that name), and the more sophisticated technique of Little Walter, reckoned by many to be the finest exponent of the 'blues harp'. The album closes with a track by the comparatively smooth stylist Little Milton. The importance of the Chess roster in the subsequent history of r&b cannot be over-emphasized. In Britain the Chess story has been lavishly packaged in three four-album boxed sets under the overall title *Genesis*, and the more commercial output of the label is represented on the eight *Chess Golden Decade* albums. This series also includes a *Chess Golden Decade Sampler* (CHESS 6830 181), containing sixteen of the label's greatest hits.

Muddy Waters

Chess Blues Masters (CHESS 2 ACMB 203: IMPORT)

Louisiana Blues/Honey Bee/I Just Wanna Make Love To You/Kind Hearted Woman/She Moves Me/Hoochie Coochie Man/Long Distance Call/She's All Right/Rolling Stone/Standing Around Crying/Too Young To Know/Walking Through The Park/Still A Fool/You Can't Lose What You Ain't Never Had/I Can't Be Satisfied/I Want You To Love Me/Rollin' And Tumblin'/Just To Be With You/You're Gonna Need My Help Some Day/Same Thing/My Life Is Ruined/Baby Please Don't Go/Got My Mojo Working Part 1

Waters (McKinley Morganfield) was 'discovered' in 1941 by folk archivists Alan Lomax and John Work, and was recorded singing the southern country blues for the Library of Congress. He was born in Mississippi in 1915, and in 1943 migrated to Chicago, holding a number of day jobs while playing in the clubs at night. Signed to the Chess label in the late forties, he has effectively become the 'father figure' of Chicago blues, translating the rural blues of his youth into an electrified urban setting. He is distinguished by his rich vocal delivery, his influential bottleneck guitar playing, and by the number of blues classics he has written. His bands of the fifties featured some of the finest musicians on the Chicago scene, including guitarist Jimmy Rogers, bass-player Willie Dixon (also a great writer of urban blues songs), harmonica-player Little Walter and pianist Otis Spann. The release of Chess material in Britain from the late fifties, and Waters' first UK tour in 1963, were the leading influences on the British 'r&b' revival (the early repertoire of the Rolling Stones, for example, was predominantly Chess blues): the music was subsequently 're-exported' back to America and led to belated recognition for the masters of the style. With *Muddy Waters – Folk Singer* (1963) Waters returned to his roots in the rural acoustic blues: he continues to record and tour, health permitting, and a successful collaboration with Johnny Winter in the late seventies, starting with the album *Hard Again*, led to the latest revival in his fortunes. The recommended album may be hard to find, but is simply one of many compilations over the years (*The Best of Muddy Waters* is another) which have offered his early and essential Chicago work.

Lightnin' Hopkins

All Them Blues (DJM DJLMD 8016)

Walkin' Blues/Baby Please Don't Go/Bad Luck Blues/Got To Move Your Baby/Shining Moon/What Did I Say/You've Got To Fan It/Mojo Hand/Don't Wake Me/Talk Of The Town/Goin' Back Home/Good Times/Sometimes She Will/Love Is Like A Hydrant/I Would If I Could/Black Mare Trot/Trouble Stay Away/Shine On Moon/Coffee For Mama/Shake It Baby/Awful Dream/Shaggy Dad/I'll Be Gone/Worried Life Blues/Have You Ever Loved A Woman

When an artist has recorded as profusely as Hopkins, who has always tended to go into a studio for anyone who offered satisfactory cash inducement, there can be no question of a 'best of' compilation. This double album of typical performances is chosen for its convenience, though the origin of the tapes seems obscure; they are reckoned to date from sessions in 1960 and 1965. Hopkins is a Texan, born in 1912, and is one of the greatest of the 'country-blues' players; though he has adapted his style to modern requirements and has a highly individual style, he typifies many aspects of the country blues. His lively, insistent boogie rhythm is a reminder that the basic function of such musicians, often itinerants in the tradition of medieval England, was to provide the dance music for rural gatherings. His meanderings from the strict blues structure and his wry, semi-improvised lyrics, drawing both on 'handed-down' and autobiographical material, are also typical. Since Hopkins has always recorded at the drop of a dollar he has not produced a masterpiece every time, but the general standard of his engaging, distinctive work is remarkably high.

Elmore James

All Them Blues (DJM DJD 28008)

It Hurts Me Too/Everyday I Have The Blues/Dust My Broom/Shake Your Moneymaker/Bleeding Heart/Pickin' The Blues/She's Got To Go/Talk To Me Baby/I Believe/Sunnyland/Stranger Blues/12-Year-Old Boy/My Baby's Gone/Find My Kinda Woman/Up Jumped Elmore/Anna Lee/I've Got A Right To Love My Baby/Mean Mistreatin' Mama/Look On Yonder Wall

There is no more exciting sound in urban blues than the relentless slide guitar and powerful voice of Elmore James. He was born in Mississippi in 1918, had his first success with a revival of Robert Johnson's 'Dust My Broom' in 1951, and subsequently moved to Chicago, where he was based until his death in 1963. These recordings date from 1959–62, and feature his regular club band: his cousin Homesick James on second guitar, Little Johnny Jones (piano), Odie Payne (drums) and J. T. Brown (tenor sax). Fierce up-tempo boogies, often derivatives of 'Dust My Broom' (featured here in one of many re-recordings), proved the most influential of James's work, and formed a staple sound of the British r&b revival. Notable among the bands who admired him were the early Fleetwood Mac, featuring Jeremy Spencer, who in the late sixties were the leading 'sneakers and blue-jeans' r&b band. Just as distinctive, however, was James's impassioned playing and singing on such slow songs as 'It Hurts Me Too'. His early death came at a time when he was just beginning to enjoy deserved recognition outside the confines of the Chicago blues clubs.

Jimmy Reed

Memorial Album, Volume 1: Big Boss Man

(DJM DJD 28033)

Found My Baby/Roll & Rhumba/You Don't Have To Go/Boogie In The Dark/Shoot My Baby/Rockin' With Reed/Come On Baby/Ain't That Loving You Baby/When You Left Me/My First Plea/You Got Me Dizzy/Do The Thing/Little Rain/Signals Of Love/Honest I Do/Odds And Ends/My Bitter Seed/Ends And Odds/A String To Your Heart/You Got Me Crying/Down In Virginia/I'm Gonna Get My Baby/Caress Me Baby/I Know It's A Sin/You In That Sack/Going To New York/Take Out Some Insurance/Big Boss Man

Reed proved a glorious exception to the rule that a 'folk music' must be sweetened and sanitized in order to enjoy commercial success. He was one of the most individual of blues performers, having like many others migrated from Mississippi to Chicago, playing a simple, langorous, insistent and sometimes rather chaotic version of electric blues, and yet for six years, commencing in 1957, he featured in the national pop charts a dozen times. His trade-marks were a loping, hypnotic, bass-heavy rhythm, a slurred, urgent vocal delivery, a strident harmonica style (he was one of the first to improvise a harness to enable him to play guitar and harmonica together) and the trading of delicate little guitar figures with his lead guitarist, usually Eddie Taylor. The recommended album covers his recorded career from its start in 1953 to its height in 1960. An increasing drinking problem led to a reputation for unreliability in the sixties, and his recordings then were largely re-makes of earlier material.

John Lee Hooker

Dimples

(DJM DJD 28026)

Unfriendly Woman/Wheel And Deal/Mambo Chillun/Time Is Marching/I'm So Worried Baby/Baby Lee/Dimples/Every Night/The Road Is So

Rough/Trouble Blues/Stop Talking/Everybody Rockin'/I'm So Excited/ I See You When You're Weak/Crawlin' Black Spider/Little Wheel/ Little Fine Woman/Rosie Mae/You Can Lead Me Baby/I Love You Honey/You've Taken My Woman/Mama You Got A Daughter/Maudie/ I'm In The Mood/Boogie Chillun/Hobo Blues/Crawlin' Kingsnake/Boom Boom

There's a brooding, loping elegance about Hooker's anarchic blues that make him one of the most distinctive artists in the field. He was for commercial reasons usually set within the discipline of a group, as on these recordings (1955–61) for the Vee-Jay company. Look out for the *Burning Hell* album as an excellent example of his work as an unaccompanied, acoustic performer. His rhythm is rock-solid, but he has always tended to stray from the rigid timing of the chord changes, and he is best when the group gives structure without swamping him, as on 'Dimples' or 'Boom Boom'. He first recorded in 1948, and this album includes impeccable 1959 re-makes of his early successes. In the early years of his recording career he was based in Detroit, making records under a variety of pseudonyms, but the tracks on this double album were produced in Chicago, with support from Jimmy Reed's second guitarist Eddie Taylor (and Reed himself on four tracks). The album ends with Hooker's major 'pop' hit from 1961, 'Boom Boom'. Two sample tracks typify Hooker's influence: the unique shuffle rhythm of 'I'm So Excited', stolen by every self-respecting r&b revivalist band of the sixties, and the dark electric guitar lines of the unadorned blues 'I See You When You're Weak'. Like Jimmy Reed, Hooker is a 'primitive' in an urban setting, producing one of r&b's archetypal sounds.

Various Artists

Sound of the City/New Orleans, Where Rock & Roll Began (UNITED ARTISTS UAS 29215)

House Party Blues (Archibald)/Sleepwalkin' Woman (Smilin' Joe)/The Bells Are Ringing (Smiley Lewis)/Great Big Eyes (Archibald)/Little School Girl (Fats Domino)/Travellin' Mood (James Wayne)/Rockin' At Cosmo's (Lee Allen)/Let The Four Winds Blow (Roy Brown)/ Ooh

Poo Pah Doo, Parts 1 and 2 (Jessie Hill)/Lipstick Traces (Benny Spellman)/I Know (Barbara George)/Over You (Aaron Neville)/Waiting At The Station (Ernie K. Doe)/Country Fool (The Showmen)/Ruler Of My Heart (Irma Thomas)

Compiled to accompany part of Charlie Gillett's still unsurpassed rock history, *The Sound of the City*, this album amply illustrates the characteristic qualities of New Orleans r&b – the relaxed yet exuberant rhythmic feel, the predominantly light-hearted mood of the songs with a consistent tinge of blues plaintiveness in the vocals. It also demonstrates the extent to which the city's musicians were working within many of the conventions of rock & roll some time before the more fully documented 'Memphis fusion' of the mid fifties. The focal point for the classic early recordings – exemplified by the first eight tracks here – was Cosimo Matassa's small studio, commemorated in saxman Lee Allen's 'Rockin' At Cosmo's'. The sessions were often the outcome of the efforts of bandleader Dave Bartholomew, who was signed up at the end of the forties as an a&r man for the West Coast label, Imperial. A second phase came in 1960–62, after the rock & roll boom had subsided and most of the record companies had begun to lose interest in New Orleans performers. Imperial got the distribution rights to the local Minit label, and – with Allen Toussaint producing, writing songs and playing piano – achieved hits with Ernie K. Doe, Irma Thomas and Benny Spellman. The revival also saw Clarence Henry, Lee Dorsey and Chris Kenner make an impression on other labels. Barbara George's 'I Know' was a hit for a new label, AFO, set up as a musicians' cooperative by pianist Harold Battiste. But the company soon collapsed, and New Orleans r&b itself entered a relatively static period.

Huey 'Piano' Smith

Rockin' Pneumonia and the Boogie Woogie Flu (CHISWICK CH 9)

Rockin' Pneumonia And The Boogie Woogie Flu, Parts 1 and 2/Little Chicken Wah Wah/Little Liza Jane/Just A Lonely Clown/Hush Your Mouth/Don't You Know Yockomo/High Blood Pressure/Don't You Just

Know It/Well I'll Be John Brown/Tu-ber-cu-lucas And Sinus Blues/ Dearest Darling/She Got Low Down/Second Line

New Orleans pianist Huey Smith was one of the star session-men at Cosimo's studios in the early fifties, but came into his own after former Specialty a&r man Johnny Vincent set up the Ace label in 1955. Accompanied by his vocal group the Clowns, whose most notable lead singer was Bobby Marchan, Smith gave the label a number of sizable hits, including 'Rockin' Pneumonia' (1957), 'High Blood Pressure'/ 'Don't You Just Know It' (1958) and 'Popeye' (1962). His rolling, shuffling rhythms – contrasting with Fats Domino's more sprightly approach – were certainly indebted to another New Orleans pianist, Professor Longhair. Combined with amusingly nonsensical lyrics and fine solo instrumental work, the sound was the basis of some of the funkiest recordings of the rock & roll period. The band accompanied several featured Ace artists, helping to create such hits as 'Sea Cruise' by Frankie Ford and 'Gee Baby' by Joe and Ann. They also backed Jimmy Clanton, the teen ballad singer of 'Just A Dream' and 'Venus In Blue Jeans' fame; but it was Clanton's success that spelt the end of Ace as a force in r&b. The company opted for the lucrative pop arena and merged with Vee-Jay of Chicago in 1962. The two-volume 'Ace Story' (CHISWICK CH11 AND CH12) contains the cream of the label's output. Huey Smith became a Jehovah's Witness in the mid sixties.

Various Artists

Another Saturday Night (OVAL 3001)

Before I Grow Too Old (Tommy McLain)/Cajun Fugitive (Belton Richard)/Try To Find Another Man (Tommy McLain and Clint West)/ Jole Blon (Vin Bruce)/Who Needs You So Bad (Gary Walker)/Oh Lucille (Belton Richard)/Another Saturday Night (Clint West)/Un Autre Soir D'Ennui (Belton Richard)/The Promised Land (Johnnie Allen)/Two Steps De Bayou Teche (Austin Pitre)/Downhome Music (Rufus Jagneaux)/Laisser Les Cajuns Danser (Belton Richard)

National phenomena like rock & roll had only a marginal impact in the swamplands of Louisiana: this area continued to produce its own readily identifiable music come what may. There are various local styles, sharing a cultural basis marked by the heritage of French-speaking settlers who arrived there in the eighteenth century. The music is sometimes known collectively as 'cajun', 'bayou' or 'zydeco'; and although the last term is usually taken to imply that the musicians are black, there is a great deal of intermixing of white and black traditions. This anthology is drawn almost entirely from the catalogue of Jin & Swallow Records, the biggest cajun specialist. It's nearly all dance music, much of it featuring a swirling accompaniment of accordions and fiddles, and ranging through waltzes, two-steps and rock & roll. While the selections cover a broad spectrum of moods and attitudes, there's a general sense of balance between good-time energy and bluesy melancholy. Cajun is one of the last American folk idioms, and there could be no more eloquent tribute to its vitality than this album.

Johnny Otis

Pioneers Of Rock, Volume 3

(EMI STARLINE SRS 5129)

Crazy Country Hop/Three Girls Named Molly Doin' The Hully Gully/ Ring-A-Ling/Telephone Baby/Hey Baby Don't You Know/Casting My Spell/All I Want Is Your Love/Mumblin' Mosie/A Light Still Shines In Your Window/Willie And The Hand Jive/Let The Sun Shine In My Life/ Bye Bye Baby

Otis has been billed, appropriately enough, in the seventies as the Godfather of Rhythm & Blues. The son of Greek immigrants, his music was nevertheless firmly rooted in black culture. He formed his travelling r&b road show at the start of the fifties when this was an unfashionable and risky course to take. In so doing, he helped keep alive big band r&b, and gave himself a sufficiently flexible framework to ensure his own continued success during the rock & roll era. His resilience was partly due to an extraordinary ability for spotting and developing new talent. Among his discoveries were Little Esther (Phillips), the Robins (later the Coasters), Willie Mae Thornton (who recorded the original version of 'Hound Dog' in 1953), Hank Ballard, Little Willie John, Jackie Wilson and Etta James. His own major rock

& roll hit was 'Willie and The Hand Jive' (1958), featuring the so-called Bo Diddley beat – although Otis himself called it the 'shave-and-a-haircut, six bits' rhythm, and insisted he'd been using it for years. Several of his other best recordings of the period are included in this collection; but it lacks his biggest British hit, a rumbustious version of 'Ma, He's Making Eyes At Me', sung by Marie Adams and the Three Tons of Joy. Otis spent most of the sixties producing, dabbled with a modern rock style featuring his guitar-playing son Shuggie towards the end of the decade, and revived his r&b revue with some success in the early '70s.

Various Artists

This is How It All Began, Volumes 1 and 2

(SPECIALTY SNTF 5002/5003)

It's Getting Late In The Evening (Chosen Gospel Singers)/By And By (Soul Stirrers)/Somebody Touched Me (Alex Bradford)/Trouble In My Way (Swan Silvertones)/Don't Trust Nobody (John Lee Hooker)/Married Woman (Frankie Lee Sims)/One Room Country Shack (Mercy Dee)/R. M. Blues (Roy Milton)/Pink Champagne (Joe Liggings)/Please Send Me Someone To Love (Percy Mayfield)/Tabarin (The Four Flames)/X-Temporaneous Boogie (Camille Howard)/The Huckle-Buck (Roy Milton)/Shuffle-Shuck (Jimmy Liggins)

Lawdy Miss Clawdy (Lloyd Price)/The Things That I Used To Do (Guitar Slim)/Dream Girl (Jesse Belvin and Marvin Phillips)/Nite Owl (Tony Allen And The Champs)/Tutti Frutti (Little Richard)/Short Fat Fannie (Larry Williams)/Keep A-Knockin' (Little Richard)/I'll Come Running Back To You (Sam Cooke)/Bony Moronie (Larry Williams)/Cha Dooky-Doo (Art Neville)/Koko Joe (Don and Dewey)/Lights Out (Jerry Byrne)

Although they are sold separately, taken together these two albums define the history of the Los Angeles label Specialty, founded in 1946 and almost immediately put on the map by Roy Milton's hugely influential 'R.M.Blues', a jump-band number that, uniquely among blues records of the time, featured a tight arrangement and carefully constructed 'riff' that made it instantly memorable among potential buyers. Volume 1 covers the roots of the Specialty label: gospel (founder Art Rupe's musical preference), country blues, city blues, ballads (including the best-known by masterly writer Percy Mayfield) and boogie. Volume 2 shows how Specialty coped profitably with the arrival of rock & roll. In the early fifties Rupe strove to broaden the label's base by going to New Orleans in search of talent: one of the early results, Lloyd Price's 'Lawdy Miss Clawdy', is now regarded as a rock & roll standard in spite of the fact that it dates from 1952. Rupe capped his success with Price when, in 1955, he released 'Tutti Frutti', the first of many hits for Little Richard. The album also includes one of the biggest of all straight blues hits, Guitar Slim's 'Things I Used To Do', one of the earliest secular records by the great Sam Cooke, and two by Little Richard's rival Larry Williams.

Clyde McPhatter

A Tribute to Clyde McPhatter (ATLANTIC K30033)

Treasure Of Love/A Lover's Question/Money Honey/Seven Days/ Honey Love/White Christmas/Long Lonely Nights/Without Love (There's Nothing)/Warm Your Heart/Such A Night/Just To Hold My Hand/Someday You'll Want Me To Want You/What 'cha Gonna Do/ Bells Of St Mary's

Listening to Clyde McPhatter today, when many of the arrangements and studio techniques can sound crude, and with gospel vocal styles long since established as part of pop's vocabulary, the break-through his singing represented may not be obvious. What is instantly apparent, however, is that McPhatter possessed one of the most remarkable voices in the history of black music: the purity, flexibility and inventiveness of his high tenor lead have rarely been matched. It was a style forged in Baptist chapels. McPhatter, the son of a minister, was born in North Carolina in 1933 and formed his own church group, the Mount Lebanon Singers, at the age of fourteen after the family had moved to New York. He entered the popular field with Billy Ward's Dominoes in 1950, showing the r&b audience how potentially exciting church singing could be with records like 'Have Mercy Baby' and 'The Bells'

In 1953 he decided to break away and form his own group, the Drifters. They immediately recorded a series of milestones for Atlantic, brimming with ingenuity and humour. The first six – 'Money Honey', 'Such A Night', 'Honey Love', 'Someday', 'White Christmas', 'What 'cha Gonna Do' – reached the r&b Top Ten, firmly establishing the commercial appeal of the new style. The run of classics came to an end in 1954 when McPhatter was drafted into the air force, and the rest of this album is drawn mainly from the years 1956–9 when Atlantic promoted him successfully as a solo performer. Although the productions made some unfortunate concessions to the pop market, McPhatter's distinctive voice remained the linchpin. This was far less often the case during later contracts with MGM, Mercury and Amy, and 'Lover Please' (1962) was his last big hit. He died in 1972.

The Drifters

Golden Hits (ATLANTIC K40018)

There Goes My Baby/(If You Cry) True Love, True Love/Dance With Me/This Magic Moment/Save The Last Dance For Me/I Count The Tears/Some Kind Of Wonderful/Up On The Roof/On Broadway/Under The Boardwalk/I've Got Sand In My Shoes/Saturday Night At The Movies

The group that took Clyde McPhatter's inspired singing into the black charts was different in all but name from the Drifters who became a key act in the rise of uptown r&b. When McPhatter's departure led to a steady loss of commercial appeal, manager George Threadwell sacked the entire line-up and chose a relatively little-known New York group, the Crowns, to fill the gap. Their first record for Atlantic was 'There Goes My Baby' (1959), produced by Leiber and Stoller. It featured an arrangement previously unparalleled in r&b, involving strings, Latin rhythms, tympani and apparent references to Tchaikovsky. The song itself was oddly disconnected, lacking rhyme; and Ben E. King's lead vocal had an unusual intensity. Yet it was a smash hit in both the r&b and the pop charts, and set the pattern for a stream of so-called 'beat concerto' successes, including 'Dance With Me', 'This Magic Moment', and – biggest of all – 'Save The Last Dance For Me'. On the strength of this, King left for a solo career, to be replaced by another fine singer, Rudy Lewis. Subsequent releases began to play down the sound of the group as a whole, aiming for a smoother effect by adding a female quartet and more elaborate orchestration, and by turning to neat formula pop songs from such teams as Gerry Goffin–Carole King and Barry Mann–Cynthia Weil. Their best records in this pop vein included 'Some Kind Of Wonderful', 'Up On The Roof', 'On Broadway' and 'Under The Boardwalk'. The last-named in particular – produced by Bert Berns – created a seductive mood of romance and fun which later incarnations of the Drifters consistently tried to revive, with the result that the group's name continued to appear in the pop charts well into the seventies.

Bobby Bland

Introspective of the Early Years

(DUKE DL 92: IMPORT)

I Smell Trouble/I Just Got To Forget You/I've Been Wrong So Long/Two Steps From The Blues/You're The One/Who Will The Next Fool Be/You're Worth It All/Blues In The Night/Sometime Tomorrow/Share Your Love With Me/Road Of Brokenhearted Men/Someday/Touch Of The Blues/That Did It/One Horse Town/Chains Of Love/Since I Fell For You/Who Can I Turn To/If I Hadn't Called You Back/Loneliness Hurts/Black Night/Blind Man/Save Your Love For Me/Ask Me 'Bout Nothing

Bobby Bland's work represents one of the most important links between blues and soul, and only B. B. King has rivalled his popularity as a post-war blues singer. Born in 1930 and raised in Memphis, he was a member of the Beale Streeters in the late forties, along with King, Johnny Ace and Junior Parker. His crisp, swinging, direct style won him a contract with the Duke label of Houston in 1954, and the first of his long succession of r & b successes, 'It's My Life Baby', came the following year. 'I Smell Trouble', 'Little Boy Blue' and the Hot Hundred entry 'Farther On Up The Road' had established him as a black star by 1957. A large part of the credit for the great early recordings is due to the consistently imaginative and vital big band arrangements; these were masterminded by Joe Scott, who was also involved in composing much of the material, and they featured the superb lead guitar of Wayne Bennett. Allied with the power of Bland's voice, the developing style ensured continuing r&b chart success in the early sixties, with 'Cry, Cry, Cry', 'I Pity The Fool', 'Stormy Monday', 'Turn On Your Lovelight', 'Call On Me' and 'Two Steps From The Blues' all outstanding. Bland built up a huge audience among blacks, but his strongly gospel-tinged approach made few concessions to the mass market, and none of his records entered the national Top Ten. As the sixties progressed, his arrangements began to show the influence of contemporary soul music, although his intensely personal delivery never mixed easily with the new feel. However, when ABC took over Duke in 1972, his *California Album* and *Dreamer*, in which the hard blues core was set in a rock and pop context, at last secured him a place in the sun.

B. B. King

Live at the Regal (ABC ABCS 724)

Every Day I Have The Blues/Sweet Little Angel/It's My Own Fault/How Blue Can You Get/Please Love Me/You Upset Me Baby/Worry, Worry/You Done Lost Your Good Thing Now/Help The Poor

No modern bluesman has had a greater direct influence on pop than B. B. King. Raised in Mississippi, his style evolved partly in Memphis and New Orleans in the late forties and the fifties; but he became extremely popular in the northern cities, including Chicago, where the peerless 'Live at the Regal' was recorded in the early sixties. While he began as a self-accompanist, learning something from his illustrious cousin Bukka White, King rose to fame playing single-string solos in front of bands. This album provides some evidence of the powerful response he could generate in black audiences, and demonstrates his emphasis on the lyricism and drama of the blues – in contrast to the more rugged approach of the Muddy Waters school. King played clean and smooth – borrowing a great deal from jazz, including the 'bent' notes which became his trademark – and bringing the gospel elements in his singing further to the fore as his career progressed. His r&b chart successes began in 1950 with 'Three O'Clock Blues', on which Ike Turner played piano. Other milestones were 'Every Day I Have The Blues' (1955), 'Sweet Little Angel' (1956) and 'Sweet Sixteen' (1960). In the white rock-blues boom of the later sixties, B. B. King's guitar was a prime model, and he was inevitably teamed with various rock superstars and session-men on record, as well as being set to strings with considerable chart success. But few of these performances stand comparison with the earlier material.

Phil Spector

20 Greatest Hits

(PHIL SPECTOR INTERNATIONAL SUPER 2307 012)

River Deep Mountain High (Ike and Tina Turner)/Then He Kissed Me (The Crystals)/Be My Baby (The Ronettes)/Why Do Lovers Break Each Others Hearts (Bob B. Soxx and the Blue Jeans)/Proud Mary (Checkmates Ltd)/Today I Met The Boy I'm Gonna Marry (Darlene Love)/Zip-A-Dee-Doo-Dah (Bob B. Soxx and the Blue Jeans)/Best Part Of Breaking Up (The Ronettes)/You've Lost That Lovin' Feelin' (Righteous Brothers)/Da Doo Ron Ron (The Crystals)/He's A Rebel (The Crystals)/Not Too Young To Get Married (Bob B. Soxx and the Blue Jeans)/Uptown (The Crystals)/Unchained Melody (Righteous Brothers)/Walking In The Rain (The Ronettes)/A Love Like Yours (Nilsson and Cher)/He's Sure The Boy I Love (The Crystals)/Ebb Tide (Righteous Brothers)/Wait Till My Bobby Gets Home (Darlene Love)/ Baby I Love You (The Ronettes)

The elaborate, multi-tracked 'Wall Of Sound' developed by Spector made him the most famous of record producers; indeed, he established the producer as an important element in the sound of a pop record. As with Hitchcock in the cinema, it was Spector's name that attracted attention to his latest release, rather than that of the performer; in spite of the distinctive vocal strengths of such singers as Ronnie Bennett of the Ronettes or Darlene Love, their voices remained just one of many factors in Spector's master-schemes, which in his heyday of the early sixties were the most ambitious pop records ever made – 'little symphonies for kids'. His techniques reached most perfect expression in the 1963 album *A Christmas Gift to You* (PSI SUPER 2307 005), although this was largely overlooked at the time since its release coincided with President Kennedy's assassination. The recommended album is a more general cross-section of his work, although it omits such apprentice master-works as 'To Know Him Is To Love Him' (The Teddy Bears), 'Pretty Little Angel Eyes' (Curtis Lee) and 'I Love How You Love Me' (The Paris Sisters). The American public's rejection of Spector's most hyperbolic work, Ike and Tina Turner's 'River Deep Mountain High' (1966) hurt him deeply, and his new reclusive nature was to be compounded by a serious car crash. In later years he has worked with artists as diverse as John Lennon and Leonard Cohen, but his megalomaniac paranoia has inhibited his restoration as a leading pop music force. The panorama of his great years is covered in the six-album series *Phil Spector Wall Of Sound*, devoted to the Ronettes, Bob B. Soxx and the Blue Jeans, the Crystals, a collection of fourteen hits and two albums of 'rare masters'.

The Shangri-Las

Golden Hits of the Shangri-Las

(PHILIPS INTERNATIONAL 6336 215)

Leader Of The Pack/Past Present And Future/Train From Kansas City/Heaven Only Knows/Remember (Walking In The Sand)/Out In The Streets/I Can Never Go Home Anymore/Give Him A Great Big Kiss/Long Live Our Love/Give Us Your Blessings/Sophisticated Boom Boom/What Is Love

Master song-writers Leiber and Stoller, noted above all for their Coasters' classics, formed the New York label Red Bird, and its subsidiary Blue Cat, in 1964, in association with veteran producer George Goldner. Many of the young 'production-line' writers who also worked with Phil Spector (and Spector himself) contributed material to the labels: Jerry Barry, Ellie Greenwich, Gerry Goffin, Carole King, Barry Mann and Cynthia Weil. A survey of Red Bird's achievement is contained on two albums, *The Red Bird Era*, Volumes 1 and 2 (CHARLY CR 30108/30109), and they include tracks by the Shangri-Las, the New Orleans girl group the Dixie Cups ('Chapel Of Love'), Alvin Robinson's two classics 'Let The Good Times Roll' and 'Down Home Girl', the

Ad Libs, the Tradewinds and the Jelly Beans. Although the Shangri-Las' biggest hits 'Remember (Walking In The Sand)' and 'Leader Of The Pack' are on Volume 1, it omits two of their lesser successes which must now be seen as two of the most extraordinary pop records of the sixties – the genuinely moving teenage soap operas 'Past Present and Future' and 'I Can Never Go Home Anymore'. Therefore the record that includes them, *Golden Hits*, has been chosen instead to represent Red Bird. The Shangri-Las were a young female quartet masterminded by writer/producer George 'Shadow' Morton, who subsequently had success with Vanilla Fudge and Janis Ian. The adolescent vulnerability of the Shangri-Las' handful of great tracks has never been equalled, even by Spector.

Rhythm & Blues: Singles

Lloyd Price: *Lawdy Miss Clawdy* (1952)

A seminal New Orleans rocker, with Fats Domino's piano and the Bartholomew band accompanying a pleading blues vocal.

Hank Ballard and the Midnighters: *Work With Me Annie* (1954)

The beginning of the Annie sequence, which established Ballard's intense style among black audiences, but was too risqué for the pop market. (Ballard's other r&b hits included the 1958 original of 'The Twist', which was basically the Drifters' 'What'cha Gonna Do' with new words.)

Johnny Ace: *Pledging My Love* (1954)

This plaintive ballad of disarming simplicity and directness hastened the mass acceptance of black styles. Ace killed himself playing Russian roulette in December 1954.

The Penguins: *Earth Angel* (1954)

One of the best-remembered vocal group hits, perfectly evoking the gentle side of rock & roll.

Little Willie John: *Fever* (1956)

A much-covered performance by one of the singers most responsible for bringing gospel depth and weight into r&b. He died in prison in 1968 serving a sentence for manslaughter.

LaVern Baker: *Jim Dandy* (1956)

A singer with a remarkable expressive range, LaVern Baker was dogged by cover versions and mediocre material until this song made her a top r&r act.

Chuck Willis: *C. C. Rider* (1957)

Willis was a fine blues, rock and ballad singer who died in 1958 after making some fifteen r&b hits. This subtle performance was a pop success.

Jackie Wilson: *Night/Doggin' Around* (1958)

Wilson, who replaced Clyde McPhatter in the Dominoes, had a dazzling vocal technique and stage act, but he frequently seemed ill-suited to his material and arrangements, lurching from wild rockers to quasi-operatic ballads. This double-sided hit shows the latter approach in 'Night', while 'Doggin' Around' gives a better indication of his soul potential.

The Clovers: *Love Potion Number 9* (1959)

As well as raw harmony ballads, the Clovers' long run of fifties r&b hits for Atlantic included novelty dance numbers, culminating in this Coasters-style smash. It became a British beat standard.

Wilbert Harrison: *Kansas City* (1959)

This seemingly effortless yet compelling version of the Leiber–Stoller song was a huge hit for Harrison, who is a durable and highly distinctive performer.

Maurice Williams and the Zodiacs: *Stay* (1960)

This group, previously known as the Gladiolas, faded away after cutting the original of 'Little Darling' in 1957, until the inimitable 'Stay', with its wailing falsetto lead, soared to Number 1.

The Shirelles: *Will You Love Me Tomorrow* (1960)

A summit of pop r&b, produced by Luther Dixon, with Goffin and King's most touching and graceful composition ideally suited to Shirley Owens's wistful lead vocal.

The Phil Upchurch Combo: *You Can't Sit Down* (1961)

One of the most exciting instrumental hits, suggesting a line of descent from the raunchy fifties playing of Bill Doggett to seventies jazz-funk.

Bobby Parker: *Watch Your Step* (1961)

An explosive gospel-blues rocker which led to the Beatles' guitar intro on 'I Feel Fine' but left Parker in obscurity until his death in 1973.

Ben E. King: *Stand By Me* (1962)

King's best solo record and a vital link between uptown r&b and the soul era.

Gene Chandler: *Duke Of Earl* (1962)

The sound of the streets at its most coarse, gimmicky and magnetic – with a future soul star taking the lead.

Tommy Tucker: *Hi Heel Sneakers* (1963)

A classically straightforward blues which has become a rock standard – although no version has matched the original's warmth, or its brilliant guitar work.

The Chiffons: *He's So Fine* (1963)

One of the most infectious uptown girl-group hits, this topped the charts in 1963 and was recognized seven years later to be the source of George Harrison's 'My Sweet Lord'.

Slim Harpo: *Baby Scratch My Back* (1966)

The southern Louisiana bluesman, whose 'I'm A King Bee' was covered by the Rolling Stones, achieved considerable pop success with this lazy, gritty novelty.

Ike and Tina Turner: *Goodbye, So Long* (1966)

'It's Gonna Work Out Fine' (1961) and 'River Deep Mountain High' (1966) are perhaps the most lauded of the Turners' many records, but this ferociously paced boogie is straight from the molten core of r&b.

IAN HOARE

Soul

In one sense, the term 'soul' has simply been a convenient label for the record industry to attach to the music that sells to young blacks, replacing earlier tags like 'race music' and 'rhythm & blues'. It has been used in the seventies to refer to an increasingly broad and diverse range of styles. But its entry into widespread usage around 1964 did coincide with a distinct shift of emphasis in the dominant stylistic approach in the black field.

This change did not consist of a sudden and unprecedented merging of gospel and blues, as is sometimes suggested. The epithets 'soulful' and 'funky' had already been applied to musical styles during the fifties, when Charlie Mingus, Cannonball Adderley, Bobby Timmons, Horace Silver and other jazz performers had sought to move away from what were seen as the over-cerebral and élitist tendencies of the avant-garde, and to re-assert the blues and church roots.

Many popular r&b records of the fifties and early sixties had also displayed gospel elements. Apart from the freakish Little Richard, these forerunners of soul included the 'rhythm and gospel' vocal groups, of which the most notable were the Drifters featuring Clyde McPhatter, and Hank Ballard and the Midnighters. There was also a strong current of 'gospel-blues' solo stars, the greatest being Bobby Bland, who continued to appeal to black audiences after the advent of soul, and Little Willie John. The man whose name later became synonymous with soul, James Brown, began recording in a gospel-blues vein as early as 1956; Sam Cooke was injecting a quasi-religious purity of feeling into pop ballads from the same time; and Ray Charles, in his work at Atlantic between 1954 and 1959, mapped out much of the musical territory of the future soul, thoroughly exploring possible permutations of sacred and secular tradition, and – perhaps most importantly – taking his new hybrid into the upper reaches of the pop charts in 1959 with 'What'd I Say'.

In many of the pioneering records of the late fifties, though, gospel vocal techniques were used randomly, as a gimmick or a spice added to conventional pop tunes or a twelve-bar format. Even after Ray Charles's breakthrough, when the melodic structures of church music began to appear more consistently in r&b, the backings generally remained out of sympathy with the musical core.

Soul emerged as a fully-fledged genre only after 1963, in the hands of arrangers in the South – particularly at the Stax studios – and black uptown r&b producers in the North, particularly at Motown. While these two streams were quite separate in many respects, their common significance lay in the commercially successful development of instrumental accompaniments and studio production styles, which complemented rather than disguised the essential qualities of the black singers.

Former Detroit assembly-line worker Berry Gordy founded his Tamla-Motown organization in 1960, and built it over the next six years into America's richest independent record company.

A roster of unknown but extraordinarily talented performers were transformed into national stars; and the operation was owned and run by blacks – a new phenomenon on this scale.

Some of the early hits, such as Eddie Holland's 'Jamie', were dressed up with strings in a typical uptown manner; and the subsequent promotion of the glamorous Supremes – twelve Number 1 pop hits between 1964 and 1969 – confirmed that Gordy always had one eye on long-established areas of mass entertainment. More remarkable, nevertheless, was the extent to which gospel-based excitement was brought increasingly to the fore after 1962 in hard, intense records like Martha and the Vandellas' 'Heat Wave'. At the same time, an integrated house production style took shape, chiefly under the guidance of Smokey Robinson and the Holland–Dozier–Holland team. The imaginative peaks became less frequent after 1967. But the golden years of the Motown sound – whether it's better described as 'soul' or 'pop' – were a gloriously exuberant moment in black musical history.

The chief contribution from Memphis was the style developed by the musicians on the Stax/Volt labels, set up (as Satellite) by Jim Stewart and his sister Estelle Axton in 1959. The house band, the Mar-Keys, made up mainly of young whites from rural areas, had an instrumental hit with 'Last Night' in 1961; and the same basic line-up, with an organ replacing the horns, succeeded a year later as Booker T and the MGs with 'Green Onions'. But it wasn't until 1963 that this relaxed yet punchy sound was employed by Stax to back performers singing in a gospel mode, with guitar or horns echoing the lead vocal in the fashion of a chapel choir, or congregation. That combination brought about the classic soul of William Bell, Otis Redding, Wilson Pickett and Sam and Dave. Pickett moved on to record at Rick Hall's legendary Fame studios near Muscle Shoals in Alabama – a state which also served as host to Percy Sledge and Joe Tex in their heyday.

These new soul records were distributed by Atlantic, based in New York, which had earlier sensed the potential of the embryonic soul style and launched Solomon Burke as its own leading contender in the field. His first hit, 'Just Out Of Reach' (1961), was a re-worked country song. Elements from white music were, in fact, compounded with the black basis throughout the formative years. And Memphis provided a melting-pot for the soul synthesis, just as it had done for rock & roll.

With the exception of Motown, the most innovative period of soul (1963–6) went largely unnoticed by the mass white audience, who were preoccupied with British beat groups playing a form of music derived to an enormous extent from the new black fusions. When soul did catch on in its own right in the later sixties, it was primarily as insistent dance music – and it's in that sense that it is most widely accepted to this day.

Dance has always been fundamental to the black tradition, but the soul explosion had a wider significance. It reflected and embodied the rapid upsurge of black social and political consciousness during the sixties, given clear expression in the civil rights movement. This aspect of the music's meaning becomes clearer if the attitudes apparent in its chief sources, blues and gospel, are taken into account. The blues was generally – though not exclusively – individualistic and fatalistic in its outlook. It was also regarded, by and large, as the music of the disreputable outsider, who found his reason for continuing the struggle for survival in hedonistic pursuits, especially sex. Gospel, by direct contrast, was respectable in terms of conventional morality; it was also a form of communal ritual, lamenting the suffering of the present but celebrating the prospect of salvation. When the two came together it was possible for a mood of hope and change – firmly rooted in *this* world, warts and all – to become a major current in black popular art.

At first, the words of hymns and spirituals were often modified only slightly to give them a sexual and romantic connotation: 'This Little Light Of Mine' became 'This Little Girl Of Mine' for Ray Charles. Sexual themes were to remain essential, changing mainly by way of a greater emphasis on analysing relationships rather than simply expressing feeling. But by 1964, records like the Impressions' 'Keep On Pushing' and Sam Cooke's 'A Change Is Gonna Come' were beginning to bring the political implications to the surface; and by 1968, James Brown was able to spell it out – 'Say It Loud, I'm Black And I'm Proud'.

It was paradoxical that an overtly ethnic and political approach should ripen at a time when black music was reaching new levels of mass acceptance. During the seventies, many performers have continued to address themselves to broadly social concerns, Curtis Mayfield and Marvin Gaye being particularly successful. But as soul's commercial currency has strengthened, more and more black artists have signed to major national companies and there has been a decline in the number of identifiable regional styles appealing specifically to black audiences. Nevertheless, the opening up of international markets for different types of pop has meant that a remarkable variety of performers have now established themselves in the eyes of the public at large as 'soul' artists.

One aspect of this has been the impact of the white rock renaissance – with Sly Stone the principal catalyst for the interaction. The 'street-funk' bands, who emerged in Sly's wake and shot to prominence in the mid-seventies disco boom, seemed partly to represent a deliberate move away from the self-consciousness of the black pride anthems, a consolidation of the non-verbal Afro-American roots. Yet they also drew on rock's guitar pyrotechnics, and understood the advantages of being self-contained units. Their playing was at least as important as their singing.

There has, in fact, been a generally increased emphasis on the instrumental side of the music, tying in with the move towards the album as the most important commercial unit. The lush orchestral funk of Isaac Hayes and Barry White is one current of this; and there has also been the phenomenon of jazz artists – including Quincy Jones, Miles Davis, Herbie Hancock, Donald Byrd and George Benson – 'crossing over' in considerable numbers to more popular areas. One effect of the plethora of new fusions has been that versatile session-men, such as the guitarists Eric Gale and Cornell Dupree, have become stars in their own right.

The album market has also helped to establish a school of 'black singer/song-writers', working in a rather more intimate and reflective vein than the classic soul of the sixties – Bill Withers, Bobby Womack and Stevie Wonder, for example.

Despite such developments in the seventies, however, soul belongs essentially to a culture rather than to individuals, to the artisan rather than the genius. Its greatest moments are often achieved by performers who hit upon the right combination just once or twice before receding into obscurity. No selection of albums can encompass this central characteristic of the soul tradition. The records reviewed below merely cover some of the most influential, representative or enduring performers.

James Brown

Solid Gold: 30 Golden Hits, 21 Golden Years (POLYDOR 2929 034)

Please Please Please/Try Me/Good Good Lovin'/I'll Go Crazy/Think/Night Train/Out Of Sight/Papa's Got A Brand New Bag/I Got You/It's A Man's Man's Man's World/Cold Sweat/There Was A Time/I Got The Feelin'/Say It Loud, I'm Black And I'm Proud/Give It Up Or Turn It Loose/Mother Popcorn/Sex Machine/Superbad/Soul Power/Hot Pants/Make It Funky/Talking Loud And Saying Nothing/Honky Tonk/Get On The Good Foot/The Payback/My Thang/Papa Don't Take No Mess/Funky President/Hot/Get Up Offa That Thing

Nobody can challenge James Brown's right to the title he assumed in the sixties and has never relinquished – Soul Brother Number 1. In a career taking in around a hundred r&b chart entries, his influence has pervaded every corner of popular black music, reaching even to Jamaica and West Africa; and his presence has run like a unifying thread through the entire development of the soul genre. Born in Georgia to a poor family in 1928, his recording debut, fronting the Famous Flames vocal group, was 'Please Please Please' for Federal of Cincinnati, in 1956. A raw, wailing gospel-blues, it was a solid regional hit and was followed by a number of similar ballads before 'Try Me' gave him a foothold in the national market in 1958. He then put together the first of his regular bands and developed a ferocious line in dance numbers – 'I'll Go Crazy' and 'Think' in 1960, 'Night Train' in 1962. At the same time, he was generating an atmosphere of evangelical frenzy at his stage shows – one of which provided the million-selling

Live at the Apollo album (1962). And he was also extending his control over the business side of his career, eventually building up a complex commercial empire. His unique and paradoxical position, as the self-made black star who never forgot that he was addressing himself to the ghettos, gave him considerable symbolic political importance as black demands for equality gathered momentum during the sixties; and this, in turn, seemed to serve as a springboard for his musical advances. 'Out Of Sight' (1964) and 'Papa's Got A Brand New Bag' (1965) were contemporaneous with the earthy sounds of Memphis but were rhythmically much more adventurous – *and* managed to reach a mass international audience. The experimental nature of his style became more pronounced as the decade progressed. Song structures were loosened, and he began using *all* the instruments percussively, in line with the rediscovery of African roots among American blacks. The fractured bass lines, choked rhythm guitar and choppy brass of records like 'Cold Sweat' (1967), 'Mother Popcorn' (1969) and 'Superbad' (1970) created the vocabulary of the seventies funk boom: it was largely ex-J.B. sidemen who formed the basis of the George Clinton school of crazed heavy funk bands who have recently risen to prominence – bands such as Funkadelic, Parliament and Bootsy's Rubber Band. But despite the burgeoning competition from his host of imitators, Brown's uncompromising aggression and individuality has continued to stand out on records like 'Get On The Good Foot' (1972), 'Papa Don't Take No Mess' (1974), 'Hot' (1975) and 'Body Heat' (1976).

Ray Charles

A 25th Anniversary in Show Business Salute

(ATLANTIC 2659 009)

It Should've Been Me/Mess Around/Don't You Know/I Got A Woman/ A Fool For You/Hallelujah I Love Her So/Drown In My Own Tears/ Rockhouse/Lonely Avenue/Ain't That Love/Swanee River Rock/Night Time Is The Right Time/Mary Ann/I Believe To My Soul/What'd I Say/ Just For A Thrill/Yes Indeed/Don't Let The Sun Catch You Cryin'/ Georgia On My Mind/Unchain My Heart/Hit The Road Jack/One Mint Julep/Ruby/I Can't Stop Loving You/You Are My Sunshine/ Born To Lose/Busted/Cryin' Time/Let's Go Get Stoned/Yesterday/

Understand/Eleanor Rigby/If You Were Mine/Don't Change On Me/ Booty Butt/Feel So Bad

Ray Charles is black music's greatest eclectic, a man of gigantic talent and imagination whose work has constantly defied categorization. He was, above all, the first artist to fuse gospel, blues and jazz in a way that brought massive commercial success while remaining true to the essential spirit. His most important recordings are criminally hard to obtain at present, but a good retailer may still have copies of this double album from 1971, which is divided between the seminal period at Atlantic, where he was first marketed as the blind 'genius', and the material recorded for ABC/Paramount, which he joined late in 1959 in order to consolidate his position as a mass entertainer. At the time of 'It Should've Been Me' (1953), Charles was still feeling the influence of the club-jazz blues of Charles Brown, and hoping to follow in the footsteps of Nat 'King' Cole. 'I've Got A Woman' (1954) represents the first major stylistic breakthrough: it set the guidelines for a succession of hot r&b recordings, featuring an increasingly wide range of gospel characteristics and reaching its zenith in 1959 when the electrifying 'What'd I Say' became a million-selling pop hit. At ABC in the sixties, he continued to turn out some fine soul-jazz recordings – 'Hit The Road Jack', 'One Mint Julep', 'Sticks And Stones', 'Unchain My Heart'. But the use of string orchestras, begun at Atlantic, was greatly extended. This produced some superb performances, including 'Georgia On My Mind' and 'Ruby'; but while the *Modern Sounds in Country and Western Music* LPs gave him such enormous hits as 'I Can't Stop Loving You' and 'Take These Chains From My Heart', they also introduced a strong element of sentimentality, and he never fully recovered the intensity of his Atlantic heyday.

Sam Cooke

This is Sam Cooke (RCA VICTOR DPS 2007)

Frankie And Johnny/You Send Me/Sad Mood/Summertime/Chain Gang/ Baby, Baby, Baby/Only Sixteen/Love Will Find A Way/Bring It On Home To Me/Twistin' The Night Away/Feel It/For Sentimental Reasons/ Another Saturday Night/Wonderful World/Having A Party/Little Red

Rooster/Cupid/Sugar Dumpling/Send Me Some Lovin'/Everybody Loves To Cha Cha Cha

Though widely underrated in rock circles, Cooke was the most important pioneer of the sweet soul ballad tradition, and many key performers of the sixties – including Otis and Smokey – acknowledged their debt to him. He was a gospel star, the handsome idol of thousands of teenage girls, before he entered the world of pop represented by this collection: from 1950 to 1956 he sang lead with top church quartet the Soul Stirrers, developing a sublime, soaring style of controlled passion and rhythmic improvisation which survived almost unscathed when he ventured tentatively into the entertainment business with lightweight pop songs on Specialty such as 'Lovable' and 'I'll Come Running Back'. At first, he tried to avoid offending his gospel following by using the name Dale Cook; but when the Keen label bought a tape of 'You Send Me' the die was cast. It was a Number 1 pop hit in 1957, to be followed into the charts by further teen ballads, including 'Only Sixteen' and 'Wonderful World' in 1959, where his vocal genius transcended the insubstantial material. He signed for RCA in 1960, and while the company predictably steered him towards cabaret, and sometimes imposed overblown arrangements or shallow songs, they also discovered that material stemming directly from the black tradition, such as 'Bring It On Home To Me' and 'Sad Mood', would sell as pop. His hits – among them 'Chain Gang', 'Cupid' and 'Having A Party' – did nothing to diminish his stature in the black community. And when he died in a shooting incident at a Los Angeles motel in December 1964, Cooke left behind 'A Change Is Gonna Come', a haunting ballad that foreshadowed the imminent flowering of black political consciousness.

Otis Redding

The Best of Otis Redding (ATLANTIC K 60016)

Shake/Ole Man Trouble/Good To Me/I Can't Turn You Loose/I've Been Loving You Too Long/Tell The Truth/Satisfaction/Cigarettes And Coffee/Down In The Valley/These Arms Of Mine/Tramp/Fa-Fa-Fa-Fa-Fa (Sad Song)/Try A Little Tenderness/Rock Me Baby/That's How

Strong My Love Is/My Girl/Love Man/A Change Is Gonna Come/Just One More Day/Respect/Pain In My Heart/My Lover's Prayer/Chain Gang/You Don't Miss Your Water/Sittin' On The Dock Of The Bay

Otis Redding was by all accounts a constant source of inspiration to the musicians he worked with, and his colleague Carla Thomas is said to have attributed the entire Memphis sound to him. Yet for an artist of his indisputable stature and influence, the quality of his recorded work is extremely varied, with the greatest performances concentrated in 1964 and 1965. His debut for the Stax subsidiary Volt was the ballad 'These Arms Of Mine' in 1962, but 'Pain In My Heart' (1963) contained the first clear signs of the dense, churning arrangements which became the Stax trade-mark. The style crystallized in 1964 with the dark power of 'Mr Pitiful' and his most poignant ballad performance, 'I've Been Loving You Too Long'. He maintained the standard with 'Respect' in 1965. Then, later that year, came 'I Can't Turn You Loose' with its raw 'gotta, gotta' exclamations and pounding beat – the first in a line of similarly frenetic dance numbers apparently aimed at the growing white audience for soul. Redding's cover version of the Rolling Stones' 'Satisfaction' (1966) was confirmation of the trend. He had gained national acceptance only months before he died in a plane crash at the age of twenty-six in December 1967, and the posthumously issued 'Dock Of The Bay' was his only million-seller.

Wilson Pickett

Greatest Hits (ATLANTIC K 60038)

In The Midnight Hour/I Found A Love/634–5789/If You Need Me/Mustang Sally/Don't Fight It/Everybody Needs Somebody To Love/It's Too Late/99½ (Won't Do)/Funky Broadway/Soul Dance Number Three/Land Of 1,000 Dances/Don't Let The Green Grass Fool You/Sugar Sugar/Get Me Back On Time, Engine Number Nine/I'm A Midnight Mover/A Man And A Half/Mama Told Me Not To Come/She's Lookin' Good/I'm In Love/Don't Knock My Love, Part 1/Hey Jude/You Keep Me Hangin' On/I Found A True Love

Wilson Pickett first made an impact when he screamed the lead vocal on the Falcons' 'I Found A Love' (1961), which is often cited as the first 'soul' record. It was distributed by Atlantic, whose interest in the singer was revived when his original version of 'If You Need Me' was competing with the more polished rendition by the label's own Solomon Burke in 1963. Pickett was signed the following year and taken to Memphis, where he teamed up with Steve Cropper and the Stax band to create the trail-blazing hit 'In The Midnight Hour' in 1965. 'Don't Fight It' followed, before he switched to recording at Muscle Shoals, achieving hits in 1966 with '634–5789', '99½', 'Mustang Sally' and 'Land Of 1,000 Dances'. 'The Wicked Pickett' was now a major star, carrying a rugged black sound to the mass market with uniquely consistent success. But his harsh exhortations to get up and move became increasingly predictable, and his better performances in the later sixties were often ballads – such as 'Hey Jude' (1968), featuring Duane Allman's guitar. Gamble and Huff's Philadelphia sound gave his career a boost – 'Engine Number Nine', 1970 – but he has not established himself as an important seventies performer.

Smokey Robinson and the Miracles

Anthology (MOTOWN M793R3)

Got A Job/Bad Girl/Way Over There/Depend On Me/Shop Around/Who's Lovin' You/What's So Good About Goodbye/I'll Try Something New/I've Been Good To You/You've Really Got A Hold On Me/A Love She Can Count On/Mickey's Monkey/I Gotta Dance To Keep From Crying/I Like It Like That/That's What Love Is Made Of/Come On Do The Jerk/Ooo Baby Baby/The Tracks Of My Tears/My Girl Has Gone/Choosey Beggar/Going To A Go-Go/I'm The One You Need/Save Me/The Love I Saw In You Was Just A Mirage/More Love/I Second That Emotion/If You Can Want/Yester Love/Special Occasion/Baby, Baby Don't Cry/Doggone Right/Here I Go Again/Abraham, Martin and John/Darling Dear/Point It Out/Who's Gonna Take The Blame/The Tears Of A Clown/I Don't Blame You At All/Satisfaction/We've Come Too Far To End It Now/I Can't Stand To See You Cry

Smokey Robinson's talent as a composer – 'America's greatest living poet' in Bob Dylan's much-quoted phrase – is legendary; but his contributions as a performer and producer have been equally important. He was Berry Gordy's first signing to Tamla and blossomed immediately as a giant creative force. The Miracles gave the label its first Top Ten hit in 1960 with 'Shop Around', and Smokey's high tenor – fragile, but amazingly supple, precise and inventive – went on to grace several beautifully crafted ballad hits later in the decade, notably 'You've Really Got A Hold On Me' (1962) and 'Tracks Of My Tears' (1965). There were also some crackling up-tempo cuts like 'Mickey's Monkey' (1963) and 'Going To A Go-Go' (1965). His songs often explored the paradoxes of romance, and the gap between appearance and emotional reality. With consummate wit and elegance, he employed extended metaphors, antithesis and irony, bringing it home with incisive opening lines in the simplest of language: 'I don't like you, but I love you.' Some of his most memorable songs were written for Mary Wells, the Temptations and Marvin Gaye, whose records he frequently produced, helping to shape the mature Motown sound of the mid sixties. Smokey left the Miracles in 1972, and his subsequent solo output – although more subdued than the sixties material and lacking its dramatic immediacy – has been nonetheless excellent.

The Temptations

Anthology (MOTOWN M782A3)

The Way You Do The Things You Do/I'll Be In Trouble/The Girl's Alright With Me/Girl (Why You Wanna Make Me Blue)/My Girl/It's Growing/Since I Lost My Baby/My Baby/Don't Look Back/Get Ready/Ain't Too Proud To Beg/Beauty Is Only Skin Deep/(I Know) I'm Losing You/All I Need/You're My Everything/It's You That I Need/I Wish It Would Rain/I Truly, Truly Believe/I Could Never Love Another/Please Return Your Love To Me/Cloud Nine/Runaway Child, Running Wild/Don't Let The Joneses Get You Down/I Can't Get Next To You/Psychedelic Shack/Ball Of Confusion/Funky Music Sho Nuff Turns Me On/I Ain't Got Nothin'/Ol' Man River/Try To Remember/The Impossible Dream/I'm Gonna Make You Love Me/Just My Imagination/Superstar/Mother Nature/Love Woke Me Up This Morning/Papa Was A Rollin' Stone

The Temptations rode on the crest of the Motown wave to become the leading black vocal group during much of the sixties. Their prolonged success was partly due to their outstanding lead singers – the formidable baritone David Ruffin, who left to go solo in 1968, and the high-pitched Eddie Kendricks, who departed three years later. They were always in the vanguard of the Detroit sound's evolution, with Smokey Robinson masterminding their early hits, including the ingenious beat ballads 'The Way You Do The Things You Do', 'My Girl' (1964) and 'It's Growing' (1965). Their studio sound, under Robinson's guidance, grew to its full stature with 'Don't Look Back' and 'Get Ready', before Norman Whitfield took the reins in 1966 to produce the fiery 'Ain't Too Proud To Beg' (1966). Whitfield steered them into rock-influenced material with ambitious arrangements and lyrics, such as 'Cloud Nine' (1968) and the chart-topping 'I Can't Get Next To You' (1969). The crowning glory of this phase was 'Papa Was A Rollin' Stone' (1972), in which psychedelic sophistication and nitty-gritty funk were fused in a stunningly dramatic production. Later records, alternating disco-funk with harmony ballads, have been considerably less striking.

Marvin Gaye

Anthology (MOTOWN TMSP 1128)

Stubborn Kind Of Fellow/Hitch Hike/Pride And Joy/Can I Get A Witness/What's The Matter With You Baby/You're A Wonderful One/Try It Baby/Baby Don't You Do It/How Sweet It Is/I'll Be Doggone/Pretty Little Baby/Ain't That Peculiar/One More Heartache/Take This Heart Of Mine/Little Darling/It Takes Two/Your Unchanging Love/You/You're All I Need To Get By/Chained/You Ain't Livin' Till You're Lovin'/I Heard It Through The Grapevine/Too Busy Thinking About My Baby/That's The Way Love Is/The Onion Song/Abraham, Martin And John/What's Going On/Mercy Mercy Me (The Ecology)/Inner City Blues/Save The Children/Trouble Man/Let's Get It On/You're A Special Part Of Me

Marvin Gaye has performed on over fifty r&b hits, working with most of Motown's top producers and touching on many styles. He's essentially a studio craftsman rather than a great virtuoso singer, possessing a fairly light voice that's adaptable to moods of vulnerability, tenderness, strength or sensuality as required. The hits began with 'Stubborn Kind Of Fellow' (1962) and its swinging, handclapping feel was maintained in the classic 'Pride And Joy' and 'Can I Get A Witness'. A second phase, with Smokey Robinson producing, led to denser sounds, including 'Ain't That Peculiar' and 'I'll Be Doggone' (1965). Gaye has also specialized in romantic duets, teaming up with Mary Wells, Kim Watson, the late Tammi Terrell – the most successful partnership – and later with Diana Ross. Norman Whitfield helped him to a huge hit in 1968 with the tense, ominous 'I Heard It Through The Grapevine'. And in 1971 he switched direction abruptly, emerging as a superb album 'auteur' with *What's Going On*, an expansive, almost meditative collection of socially oriented ballads. He capped this with the spacious, sinuous eroticism of 'Let's Get It On' (1973), and while his output has diminished since then, 'Got To Give It Up' (1977) re-affirmed that he's still liable to come up with a fresh, vigorous sound at any time.

Curtis Mayfield

His Early Years with the Impressions

(PROBE GTSP 201)

Gypsy Woman/Amen/Keep On Pushing/I'm So Proud/People Get Ready/ We're A Winner/It's All Right/Woman's Got Soul/We're Rollin' On/ Never Let Me Go/Grow Closer Together/You Must Believe Me/Sad, Sad Girl And Boy/Talking About My Baby/I'm The One Who Loves You/Ridin' High/Emotions/Can't Work No Longer/Sometimes I Wonder/ Get Up And Move

In 1958, the solemnly devotional ballad 'For Your Precious Love', by the teenage Jerry Butler and the Impressions from Chicago, opened up new possibilities for the vocal group record. Its success took Butler off on a solo career to which one of the Impressions, Curtis Mayfield, contributed some compositions and guitar accompaniments. Then, in 1961, Mayfield did the trick for the Impressions themselves with the mellow exoticism of 'Gypsy Woman'. He went on to become the premier figure in northern city soul outside Detroit. Apart from the Impressions' sixties recordings represented by this LP, Mayfield supplied material for Major Lance and Gene Chandler; and in his collaboration on the production side with Johnny Pate and Carl Davis, a distinctive 'Chicago soul' sound was forged. It was a cool, graceful, finger-poppin' synthesis, dominated by taut vocals and stately brass riffs – a counterbalance to the more aggressive approach associated with Motown. At the same time, Mayfield's song-writing evolved to capture the essential mood of soul in the later sixties. The Impressions' 'It's All Right' (1963) was seminal, using a colloquial phrase that focussed social, religious and romantic meanings, and referred simultaneously to the music itself as a unifying force. He created what he called 'songs of faith and inspiration' – 'Keep On Pushing' (1964) and 'People Get Ready' (1965) – eventually making the black political element explicit in 'We're A Winner' (1968), 'Choice Of Colours' and 'Mighty Mighty Spade And Whitey' (1969). He went solo in 1970, and while some of his work since then has been less economic and acute, the *Superfly* sound-track (1972) was a masterpiece of ghetto song-sketches.

Sly and the Family Stone

Stand (CBS 63655)

Stand!/Don't Call Me Nigger, Whitey/I Want To Take You Higher/Somebody's Watching You/Sing A Simple Song/Everyday People/Sex Machine/You Can Make It If You Try

Sly Stone instigated a whole new current of soul by way of a manic exploration of the possibilities of black–white cultural interaction. This 1969 LP was both a peak and a turning point in his career. The ritualistic 'I Want To Take You Higher' summed up his interpretation of the spirit of the boogie – the end of a road that began with the volatile mixture of the number 'Dance To The Music' in 1967. His bass/drum dynamics owed something to James Brown, but the sound was spacier, peppered with wild interjections on sax and guitar. And the voices butted in unpredictably – black and white, male and female – modifying doo-wop and gospel, wailing the blues or delivering blunt choral chants. In songs like 'Life' and 'M'Lady', the bright colours of psychedelia mingled with the earthy solidity and emotionalism of the black sixties mainstream in a celebration of music as the great integrator. But *Stand* also contained hints of the tougher, more sardonic vision to come. A new Sly emerged late in 1971 on *There's A Riot Going On*, a record of low-key hypnotic rhythms and oblique self-questioning: 'Feel so good/Don't wanna move.' But while *Riot* was a salutary event in modern pop, his earlier stylistic adventures probably had a more lasting influence on other performers.

Aretha Franklin

Ten Years of Gold (ATLANTIC SD 18204)

I Never Loved A Man (The Way I Love You)/Respect/Baby I Love You/ A Natural Woman/Think/See Saw/Spanish Harlem/Rock Steady/Day Dreaming/Angel/Until You Come Back To Me/Something He Can Feel

It was Atlantic that first did justice to the majesty of Aretha Franklin, and this album brings together twelve of her most successful singles for the company. She signed late in 1966 at the age of twenty-four, after starting with gospel – her father was a prominent Baptist preacher in Detroit – and then spending six years with Columbia, fruitlessly seeking an appropriate setting for her chillingly intense vocals. Atlantic's Jerry Wexler then took her to Muscle Shoals, where she cut the song that established her – Ronnie Shannon's 'I Never Loved A Man (The Way I Love You)'. To an austere and meticulous accompaniment, she ran the emotional gamut, from a fierce pride to anguished vulnerability and desire, in a three-minute re-definition of soul. Other hits followed quickly, with 'A Natural Woman', 'Baby I Love You', 'Think' and a strutting version of 'Respect' standing out. Her subsequent career has been uneven, dogged by personal crises and lapses into the style of Las Vegas. There have nevertheless been many superb recordings during the seventies, including worth-while collaborations with Quincy Jones and Curtis Mayfield. Her fire and spirit are nowhere more apparent than on the *Amazing Grace* gospel album, recorded live in church in 1972.

Isaac Hayes

Chronicle

(STAX/EMI STM 7003)

Theme From Shaft/*Walk On By*/*Ain't That Lovin' You*/*Theme From* The Men/*I Stand Accused*/*Do Your Thing*/*Never Can Say Goodbye*/*Let's Stay Together*/*Joy, Part 1*/*By The Time I Get To Phoenix*

Hayes was one of the stalwarts of Stax during its sixties golden age. He played keyboards on many hits, and was producer and writer of others – notably in partnership with David Porter in the long run of dazzling Sam and Dave singles. But it was the unprecedented format of the *Hot Buttered Soul* LP in 1969 that made him a star in his own right. The set contained only four tracks – one of them, 'By The Time I Get To Phoenix', nearly nineteen minutes long. It was a huge commercial success, and in the years up to 1974 covered by this collection, Hayes refined and extended this new approach, with the chattering wah-wah and staccato brass of the *Shaft* sound-track marking the summit of his international fame, and providing the model for countless Hollywood themes. Hayes had an immense impact on the direction of soul, though it wasn't all to the good. On the one hand, his use of large orchestras and extended monologues led to the vapid Barry White school of sophistisoul. But he also created space for soul artists to extend their musical ideas on record, and gained wider acceptance for styles derived from jazz. He left Stax in 1974 after a royalties row, and his later work for ABC has been largely disco-oriented.

Al Green

Greatest Hits

(LONDON SHU 8481)

Sha La La/*Here I Am*/*I'm Still In Love With You*/*You Ought To Be With Me*/*Call Me*/*Let's Stay Together*/*How Can You Mend A Broken Heart*/*Look What You Done For Me*/*I Can't Get Next To You*/*Let's Get Married*/*Tired Of Being Alone*

Willie Mitchell's Hi studios generated another Memphis sound to stand alongside Stax, providing the framework for Al Green to climb to stardom in the early seventies. The economy and restraint of the style contrasted sharply with the priorities of much popular soul at the time. The first of his many hits was a tense, insidious version of the Temptations/Norman Whitfield song 'I Can't Get Next To You' (1970), in which the big-city production job was replaced by the musical equivalent of a pressure-cooker. Green's vocal acrobatics were clearly gospel-based, but he always kept well short of catharsis; and while the Hi formula was beginning to sound a little stale by the latter part of the seventies, it is a classic branch of southern soul. Other performers who have made excellent records with Mitchell include Ann Peebles – especially the slow-burning 'I'm Gonna Tear Your Playhouse Down' – and Syl Johnson.

The Staple Singers

Bealtitude: Respect Yourself (STAX 2325 069)

This World/Respect Yourself/Name The Missing Word/I'll Take You There/This Old Town/We The People/Are You Sure/Who Do You Think You Are? (Jesus Christ The Superstar)/I'm Just Another Soldier/Who

The Staples epitomize the gospel essence of soul, and this album – released in 1972 – was their definitive statement. It consummated the movement by which the music came to transcend its earlier limitations of subject-matter and address itself to the whole experience of black Americans. The group had been recording for fifteen years as a church quartet before they began making 'soul' hits for Stax in 1968. They featured the guitar of Roebuck 'Pops' Staples and the jagged, kaleidoscopic lead vocals of his daughter Mavis, supported by her sisters Cleotha and Yvonne. Both 'Respect Yourself' and 'I'll Take You There' went high in the singles charts. And in later recordings such as 'If You're Ready' (1973) and 'City In The Sky' (1974), they retained their special blend of the devout, the angry and the sensual. They went on to collaborate with Curtis Mayfield.

Various Artists

Phillybusters: The Sound of Philadelphia

(PHILADELPHIA INTERNATIONAL PIR 65869)

Back Stabbers (O'Jays)/Dirty Ol' Man (Three Degrees)/Family Affair (MFSB)/I'll Always Love My Mama (Intruders)/If You Don't Know Me By Now (Harold Melvin and the Blue Notes)/Me And Mrs Jones (Billy Paul)/I Miss You (Harold Melvin and the Blue Notes)/I Can't Quit Your Love (Bobby Taylor)/Tossin' And Turnin' (Bunny Sigler)/It's Forever (Ebonys)/Slow Motion (Johnny Williams)/Love Train (O'Jays)

The Philadelphia producers and arrangers, Kenny Gamble, Leon Huff and Thom Bell, have been the pacesetters in northern production soul in the seventies. A coherent Gamble–Huff style first emerged in their work with Jerry Butler in the late sixties, but it was when they formed Philadelphia International Records in 1971, in a tie-up with Columbia, that their golden period of national hits got fully under way. Their characteristic strength was in blending huge, shimmering orchestrations with the tight, funky core of the MFSB band in a way that seemed to reinforce rather than detract from the power and soulfulness of their brilliant roster of performers. The *Phillybusters* set – issued in 1974 – shows the approach at its commercial and artistic peak, including some of the finest recordings by the O'Jays and the Blue Notes together with less renowned gems such as the Johnny Williams and Ebonys tracks. Bell, who often worked for PIR, specialized in providing lush yet incisive arrangements for vocal groups working in an updated doo-wop vein, and enjoyed enormous success with the Delfonics and the Stylistics. His greatest achievements, however, were at Atlantic in 1972–6 with the ex-Motown group the Spinners.

Kool and the Gang

Greatest Hits (POLYDOR 2310 401)

Funky Stuff/Jungle Boogie/Hollywood Swinging/The Gang's Back Again/Let The Music Take Your Mind/Kool And The Gang/Higher Plane/Rhyme Time People/Rated X/Good Times/Music Is The Message/ Funky Man

Among the more inventive of the 'street-funk' bands who sprang up in the wake of Sly and James Brown were the Ohio Players, Graham Central Station and the early Fatback Band, with the Commodores eventually coming through as Motown's smoother contenders in the field. But Kool and the Gang were perhaps the most representative, and arguably the best. They emphasized their self-contained precision, their power and the pursuit of fun. Incorporating jazz inflections and chords – they started out in New Jersey as the Jazziacs – the Gang declared with every move that black pop performers need not be dominated by producers and session-men. Lyrics and tunes were played down; they were primarily interested in ensemble horn sounds and danceability, with Robert 'Kool' Bell's pile-driving bass controlling and directing the proceedings. Beginning with Sly imitations such as 'Let The Music Take Your Mind' (1970), they gradually developed an original style, and the raw excitement of the hits from 'Funky Stuff' (1973) to 'Spirit Of The Boogie' (1975) were essential to the disco boom.

Stevie Wonder

Innervisions (MOTOWN STMA 8011)

Too High/Visions/Living For The City/Golden Lady/Higher Ground/ Jesus Children Of America/All In Love Is Fair/Don't You Worry 'Bout A Thing/He's Misstra Know-It-All

Stephen Judkins was earmarked for genius status from the time he joined Motown at the age of eleven, and was promoted as a kind of pocket Ray Charles (another blind musician) under the name Little Stevie Wonder. After topping the charts with the rousing 'Fingertips, Part Two' in 1963, he succeeded with formula dance material like 'Uptight' (1965) and more romantic songs like 'I Was Made To Love Her' (1967). But it wasn't until 1970 that his moment really arrived. The idiosyncratic *Where I'm Coming From* LP pointed the way to a style which crystallized in 'Music Of My Mind' (1972). Heavily influenced by psychedelic rock and Latin rhythms, playing virtually all the instruments himself – notably electronic keyboards – and making full use of sophisticated production techniques, he used his firm Detroit foundations to build a singular form of 'black singer/songwriter rock' which was both commercially successful and won over the white critics. *Talking Book* (1972) has received the most acclaim of the seventies albums, but its successor *Innervisions* is a slightly sharper, tougher set, benefitting from the use of excellent sidemen and including some of his most durable songs. The album is also relatively sparing with the half-realized quasi-mystical lyrics which particularly marred parts of *Fulfillingness' First Finale* (1974). The long-awaited *Songs in the Key of Life* appeared in 1976 after he'd signed a new contract for the biggest ever advance – $13 million.

Millie Jackson

Caught Up (SPRING/POLYDOR 2391 147)

If Loving You Is Wrong I Don't Want To Be Right/The Rap/All I Want Is A Fighting Chance/I'm Tired Of Hiding/It's All Over But The Shouting/It's Easy Going/I'm Through Trying To Prove My Love To You/Summer (The First Time)

Millie Jackson's early singles for Spring – including 'Child Of God' (1972) and 'It Hurts So Good' (1973) – showed her to be a uniquely powerful vocalist with an emphatically populist stance. But it was this 1974 'concept' album – a comparative rarity in soul – that confirmed her stature as the most important female singer of the genre to emerge in the seventies. Following in the path of the Soul Children's *Friction* set, issued on Stax a few months earlier, she proved that it was possible to introduce an extended semi-narrative structure without losing any of the bite of the traditional three-minute format of hard-core r&b. It consists of a cycle of songs, old and new, and prolonged 'raps', all on the time-honoured theme of marital infidelity. Over the pithy but spacious backdrop supplied by the Muscle Shoals band she acts out moods ranging from the hilarious, to the raunchy, to the desperately passionate, in a tour-de-force vocal performance. Her later career has been less strikingly inventive but remarkably consistent, and included a fine set in 1978, *Get It Outcha System.*

The Isley Brothers

Forever Gold (EPIC 86040)

That Lady/Live It Up/Hello It's Me/(At Your Best) You Are Love/ Fight The Power/For The Love Of You/Hope You Feel Better Love/ The Highways Of My Life/Harvest For The World/Summer Breeze

Rudolph, Ronald and Kelly Isley had been a successful act for nearly fifteen years before they began making the rock-soul hits compiled here. 'Shout' (1959) and 'Twist And Shout' (1962) were gospel-r&b milestones, and at Motown they had performed on the Holland–Dozier blockbuster 'This Old Heart Of Mine' (1966). They left Motown in 1969 to revive their own company, T-Neck, and augmented their line-up with two younger brothers – Ernie on guitar and Marvin on bass – plus Chris Jasper on keyboards. The Isleys then set about creating some of the most imaginative black pop music of the seventies. 'That Lady' (1973) set the pace, with Ernie's spectacular synthesized lead suggesting he'd learned something from a former sideman of the group, Jimi Hendrix. Several dance hits followed, including 'Live It Up' (1974) and 'Fight The Power' (1975), with the hard funk of the rhythm section balancing the sweet, high-pitched vocals. They've also produced some of the best romantic ballads of recent years, particularly 'Summer Breeze'. In 1978, 'Take Me To The Next Phase' proved their ability to refresh their style when the need arose and gave them another million-seller.

Joe Tex

Bumps and Bruises (EPIC 81931)

Ain't Gonna Bump No More/Leaving You Dinner/Be Cool (Willie Is Dancing With A Sissy)/I Mess Up Everything I Get My Hands On/We Held On/I Almost Got To Heaven Once/Hungry For Your Love/Jump Bad/There's Something Wrong

Joe Tex rose to prominence in the mid sixties with an inimitable series of tongue-in-cheek, sermonizing ballads, recorded principally in Muscle Shoals and including 'Hold What You've Got' and 'A Sweet Woman Like You'. His slightly detached stance – paralleling, in some ways, Chuck Berry's relationship to rock & roll – worked for him again in 1976 when he returned from a period as a Muslim preacher to achieve a huge hit with 'Ain't Gonna Bump No More (With No Big Fat Woman)'. 'She knocked me down, she broke ma hip,' he alleges, to the accompaniment of a driving pop-disco rhythm. The record injected a much-needed dose of energy and wit into an increasingly stereotyped area, and the rest of the LP confirms that his ebullience and sly charm remain largely intact. It was recorded in Nashville, reflecting the strong current of country music that's always been present in his material.

Soul : Singles

Gladys Knight and the Pips: *Every Beat Of My Heart* (1961)

One of the greatest female soul voices with her earliest and perhaps loveliest hit, written by Johnny Otis.

Booker T and the MGs: *Green Onions* (1962)

The forceful yet easy sound of the group at the heart of Stax.

Major Lance: *Um Um Um Um Um Um* (1963)

A landmark of Mayfield's Chicago school, obliquely re-stating the notion that soul can't be understood through explanation, only through feeling.

Solomon Burke: *Everybody Needs Somebody To Love* (1964)

'The King of Rock and Soul' at his testifying best.

Sam and Dave: *You Don't Know Like I Know* (1965)

The duo's vibrant vocal interplay is given full weight by a pile-driving Hayes–Porter production. Their peak.

Darrell Banks: *Open The Door To Your Heart* (1966)

A masterpiece of grinding, shuffling southern funk, considerably more complex rhythmically than the average Stax single of the day.

Percy Sledge: *When A Man Loves A Woman* (1966)

The aching vocal, a vividly precise lyric, and the lean Muscle Shoals backing featuring chapel-inspired organ, make this one of the purest of soul classics.

The Four Tops: *Reach Out, I'll Be There* (1966)

The stunning climax of the work of the Holland–Dozier–Holland team. Definitive Motown.

Laura Lee: *Dirty Man* (1967)

The performer whose scorching vocals and earthy wit set a pattern for Millie Jackson; here at her peak in Muscle Shoals.

The Radiants: *Hold On* (1969)

A manic, crashing beat and searing vocals make this an evergreen of Chicago dance soul.

Jackson Five: *I Want You Back* (1969)

Simply one of the most exciting and imaginative pop records ever made. It launched the group as major stars.

Donny Hathaway: *The Ghetto* (1970)

At one time, Hathaway's multi-faceted talent – especially his keyboard work – seemed at least as substantial as Stevie Wonder's. He faded into obscurity, but this still sounds magnificent. He died in 1979.

Bill Withers: *Ain't No Sunshine/Grandma's Hands* (1971)

Withers' first single showed the directness, warmth and intelligence which made him an important seventies figure, best heard in the Carnegie Hall live album.

Betty Wright: *Clean Up Woman* (1971)

A superb example of the influential records put out on the TK group of labels in Florida, with the stylish teenage singer supported by some amazing guitar licks from Willie 'Little Beaver' Hale.

Linda Jones: *For Your Precious Love* (1972)

Lorraine Ellison's 'Stay With Me' is sometimes cited as the quintessential 'deep soul' record, but this spine-chilling piece of histrionic desolation has the edge.

The Chi-lites: *Have You Seen Her?* (1972)

The eccentric ingenuity of producer/lead singer/song-writer Eugene Record enabled this superficially corny hit to transcend camp and be genuinely touching.

Johnnie Taylor: *I've Been Born Again* (1974)

A sublime and immaculately played example of pure southern soul from one of the most consistent Stax performers, now with Columbia.

Don Covay: *It's Better To Have (And Don't Need)* (1974)

A sizzling renaissance for the man responsible for such earlier classics as 'Mercy Mercy' and 'See Saw'.

The Emotions: *Best Of My Love* (1977)

An exuberant smash-hit from the ex-Stax female vocal group, with producer Maurice White demonstrating that a disco orientation need not stifle musical ideas.

Funkadelic: *One Nation Under A Groove* (1978)

'The funk, the whole funk, nothing but the funk.' George Clinton's demonic bunch take J.B./Sly basics to the merry outer limits of sanity and the top of the r & b charts.

JOHN COLLIS

Country

Country music, developing from Anglo-Celtic immigrant origins, has become so diversified that perhaps we must fall back on Kris Kristofferson's definition, which precedes his recording of 'Me and Bobby McGee': 'If it sounds country, man, that's what it is – a country song.' In other words, you know it when you hear it. Some can hear it in the ballads of black soul singers Percy Sledge and Solomon Burke, or in the rock & roll of long-haired Texan bar-bands. At another extreme it can simply be a repository of blue-collar, right-wing moralizing. This political aspect cannot be ignored, though its dilution is one of the beneficial aspects of the spread of the music. Country grew from the home-made music of poor, hard-working, uneducated southern whites, and if they were lucky enough to grasp the opportunity of pursuing the American Dream, their grasp was inevitably a self-centred and defensive one. Southern culture and economics were originally based on the exploitation of slave labour. It was because of this, indirectly, that the music took root in the South: settlers from the British Isles landed in other parts of America as well, bringing their ballads and folk songs with them, but in the South they developed an inward-looking, protective character which deliberately isolated them from the rest of the country, and prevented the immediate dispersion of their indigenous music. Even now, southerners find themselves ranged against northerners, intellectuals, sophisticates, other minority groups – anyone who isn't them, and somehow threatens them. Inevitably country music has become in part a defiant expression of southern pride, standing by to repel boarders. But as its followers have migrated in search of work – to the fruit-growing West during the Depression, to the farms of the Mid-west, and to the industrial North – they have taken their music with them.

The music of the South is polyglot: to those Anglo-Celtic ballads which can be taken as the basis of 'hillbilly' music must be added, for example, the jazz and rhythm & blues of New Orleans, the French-Canadian music of Louisiana, the polkas of German settlers a little further west, the blues of Texas and the Mississippi Delta, and the Spanish music of Mexico. The development of Western Swing in the Texas of the twenties symbolizes this: it is now seen as a form of country music, but it has equally strong elements of big-band jazz and urban blues.

The original hillbillies were untouched by these influences, which only began to filter in during the early years of this century. When they settled as pioneering farmers in the hills of Virginia, the Carolinas, Kentucky and Tennessee, they sang their British narrative songs to the accompaniment of home-made fiddles and dulcimers. As the songs became adapted to reflect their new life, so other stringed instruments were introduced, particularly guitar, banjo and mandolin. 'Bluegrass' music is directly derived from these early rural string bands.

As the descendants of the early settlers travelled further south and west, before the spread of radio, they would pick up other influences – black guitar styles and the jazz of the cities, for example – and learn new songs. The 1920s, with the arrival of both radio and gramophone, enabled the music to be instantly, and commercially, disseminated for the first time. Of the radio shows that came into being, the most famous is 'The Grand Ole Opry', which started in Nashville, Tennessee in 1925, and still exists. It has always been broadcast live as a sponsored concert, acting as a magnet for fans of the music, and must be one of the major reasons why Nashville has become the commercial centre of country & western. The record companies, too, moved in to exploit the music, just as they were beginning to do with Negro blues ('race music') and as a result a tubercular ex-railroad man from Mississippi, Jimmie Rodgers, became country music's first 'superstar' by the end of the decade. The Carter Family, too, were profusely recorded, playing the pure 'mountain music' of Virginia (see 'Folk & Blues'): thus the 'ethnic' basis of country music was preserved in unsullied form.

Although still confined largely to the South, and to the South-west as a result of migration, country music was now a business, in spite of the Depression, and soon lost its exclusively home-made character. Performers could now be paid for appearances on record and radio, and on travelling road-shows. This growth continued throughout the thirties, together with the progressive infiltration of other regional musical influences.

Another significant change in the organization of this new 'industry' occurred in 1939. In order to make a living from his songs, a writer has to be affiliated to a body which 'licenses' his music, monitors its use, and collects the royalties for broadcast performances. Until this time, there was only one such organization, the American Society of Composers, Authors and Publishers, which, being northern orientated, had proved resistant to 'hillbilly' music. In 1939 they increased their licensing rates to radio stations to an unacceptable degree, which led to the formation of a rival organization, Broadcast Music Incorporated. BMI were more receptive to the song-writers of the South, who suddenly found available the revenue-collecting set-up they had previously been denied. No doubt ASCAP would eventually have broadened their outlook without this breaking of their monopoly, but the 1939 confrontation resulted immediately in potentially nation-wide exposure for country performers, at a time when ever-increasing migration was spreading the demand for them. Furthermore, the war brought people from different parts of the continent together, exposing many of them to country music for the first time.

The second 'great' of c&w came to prominence in the late forties, by which time its regional nature had been broken down enough for him to become a national star. Hank Williams came from Alabama, and like Jimmie Rodgers had learnt as much from the black musicians he knew in his youth as from the hillbilly music on the radio. His first hit, 'Lovesick Blues' in 1949, was not one of his own compositions, but during his short career he was to write more 'standards' than anyone. His life has unfortunately become a musical blueprint – the country boy suddenly presented with money and fame, fatally destroying his career with alcohol and pills. It would seem that Williams was one of those with a low resistance to narcotics, with the result that he was blacklisted by promoters as unreliable at the very time that his fame was at its height.

Although the c&w industry could remain immune to the early stirrings of rock & roll, particularly in its urban and northern manifestations, and shrug it off as 'nigger music', it was ironically a young hillbilly who became the figure-head of the revolution in the mid fifties. On

Presley's early records – while he was still a local phenomenon causing a sensation on 'Louisiana Hayride', a rival to 'The Grand Ole Opry' – one of his re-interpretations of a black song would be carefully coupled with a hillbilly number, for Tennessee consumption. Rock & roll, bringing with it the cult of youth and rebellion, hit the traditional country artists hard.

As a result of rock & roll, the young generation of country performers adopted the new style to a varying degree – Carl Perkins, Jerry Lee Lewis, Gene Vincent, the Everly Brothers – and the galloping expansion of country music, by now firmly centred on Nashville, was contained for almost a decade. Of this generation, only Johnny Cash became hugely successful in a more traditional style, and as a result of his persistence is now seen as the third of the very great artists, in company with Rodgers and Williams. Many of the older artists made attempts to accommodate the youthful music with varying degrees of success; others just waited resentfully for it to blow over.

Of course the revival came, and many of the rock & rollers (Perkins, Lewis and the Everlys as well as many lesser lights such as Conway Twitty) drifted back to country music. I would argue that one of the major turning-points was the curious decision by Ray Charles, in 1962, to record two albums of country & western standards. Charles, with his unique and influential fusion of gospel and blues, was as revolutionary an influence on black rhythm & blues music in the fifties as was James Brown, and yet he suddenly grabbed a handful of hillbilly tunes and surrounded them with lush arrangements. But if anyone could indicate, to those with ears to hear, the essential similarities between rhythm & blues and country, it had to be Charles: he had a huge following who would never have listened to c&w, and he had the interpretive genius to draw the best from the songs. His 'betrayal' was shocking, but many blues fans had their minds broadened.

Perhaps the 'British invasion' helped country & western back to its feet. The raw power of early rock & roll had long been neutralized, and many Americans turned back to their own musical tradition. The sixties saw a huge expansion in the number of country-music radio stations, and the industry in Nashville, and to a lesser degree in other cities such as Bakersfield in California ('Nashville West'), expanded to feed the demand. The television companies woke up to this, and more and more country stars found themselves hosting networked shows. Inevitably, at this time the definition of a 'country song' became broader, to take in the simple, gut-bucket style of the early fifties, the harder edge of the rock & roll generation, the syrupy patriotism fuelled by the Vietnam War, shimmering violins, the contemporary 'folk' style that had developed in the coffee-houses and the foot-stamping dexterity of bluegrass, as well as Bob Dylan and the Byrds.

The dominant sound emanating from Nashville in the late sixties and early seventies was one of entrenchment, of nostalgia for understandable values in a world that was clearly changing. Kennedy's America had changed to Nixon's, but in the meantime people had had their automatic beliefs rudely questioned – there were even troublemakers doubting the imperial righteousness of conducting a squalid war in a tiny country halfway across the world. Mainstream country became a comforting cocoon of schmaltz, and an ever-widening audience was ready for it. Producer and writer Billy Sherrill tapped this mood perfectly via Tammy Wynette; her songs were only concerned with marriage and its problems, problems comprehensible to a vast audience confused by wider issues. The best popular music is almost invariably about sex, but the successful country records of the time limited their points of reference to those of a particular listenership: the proud and ambitious lower middle class. They required old-fashioned 'sincerity' with new, sweet production techniques. It is noticeable that the other large record-buying section of the population, the young and educated, had themselves turned, by the mid seventies, to slick, bland, inoffensive music, much of it distantly originating in country & western; music that is usually gutless, but immaculately performed and produced.

The dominance of Nashville as the centre of country-music activity has not seriously been challenged. Bakersfield remains largely based on the success of its two stars, Merle Haggard and Buck Owens, and the Texas city of Austin did not develop an industry. The importance of Austin grew in the early seventies; it had an attractive atmosphere and a local folk/country scene based around the university. Performers from outside drifted to the city – Doug Sahm, Jerry Jeff Walker and notably Willie Nelson (who by his move was consciously rejecting the direction in which Nashville was going) – but it would seem that the 'business side', record companies, recording studios and entrepreneurs, did not follow the artists to a sufficient degree. However, much of the vitality of contemporary country music does come from Texas, while the performers in Nashville continue to look for ways to broaden their appeal and increase their income – 'a race for Las Vegas', as one producer puts it, which inevitably threatens to enervate the genre. But while Dolly Parton and Bill Anderson pioneer 'country disco', there are still bands like that of Joe Ely, musicians who grew up with rock & roll, who are injecting a much-needed dose of vitality into the continuing tradition of country music.

Country : Albums

Jimmie Rodgers

A Legendary Performer (RCA PL 12504)

Sleep Baby Sleep/T For Texas/In The Jailhouse Now No. 2/Ben Dewberry's Final Run/You And My Old Guitar/Whippin' That Old TB/TB Blues/Mule Skinner Blues/Old Love Letters/Home Call

A sample album illustrating the quaint artistry of Rodgers is included here for the sake of historical completeness: he is often referred to as 'the father of country music', becoming famous during the years of the Depression. 'The Singing Brakeman', so called because of his love of the railroads which provided the subject matters of many of his songs, was born in Meridian, Mississippi, in 1897, and died after a long battle with TB in 1933. His songs usually had a blues base, a reminder that he, like so many subsequent country performers, was taught to play the guitar by blacks. His simple strumming style is reminiscent of the great black artist Leadbelly, but without echoes of the latter's forceful personality. His songs were usually sentimental, often featuring his yodelling 'trade-mark', though the recommended album includes two defiant songs about the TB that was killing him. He can have little appeal to the contemporary country audience, but was a giant of the early recording industry who is naturally remembered with pride by the traditional country fraternity.

Hank Williams

40 Greatest Hits

(MGM 2683 071)

Move It On Over/A Mansion On The Hill/Lovesick Blues/Wedding Bells/Mind Your Own Business/You're Gonna Change/Lost Highway/ My Bucket's Got A Hole In It/I Just Don't Like This Kind Of Living/ Long Gone Lonesome Blues/My Son Calls Another Man Daddy/Why Don't You Love Me/Why Should We Try Anymore/They'll Never Take Her Love From Me/Moanin' The Blues/Nobody's Lonesome For Me/ Cold Cold Heart/Dear John/Howlin' At The Moon/I Can't Help It/Hey Good Lookin'/Crazy Heart/Lonesome Whistle/Baby, We're Really In Love/Ramblin' Man/Honky Tonk Blues/I'm Sorry For You My Friend/ Half As Much/Jambalaya/Window Shopping/Settin' The Woods On Fire/You Win Again/I'll Never Get Out Of This World Alive/Kaw-Liga/ Your Cheatin' Heart/Take These Chains From My Heart/I Won't Be Home No More/Weary Blues From Waitin'/I Saw The Light

After Jimmie Rodgers, Williams was the second 'giant' of country music, and most would agree that he is the genre's greatest figure. He achieved this in a very short time, dying of booze and drugs at the age of twenty-nine, on New Year's Day 1953, having been almost single-handedly responsible for the boom in country music immediately after the war. The nasal voice, Hawaiian guitar and droning fiddles may sound rather old-fashioned nowadays, but the power of Williams's singing and his extraordinary ability to synthesize emotions into simple, memorable songs ensure that his appeal is still apparent. Williams was the first country artist whose fame spread beyond the southern states, and during his lifetime such mainstream singers as Tony Bennett and Jo Stafford had national hits with his songs. This laid the basis for country music's progressively broadening appeal, to the point where, now, an originally 'pure' country singer like Dolly Parton can become an international star. Williams started this process, however, without compromising his music. It is worth noting that the first song on the album, 'Move It On Over', would now be recognized as pure rockabilly, though it was recorded in 1947.

Johnny Cash

Old Golden Throat (CHARLY CR 300005)

Big River/Luther's Boogie/You Are My Baby/Folsom Prison Blues/Hey Porter/Next In Line/Oh Lonesome Me/Belshazah/Get Rhythm/Rock Island Line/Country Boy/Train Of Love/I Walk The Line/Katy Too/ Ballad Of A Teenage Queen/Mean Eyed Cat

Of the living country singers, Cash is the 'biggest', though the distinctiveness of his style and the unusual timbre of his voice have limited his direct influence on those who have come afterwards. He started his career on Sun in 1955, having formed a trio in Memphis with bassist Marshall Grant and guitarist Luther Perkins, the 'limitations' of whose style in fact helped to give early Cash records their unique sound. With 'Guess Things Happen That Way' (1957) Cash moved into the national pop charts, as well as the localized country listings, and successive records like 'Ways Of A Woman In Love' were also pop hits. His career then faded slightly, perhaps due to the similar sound of his records, and he moved to the Columbia label for a new period of success in 1958. His career took another dip in the early sixties, aggravated by his growing addiction to pills, but revived in 1963 with 'Ring Of Fire'. He was eventually cured of his addiction through his relationship with June Carter, whom he married in 1967, and when he recorded an album live at Folsom Prison in the following year he was re-established in the top position that he has occupied since. There is a profusion of Cash albums available: the recommended one is a sample of his early Sun work, but 'Folsom Prison' (CBS 63308) is equally important. In common with many country stars Cash puts out too many albums, with the inevitable quota of 'filler material', but in 1976 he released *One Piece at a Time* (CBS 81416), which gives a startling display of his range and is one of the best 'mainstream' country records of the decade.

Nitty Gritty Dirt Band

Will the Circle be Unbroken

(UNITED ARTISTS UAS 9801)

Grand Ole Opry Song/Keep On The Sunny Side/Nashville Blues/You Are My Flower/The Precious Jewel/Dark As A Dungeon/Tennessee Stud/Black Mountain Rag/Wreck On The Highway/The End Of The World/I Saw The Light/Sunny Side Of The Mountain/Nine Pound Hammer/Losin' You/Honky Tonkin'/You Don't Know My Mind/My Walkin' Shoes/Lonesome Fiddle Blues/Cannonball Rag/Avalanche/Flint Hill Special/Togary Mountain/Earl's Breakdown/Orange Blossom Special/Wabash Cannonball/Lost Highway/Way Downtown/Down Yonder/Pins and Needles/Honky Tonk Blues/Sailin' On To Hawaii/I'm Thinking Tonight Of My Blue Eyes/I Am A Pilgrim/Wildwood Flower/Soldier's Joy/Will The Circle Be Unbroken/Both Sides Now

This remarkable triple-album project is perhaps the first record that the newcomer to country music should consider buying. Country-rock band the Nitty Gritty Dirt Band moved into Nashville, overcame the prejudice among the old country performers against 'long-hairs', and acted as backing band to an impressive list of the country 'greats', including Mother Maybelle Carter, Earl Scruggs, Doc Watson, Roy Acuff, Merle Travis and Jimmy Martin. The result is a kaleidoscopic anthology of country music. It climaxes on a version of A. P. Carter's classic 'Will The Circle Be Unbroken' which features everyone involved in the project, and then ends provocatively with an instrumental version of Joni Mitchell's 'Both Sides Now', performed by Earl Scruggs' guitarist son Randy. On the long journey through the album we have heard the masters revive their hits, with some spellbinding examples of instrumental country picking, and occasionally revealing snippets of studio conversation. It hardly matters that such veterans as Roy Acuff and Maybelle Carter are no longer in perfect voice; this ambitious exercise is a success only qualified by the infuriating complexity of the album packaging.

Bill Monroe

Best of Bill Monroe and His Blue Grass Boys (MCA MCF 2696)

Mule Skinner Blues/Devil's Dream/Walking In Jerusalem/Roanoke/I'm Travelling On And On/Blue Moon Of Kentucky/I Saw The Light/Get Up John/McKinley's March/Whitehouse Blues/Uncle Pen/Rawhide/Footprints In The Snow/I'm Going Back To Old Kentucky/Kentucky Mandolin/Molly And Tenbrooks/I'm Working On A Building/My Little Georgia Rose/Don't Put Off 'Til Tomorrow/I'm On My Way Back To The Old Home

Bluegrass is a derivative of one of the oldest American musical forms, that of the rural string bands. Emphasis is not so much on the guitar, which features as a backing instrument, as on banjo, fiddle and mandolin: bluegrass is a heavily syncopated style often played at breakneck speed, which in large doses can sometimes sound mechanical to the unconverted. The 'father' of the style is Bill Monroe, born in 1911 and still performing regularly, who plays both fiddle and mandolin. Of the musicians who have passed through his band, the best-known are Lester Flatt and Earl Scruggs, guitarist and banjoist respectively, who left the Blue Grass Boys in 1948 and performed as a duo until 1969. The recommended sampler covers the years 1950–71, and includes a re-recording of Monroe's 1946 hit 'Blue Moon Of Kentucky' that was released to compete with Elvis's version in 1954. Examples of the work of Flatt and Scruggs can be found on *Foggy Mountain Breakdown* (PHILIPS 6336 255).

Bob Wills and His Texas Playboys

The Bob Wills Anthology (CBS EMBASSY 31611)

New Osage Stomp/Maiden's Prayer/Steel Guitar Rag/Blue Yodel No. 1/Silver Bell/That's What I Like 'Bout The South/The Waltz You Saved For Me/Corrine Corrina/Time Changes Everything/Big Beaver/Take

Me Back To Tulsa/New San Antonio Rose/I Knew The Moment I Lost You/Twin Guitar Special/Roly Poly/Brain Cloudy Blues

Western Swing was a Texan form of country developed by Bob Wills; reaching its peak in the years around World War II, it was an eclectic style, based on a solid dance beat, and drawing on big-band and traditional jazz, blues, hillbilly and country fiddling, welding them together into an irresistible good-time swing music. The instrumental emphasis can vary from tune to tune, but the most characteristic line-up has two or even three fiddles, one played by Wills, and a steel guitar. It was Wills's electric steel player, Leon McAuliffe, who pioneered the instrument; 'Steel Guitar Rag' illustrates both this and Wills's familiar habit of introducing and urging on his soloists.

Wills was born in 1905, began playing fiddle on local radio stations in his late teens, and formed his first band in 1933, recording profusely from then until his death in 1975: a version of his band, including several originals, has survived him. The recommended record, a distillation of an American double album, comes from the years 1935–46, when he was at the peak of his popularity. Asleep at the Wheel, the best of those bands who have translated Western Swing into a contemporary context, is well represented on *Comin' Right At Ya* (SUNSET SLS 50415), and a sampler featuring both bands, together with Willie Nelson and Freddy Fender, is also recommended: *Texas Country* (UNITED ARTISTS UA-LA574-H2).

George Jones

Greatest Hits

(MERCURY 20107 MCL)

Eskimo Pie/Money To Burn/Just One More/Aching, Breaking Heart/Wandering Soul/Big Harlan Taylor/Seasons Of My Heart/You're Still On My Mind/If I Don't Love You, Baby (Grits Ain't Groceries)/When My Heart Hurts No More/Cup Of Loneliness/Tarnished Angel

In twenty-five years Jones has moved from being a young rockabilly hopeful to one of the biggest stars in country music, and the quality above all which has established him is his remarkably supple voice, which still retains its twanging Texan tenor quality. He has moved from label to label over the years, and unfortunately no single album has assembled his greatest moments: in the end I've chosen my favourite, though it is a long-deleted collection from 1965. His earliest years, on Starday, can be found on the Ace album *White Lightnin'* (ACE CH 13): the title track, written by the Big Bopper, was Jones's first classic. Tracks from his time with United Artists are on the imported double *Superpak* (UA UXS 85), and from Musicor in the second half of the sixties on *Famous Country Music-makers* (RCA DPS 2056). The early seventies are represented by *The Best of George Jones* (EPIC EPC 80847), and in 1977 he released *All-time Greatest Hits*, Volume 1, on CBS 31567, which features re-recordings of hits from his first record 'Why Baby Why' onwards. In terms of titles alone, this is the most representative album. Although Jones has a light, confident up-tempo style, it is the 'honky-tonk weepies' that show him at his strongest: such numbers as 'The Window Up Above', 'She Thinks I Still Care', 'Seasons Of My Heart' and, above all, 'Tarnished Angel'.

Willie Nelson

Shotgun Willie (ATLANTIC SD 7262: IMPORT)

Shotgun Willie/Whiskey River/Sad Songs And Waltzes/Local Memory/Slow Down Old World/Stay All Night (Stay A Little Longer)/Devil In A Sleepin' Bag/She's Not For You/Bubbles In My Beer/You Look Like The Devil/So Much To Do/A Song For You

Nelson, a Texan, started as a DJ and song-writer, and such subsequent standards as 'Funny How Time Slips Away', 'Crazy' and 'Hello Walls' preceded his first hit as a performer, 'Touch Me', in 1962. There are several elements of individuality in his style: a perfect 'crooner's' voice, both light in pitch and rich in texture, his use of a gut-stringed guitar, and the jazz influence in his chord structures and solos. His early compositions are collected on *Famous Country Music-makers* (RCA DPS 2062), but *Shotgun Willie* (1973) has been selected because it illustrates several of the broadening influences creeping into country music at the time. The bulk of the recording was done in New York rather than Nashville; of the three credited producers, two (Arif Mardin and Jerry Wexler) are more usually associated with black music; the soul session group the Memphis Horns are present on one track and on another the string arrangement is by Donny Hathaway; and the background presence of such Texan friends as Waylon Jennings and Doug Sahm points the way to the communal 'outlaw' movement. With subsequent records, *Phases and Stages* and *Red-headed Stranger*, Nelson also introduced the 'concept album' to country music.

Waylon Jennings

Dreaming My Dreams (RCA LSA 3247)

Are You Sure Hank Done It This Way/Waymore's Blues/I Recall A Gypsy Woman/High Time (You Quit Your Low Down Ways)/I've Been A Long Time Leaving (But I'll Be A Long Time Gone)/Let's Help All The Cowboys (Sing The Blues)/The Door Is Always Open/Let's Turn Back The Years/She's Looking Good/Dreaming My Dreams With You/ Bob Wills Is Still The King

It is rare that one of the giants of country music produces an 'almost perfect' album: so faithful is their following that there is a strong temptation to get a couple of good tunes (to take care of hit singles during the album's life) and pad out the rest. But Cash did it with *One Piece at a Time*, as did Waylon in 1976 with *Dreaming My Dreams* – from rabble-rousing country-rock through the blues to reflective ballads, the backings spare and subtle. Jennings started as a DJ in Lubbock, Texas, which led to a job as Buddy Holly's bass-player. After Holly's death he continued to work locally before signing with RCA in 1965. His stature has increased progressively to the point where he is now one of the music's very biggest stars. In the seventies he became identified, with others such as Willie Nelson and Tompall Glaser, as a so-called 'outlaw', which implied a rejection of certain Nashville conventions. Even if this meant little more than swapping short hair for long, spangled cowboy suits for jeans, and rehearsed 'sincerity' for a more casual stage approach, it had some impact on the hidebound country scene. By the mid seventies, however, the 'outlaws' were in danger of becoming a self-congratulatory in-crowd, and in 1978 Jennings was singing 'don't you think this outlaw bit's done got out of hand?'

Merle Haggard

Songs I'll Always Sing (CAPITOL CAPSP 101)

Okie From Muskogee/The Emptiest Arms In The World/Mama Tried/Swinging Doors/Uncle Lem/The Fightin' Side Of Me/Sing Me Back Home/Silver Wings/Sing A Sad Song/Honky Tonk Night Time Man/Kentucky Gambler/I'm A Lonesome Fugitive/Things Aren't Funny Anymore/Daddy Frank/I Forget You Every Day/Workin' Man Blues/Love And Honour/Branded Man/Someday We'll Look Back/I Take A Lot Of Pride In What I Am

Haggard comes from the Californian centre of country music, Bakersfield, and caused something of a stir when he broke through into the pop charts in 1969, at a time when political attitudes had been polarized in America by the Vietnam War, with two uncompromising records, 'Okie From Muskogee' and 'The Fightin' Side Of Me', which appealed to the self-satisfied, unquestioningly patriotic right wing. Only Haggard knows if they were honest expressions of opinion or a clever exploitation of 'hard-hat' feelings. Less controversial is the simple, sentimental beauty of such songs as 'Sing Me Back Home' and 'Silver Wings', which show Haggard at his best: a tough, clear voice over precise backings. Haggard's image has obvious appeal to a large part of the American population; the ex-convict who 'made good' without losing his taste for simple pleasures, singing songs which cunningly balance masculinity and vulnerability. Such numbers as 'Honky Tonk Night Time Man' again emphasize that the border between country & western and blues is a hazy one, as well as giving a chance for Haggard's guitarist Roy Nicholls to display his remarkable skill. A slightly different selection of Haggard's best songs is available on the sixteen-track album *The Very Best Of* (CAPITOL EST 23234), but the featured double has twenty tracks.

Bakersfield's other famous country son, Buck Owens, is best represented on *The Best of Buck Owens*, Volume 2, re-released on the budget label Music for Pleasure as *12 Great No. 1 Country Hits* (MFP 50357). His lively style, close to rockabilly, is less impressive in depth than that of Haggard.

Jerry Lee Lewis

She Still Comes Around (To Love What's Left of Me) (MERCURY 20147 SMCL)

To Make Love Sweeter For You/Let's Talk About Us/I Can't Get Over You/Out Of My Mind/Today I Started Loving You Again/She Still Comes Around (To Love What's Left Of Me)/Louisiana Man/Release Me/Listen, They're Playing My Song/There Stands The Glass/Echoes

Although he will never break the rock & roll habit, in this case storming through 'Let's Talk About Us', Lewis has for some years been regarded primarily as a country singer; such is his effortless and distinctive mastery of both styles that he demands to appear in both categories. Lewis is strongest at sentimental ballads, reflecting on some aspect of marital relationships, but the virtuosity of his performance nullifies any accusation of being maudlin. At the end of the sixties he had a series of hits with such material; among the best not included here are 'What's Made Milwaukee Famous', 'She Even Woke Me Up To Say Goodbye' and 'When He Walks On You (Like You Walked On Me)'. The split between the rocking and country sides of Lewis's style is reflected in the fact that he then succeeded with re-makes of up-tempo oldies such as 'Chantilly Lace', 'Lonely Weekends' and 'Drinking Wine Spo-De-O-Dee' in the early seventies, and nowadays in concert he switches bewilderingly between the two tempos, often with little concern for the preferences of the particular audience. The antidote to disappointment is to recognize his supreme command of both styles.

Bob Dylan

Nashville Skyline (CBS 63601)

Girl From The North Country/Nashville Skyline Rag/To Be Alone With You/I Threw It All Away/Peggy Day/Lay Lady Lay/One More Night/

Tell Me That It Isn't True/Country Pie/Tonight I'll Be Staying Here With You

More than any other album, with the possible exception of the Byrds' *Sweetheart of the Rodeo*, this made the sixties rock & roll generation aware of country music; after Dylan had set his seal of approval on Nashville, a succession of artists made the pilgrimage to the studios there. The top Nashville session-men are among the richest performers in music; they can work three sessions a day 'and still eat with the family every night' so it takes a lot to tempt them out on the road. Rarely reading from sheet music, they work out 'head arrangements' on the spot, and achieve their unique sound with the minimum of takes. *Nashville Skyline* has a delightfully improvised sound: producer Bob Johnston and session-men Kenny Buttrey, Charlie McCoy, Pete Drake, Norman Blake, Charlie Daniels and Bob Wilson, names only known to those who read sleeve-credits, turned out a two-day masterpiece. Dylan's writing is at its sparest: a simple collection of beautifully crafted love songs. Those looking to Dylan for complex imagery and hard-edged backings saw this album as yet another betrayal, but he was a step ahead as usual, and the warm, uncluttered charm of the songs has survived magnificently.

Gram Parsons

GP (REPRISE K 44228)

Still Feeling Blue/We'll Sweep Out The Ashes In The Morning/A Song For You/Streets Of Baltimore/She/That's All It Took/The New Soft Shoe/Kiss The Children/Cry One More Time/How Much I've Lied/Big Mouth Blues

Parsons was a rich boy who adopted the fantasies of country music, and burned himself up in doing so; he was an influential propagandist for the virtues of c&w among the young West Coast musicians, and a dominant member of that family of bands with the Byrds at its centre. In leading these musicians towards country, a process which found best expression in The Byrds' *Sweetheart of the Rodeo* (CBS S 63353), Parsons was of more importance than he was as a country singer, when he had considerable trouble pitching the notes correctly. His friend and harmony-singer, Emmylou Harris, has a better voice, though its limitations are exposed in the course of a whole evening. Her best album is *Elite Hotel* (REPRISE K 54060), which features the first version of her group the Hot Band, with ace veterans James Burton on guitar (late of Ricky Nelson and Elvis) and ex-Cricket Glen D. Hardin on piano. Parsons' second solo album, featuring his aching version of 'Love Hurts', was *Grievous Angel* (REPRISE K 54018).

Kris Kristofferson

Me and Bobby McGee (MONUMENT MNT 64631)

Blame It On The Stones/To Beat The Devil/Me And Bobby McGee/The Best Of All Possible Worlds/Help Me Make It Through The Night/The Law Is For The Protection Of The People/Casey's Last Ride/Just The Other Side Of Nowhere/Darby's Castle/For The Good Times/Duvalier's Dream/Sunday Mornin' Comin' Down

Although successive albums have suggested that Kristofferson said all that he had to say early on in his late-starting career (realization of which may have prompted his lucrative move into films), this album is a strong candidate to represent the 'new breed' of country song-writers. All writers hope that they'll come up with a song that will pay the rent for years on the strength of cover versions, but this album spawned at least four: the title track, which cast the 'aimless drifting' theme in a new, tender light; the seductive love song 'Help Me Make It Through The Night'; the reflective 'For The Good Times'; and the anthem of emptiness, 'Sunday Mornin' Comin' Down'.

Since the war Nashville has acted as a magnet to young hopefuls, who invest their savings in a shot at stardom, and tramp Music Row trying to peddle their songs. One of the models they now bear in mind is Kristofferson, who went from sweeping up in the studios to super-stardom. But, as Johnny Cash points out in his liner-note: 'His songs covered everyone's floor/From five years of sending his demo's/And leaving them at every door'. As Nashville has grown, overnight stardom has become a thing of the past.

Dolly Parton

The Best of Dolly Parton, Volume 2

(RCA LSA 3236)

Jolene/Traveling Man/Lonely Comin' Down/The Bargain Store/Touch Your Woman/I Will Always Love You/Love Is Like A Butterfly/Coat Of Many Colors/My Tennessee Mountain Home/When I Sing For Him

Parton has now travelled the entire route from the 'pure', home-made music of the Appalachian mountains to international, middle-of-the-road fame; there have of course been musical losses as well as personal gains along the way. She first came to notice in the mid sixties when she joined the Porter Wagoner show, a country revue headed by a rather bland, mainstream country star. Her unusually expressive voice, song-writing talent and physical beauty soon indicated a solo career. She has not achieved a totally satisfying album; her affecting sentimentality can tip over into the maudlin, and her growing fame has perhaps led her to record too much in recent years. The recommended album, however, is a collection from the period that, so far, represents her creative peak. The jaded irony of 'The Bargain Store', the defiant jealousy of 'Jolene', the sentimental autobiography of 'Coat Of Many Colors' and, above all, the emotion of 'I Will Always Love You' (one of the most beautiful love songs ever recorded) indicate her range, and are served by the tightest of Nashville backings. 'Love Is Like A Butterfly', however, is a reminder of how easily her style can lead to cloying whimsy.

John Fogerty

The Blue Ridge Rangers

(FANTASY FT 511)

Blue Ridge Mountain Blues/Somewhere Listening/You're The Reason/Jambalaya/She Thinks I Still Care/California Blues/Workin' On A Building/Please Help Me I'm Falling/Have Thine Own Way, Lord/I Ain't Never/Hearts Of Stone/Today I Started Loving You Again

Purporting to be by a five-piece band, all of whom look suspiciously like Fogerty, this is in fact a multi-tracked one-man effort released in 1973, after Fogerty's band Creedence Clearwater Revival had broken up. Rarely can an album of cover versions have had such power; he selects twelve songs covering the history of country music from Jimmie Rodgers to Merle Haggard, and often the originals seem pale by comparison. The conservatism of country music over the years has tended to bury outstanding songs in cornball arrangements, and it has sometimes been left to children of rock & roll to rediscover the power of the best c&w (Leon Russell did a similar anonymous album, *Hank Wilson's Back*, illustrated by a picture of Hank Wilson's back). There are those who will always be allergic to the basic sound of country music, and this album would be a good test, since Fogerty's loving reconstructions have a core of contemporary rock & roll.

Commander Cody and His Lost Planet Airmen

Lost in the Ozone (PARAMOUNT SPFL 276)

Back To Tennessee/Wine Do Yer Stuff/Seeds And Stems (Again)/Daddy's Gonna Treat You Right/Family Bible/Home In My Hand/Lost In The Ozone/Midnight Shift/Hot Rod Lincoln/What's The Matter Now?/20 Flight Rock/Beat Me Daddy Eight To The Bar

In the early seventies the Cody band appeared from Michigan playing a selection of music that went completely against the trend of the time, as if Bowie had never existed. A mixture of standards and originals, it was solidly based on country, spreading out from there to embrace rock & roll, rockabilly and boogie-woogie. The country material varies from the sentimentality of 'Family Bible' to their subsequent obsession with tough trucking songs, best exemplified on the album *Hot Licks, Cold Steel and Truckers Favorites.* The strength of the band lay in its musical diversity: in Andy Stein they possessed a virtuoso on both fiddle and sax; the saxophone could occasionally be augmented with further brass; they also added piano, pedal steel and sometimes harmonica to the basic group line-up; and the lead vocals came from three directions. Perhaps the band was too sprawling to last, particularly playing 'unfashionable' material; on their last visit to Britain, the internecine fights seemed to be only just confined to the off-stage area. Cody reappeared with a new line-up, but his adoption of a more modish 'funk' style gave his music less distinction.

Amazing Rhythm Aces

Stacked Deck (ABC ABCL 5152)

Third Rate Romance/The 'Ella B'/Life's Railway To Heaven/The Beautiful Lie/Hit The Nail On The Head/Who Will The Next Fool Be/Amazing Grace (Used To Be Her Favourite Song)/Anything You Want/My Tears Still Flow/Emma-Jean/Why Can't I Be Satisfied/King Of The Cowboys

The younger generation of southern bands are no respecters of categories; though the country feel is never more than a track away on an Aces' Album, they also play straight r&b and rock & roll, New Orleans and Latin American and the jazz/blues/country fusion of Charlie Rich. Furthermore, this album was recorded in the Memphis studio of Sam Phillips, who pioneered rockabilly on his Sun label. In Russell Smith, the Aces have one of the finest contemporary writers and interpreters; a strong sense of irony and humour balances the sentiment in his songs, and in the course of a syllable his voice can soar from a meditative croak to an anguished falsetto. Musically, the band achieves a particularly crisp balance of acoustic and electric guitar, and exploits the underused interplay of piano and organ. As with Joe Ely, the Aces may be but representative of dozens of less exposed bands, but it is they who have managed to build up such a comprehensive recorded survey of modern southern music. They are still, however, to surpass the consistent achievement of their debut album, *Stacked Deck*.

Joe Ely

Joe Ely

(MCA MCF 2808)

I Had My Hopes Up High/Mardi Gras Waltz/She Never Spoke Spanish To Me/Gambler's Bride/Suckin' A Big Bottle Of Gin/Tennessee's Not The State I'm In/If You Were A Bluebird/Treat Me Like A Saturday Night/All My Love/Johnny Blues

If Ely represents a future for country music, then all is well for those of us who feel uncomfortable with both ends of the c&w spectrum: the wailing hillbillies on the one hand, the middle-of-the-road, over-orchestrated 'cross-over' smoothies on the other. Ely plays country music of the rock & roll generation, in a form that could only come from Texas (he was born in Lubbock, like Buddy Holly); as such it is inflected with Mexican, cajun, blues and rock influences. This debut album (1977) consists, encouragingly, not only of original tunes, but tunes written either by Ely or one of his friends. The empathy within the band seems honed by years of playing honky-tonks before entering the studio, and this is another of the album's strengths; the music comes from a 'road band', not from the usual Nashville session-men, and it thus gains in cohesiveness. Ely quickly followed this album with the equally impressive *Honky Tonk Masquerade* (MCA MCF 2832), and makes us hope that more of these young country bands will emerge from the Texas bars and gain wider exposure.

Various Artists

Stars of the Grand Ole Opry 1926–1974

(RCA CPL2 0466)

Railroadin' And Gamblin' (Uncle Dave Macon)/San Antonio Rose (Pee Wee King)/Orange Blossom Special (Bill Monroe)/Jealous Hearted Me (Minnie Pearl)/Anytime (Eddy Arnold)/Father's Table Grace (Lester Flatt)/I'm My Own Grandpa (Lonzo and Oscar)/Yakety Axe (Chet Atkins)/I Don't Hurt Anymore (Hank Snow)/I'm Thinking

Tonight Of My Blue Eyes (The Carter Family)/Down Yonder (Del Wood)/Satisfied (Martha Carson)/Ashes Of Love (Johnnie and Jack)/ Old Blue (Grandpa Jones)/How Far Is Heaven (Kitty Wells)/Four Walls (Jim Reeves)/Carroll County Accident (Porter Wagoner)/I Can't Stop Loving You (Don Gibson)/Trouble In The Amen Corner (Archie Campbell)/The End Of The World (Skeeter Davis)/Early Morning Rain (George Hamilton IV)/Send Me The Pillow You Dream On (Hank Locklin)/Young Love (Sonny James)/Morning (Jim Ed Brown)/The Three Bells (The Browns)/Country Girl (Dottie West)/Four Strong Winds (Bobby Bare)/Ribbon Of Darkness (Connie Smith)/Mule Skinner Blues (Dolly Parton)/Just A Little After Heartaches (Jeanne Pruett)

The historical scope of this compilation recommends it, since by selecting examples of country records from 1926 onwards (Uncle Dave Macon was the Opry's first star), it shows the gradual change in the basic sound of mainstream Nashville. However, it should be approached with care, perhaps only as a sampler to suggest further investigation, since some fool has decided to include an unctuous smattering of commentary and a loop of canned applause at the start of each track. The commentary would have served better as a liner note, and the applause is an insult. It should easily be possible for a major company, particularly by licensing individual tracks from other labels, to do the same job better, but in the meantime the range of this collection has not been bettered.

Country: Singles

The Delmore Brothers: *Blues Stay Away From Me* (1949)

The harmonies are 'country', but the title and mood are another reminder of how close the hillbillies were to their black neighbours, though few could admit it.

Hank Snow: *I'm Movin' On* (1950)

As above: when later arranged by Ray Charles, this driving railroad song became a rhythm & blues classic. Snow, a Canadian, has proved one of the longest-surviving country stars.

Hank Thompson: *The Wild Side Of Life* (1952)

Honky-tonk meets Western Swing in a standard with the unforgettable line 'I didn't know God made honky-tonk angels', which was immediately and successfully contradicted by Kitty Wells – it was the feckless male who made them.

Sonny James: *Young Love* (1956)

The teenager arrives in country music, via the familiar C–Am–F–G chord sequence, and provided an international pop hit for both James and actor Tab Hunter.

Wink Martindale: *Deck Of Cards* (1959)

The 'po-faced moralizing' school of country music in monologue form: war, patriotism and, above all, God, unfortunately successful worldwide. But it can't be ignored.

Marty Robbins: *El Paso* (1959)

That other c&w stand-by, death, features in the greatest of the cowboy songs (Tex Ritter was too bad a singer for 'High Noon' to compete), dressed in Spanish rhythms from just over the border.

Webb Pierce: *I Ain't Never* (1959)

A relentless rhythm and the line 'You've got me living in a haunted dream' gave a durable star his most appealing hit, still worth reviving.

Jim Reeves: *He'll Have To Go* (1959)

He had a voice like cocoa and flew into a mountain, but the king of schmaltz overcame disrespect with this desperate song – he's on the phone and his rival's on the job.

Patsy Cline: *I Fall To Pieces* (1961)

Or 'Crazy', or especially 'She's Got You' – the late Miss Cline conveyed a convincing brand of sexual angst.

Bobby Edwards: *You're The Reason* (1961)

A lilting and hypnotic melody over simple chords, with above-average lyrics, this was also a hit at the time for Hank Locklin and Joe South, and was successfully revived in 1967 by Johnny Tillotson.

Don Gibson: *Sea Of Heartbreak* (1961)

Few, apart from the obvious Hank Williams, have written more classics than Gibson; his wistful songs combine a dry voice, strong acoustic guitar and immediately appealing melodies. Among the others are 'Oh Lonesome Me', 'I Can't Stop Loving You' and 'Sweet Dreams'.

Leroy Van Dyke: *Walk On By* (1961)

A reverberating and catchy lead-guitar line cannot fail, especially when allied to that most pressing of country-music problems, adulterous guilt.

Skeeter Davis: *The End Of The World* (1962)

A gauche but perfectly pitched voice and a hollow production suggest that the world did indeed end when we said goodbye.

Claude King: *Wolverton Mountain* (1962)

King went on having country hits, but he also briefly became a pop star with this curiosity: it sold on the background yodelling, its melody and unusual story-line.

Ned Miller: *From A Jack To A King* (1962)

Love found (rather than the more usual love lost) produced an international hit, thanks to a rhythm which sounds suspiciously like West Indian blue-beat.

Dave Dudley: *Six Days On The Road* (1963)

The truck-driver has succeeded the cowboy as c&w hero, never more successfully than in this subsequent country/rock & roll standard.

Tammy Wynette: *Stand By Your Man* (1968)

Tammy, dressed in a housecoat and covered in kids, would never have cheated on her man in the late sixties, though D-I-V-O-R-C-E could be discussed among adults. Usually, however, she stood by her man and spoke to southern women who would understand.

Doug Kershaw: *Diggy Liggy Lo* (1969)

The cajun music of the displaced French-Canadians, who were expelled from Acadia by the British and migrated round the coast to Louisiana, provides one of the most fertile and unsullied of southern music styles: this example crept into the c&w charts.

Charlie Rich: *Life's Little Ups And Downs* (1969)

After years of dues-paying, starting as a Memphis rocker with a unique jazzy sound, Rich finally broke through in 1973 with 'Behind Closed

Doors'. 'Ups and Downs', a smaller and earlier hit written by his wife, is a perfect vehicle for his soaring voice.

Jerry Reed: *When You're Hot You're Hot* (1971)

An example of one of Reed's best singles, which invariably combine staggering guitar technique with cocky, humorous vocals.

MICK HOUGHTON

British Beat

In the late fifties, the only development in British pop to show any semblance of originality was skiffle, and even this was directly descended from American folk roots in blues and 'jug-band' music. Otherwise, the British version of rock & roll was *precisely* modelled on the American one, exemplified in 1956 by Britain's lone Elvis imitator, Tommy Steele. Within a year Steele had set the precedent whereby any tough image – in Steele's case scarcely detectable – was soon dropped in favour of all-round appeal.

1958, however, was Britain's most memorable rock & roll year. Cliff Richard emerged with the first genuinely exciting British rock ('Move It'), though he too was quickly groomed to be acceptable to young and old alike. Cliff's emergence had been greatly boosted by Jack Good's TV rock show 'Oh Boy', which ran for eleven months from June 1958, and introduced many of the home-grown rockers. Two of the finest, Billy Fury and Marty Wilde, had been renamed by the first entrepreneur of British pop, Larry Parnes. Parnes handled a host of artists, each with a descriptive surname: Johnny Gentle, Vince Eager, Duffy Power, even Georgie Fame and, breaking the sequence, Joe Brown. Brown, like Tommy Steele a cheery cockney, didn't achieve a hit until 1962, but he did contribute the lead guitar work to perhaps the most extraordinary and lasting recording of the British rock & roll era, Billy Fury's *Sound of Fury*. An 'authentic' rockabilly-sounding album, all the songs were nonetheless written by Fury himself. He went on to record a string of impressive big ballads that kept him in the charts until 1965.

Although 1958 was Britain's most convincing year for rock & roll, British pop music thereafter fell into something of a deep sleep. That something akin to rock & roll should reawaken, five years later, on the British side of the Atlantic, was quite unprecedented. Yet what occurred in Britain between 1963 and 1967 amounted to a rekindling of the spirit of the first rock era, while the parallel development of a youth culture was even more far-reaching in its effect than that accompanying the earlier era.

The British pop revolution took the form of a series of local movements, completely independent of one another at first, and establishing firm identities, especially in the major cities. Liverpool, of course, provides the definitive example. Each local scene generated a fierce sense of 'belonging' which focussed on the music at its heart, though that music did not necessarily represent a common local style, except in Liverpool. Essentially derivative, but fast and loud – these had been the basic qualities of British pop since the fifties; but not until now was a new stylistic element forged, strong enough to create a genuinely original article that went beyond mere imitation.

While one should not forget the crucial role of Merseybeat in the British pop explosion of the sixties, its chief significance lay in drawing attention to the existence of an extensive grass-roots pop network in Britain. This didn't just spring up in the wake of Merseybeat, nor was beat music the first grass-roots pop to develop in Britain. Skiffle had spread like wildfire following Lonnie

Donegan's chart hits in 1956. The do-it-yourself skiffle was, however, too limited and unsatisfying to last, but it did create a guitar/group consciousness that long outlived the boom. The significance of the skiffle craze lay not in the charts but in the coffee bars, church halls and other temporary venues where thousands of kids formed skiffle groups and were hooked on playing this ersatz form of rock & roll. The essential flaw in skiffle was its lack of power; with the arrival of hire-purchase in 1960, electric guitars, thirty-watt amplifiers and the basic drum kit were no longer unattainable.

If skiffle laid the foundation, then the Shadows were the catalyst in the new electric phase of nascent British pop. Their string of hits between 1960 and 1963 made them the most successful pre-Beatles group. Adopting a clean sound, with each instrument clearly distinguishable, they provided the ideal model for aspiring lead guitarists in particular, but also for drummers and bass and rhythm players. Like skiffle, the Shadows' style was constricting, and the new beat groups went back either to American rock & roll or to r&b for inspiration.

Apart from the expected influences of Chuck Berry, Eddie Cochran, Little Richard and Buddy Holly, the local groups in Liverpool found particular inspiration in contemporary vocal groups such as the Drifters, the Marvelettes, and the Shirelles, and in obscure singles that came into the city via ships docking in the port from America. Liverpool, with its well-established club set-up, evolved the most complete and singular style of all the cities where a beat scene, in some form, was in existence. There is no doubt that in most of the major cities – Birmingham, Newcastle, Manchester, Belfast, Glasgow and London – all, save one, ports, group scenes had been steadily evolving since the very early sixties. Merseybeat, following a run of chart successes by the Beatles,

Gerry and the Pacemakers, Billy J. Kramer, the Searchers *et al.*, first drew attention to this grass-roots activity throughout Britain and then offered an immediate and simply adopted stylistic bandwagon to jump aboard. The majority of local groups soon latched on to Merseybeat but they were invariably short-lived. When one looks back to the groups which survived the boom from 1963 to 1965, they were clearly those that went their own way. What they had in common was the basic umbrella style, r&b.

London, particularly after the chart break-through by the Rolling Stones in 1964, was a major influence in the large-scale shift of emphasis from beat to r&b. But r&b was open to different interpretations. Even in London, although the Stones' blueprint was widely adopted (the Yard-birds, the Pretty Things, Downliners Sect), it was in direct competition with the Flamingo style, the jazz-horn riffing of Alexis Korner's Blues Incorporated or the jazz organ-based style of the Graham Bond Organization, while others remained outside even these broad categories. Manfred Mann, for example, was one of the earliest r&b groups in London who, in their early days, couldn't decide between r&b and jazz and, later on, couldn't decide between this hybrid and straight pop. Rhythm & blues groups in the provinces also developed individual styles in total isolation from one another. The Animals (New-castle), Them (Belfast), Alex Harvey's Big Soul Band (Glasgow), John Mayall's Blues Syndicate (Manchester); none exactly fit the London pat-tern.

The impact of r&b could never be measured against a yardstick of chart success. In fact, looking at the charts for 1965, the year that the Rolling Stones, Them and the Pretty Things were rearing their heads as the delinquents of pop, beat was clearly running out of steam; the ever-youthful Cliff Richard was scoring his first

Number 1 since Beatlemania, Ken Dodd topped the charts for over a month with 'Tears', while the biggest new group to emerge, adjudged by chart success, was the Seekers.

Yet British pop wasn't in as sorry a state as the charts reflected; the excitement remained but had reverted to the clubs. In a network that traversed the country, r&b was still the reagent and, while club acts rarely broke into the singles charts, some produced albums which sold remarkably well. Both the John Mayall with Eric Clapton *Blues Breakers* album and Geno Washington's *Hand Clappin' – Foot Stompin' – Funky Butt – Live* enjoyed unheard-of album sales.

The healthy club circuit was also reflected by the pirate radio stations, at their peak between 1965 and 1967. Stations like Radio Caroline and Radio London were responsible for many of the period's more unlikely hits. But the true arbiter of the club punter's taste was the TV rock show 'Ready Steady Go'. It was the epitome of all that was thrilling about British pop, drawing heavily on Jack Good's ideas in 'Oh Boy'. 'RSG' eventually acknowledged the role of the club acts by going live to capture them at their most exciting.

By 1966, soul music was finding particular favour, especially with the black and mod audiences, but the soul-orientated groups, whether they had a horn section – like the Flamingo groups, Georgie Fame's Blue Flames, Zoot Money's Big Roll Band, or the more Stax-styled Alan Bown Set and Jimmy James and the Vagabonds – or whether they simply used soul as one facet of their style – like the Artwoods, the Action and Steampacket – came up against the same problem. Their recreations of black music sounded tremendous in the atmosphere of the clubs, but their recordings could never compete with the originals. The club-goers naturally bought the original article, so the likes of Chris Farlowe, Zoot Money and Cliff Bennett notched up few hits. Most of the club groups failed to score at all. Ultimately, this attitude fostered the proliferation of discotheques. Both cheaper and easier to run, the discos began to encroach more and more on live music.

The discotheques were the final nail in the coffin; the heyday of British beat was over by the beginning of 1967. When, in that year, the underground movement caught on outside London, it briefly gave some of the clubs a new lease of life. In its original form, mostly a London affair, the underground was a short-lived phenomenon. The key founding spirits were groups such as Pink Floyd, Soft Machine, Tomorrow, and the Crazy World of Arthur Brown, but as the year grew older other groups came under the underground umbrella. They were a motley collection: the Move, essentially a pop group, seemed out of place; as did that arch-looner Zoot Money, riding his Dantalian's Chariot like a man possessed. He shed his earlier Flamingo identity (as did many other old bluesers) without even pausing for breath. The individuals in the Nice typified the process whereby apparently new groups sprang up; three of them, David O'List, Keith Emerson and Brian Davison, had previously been with stalwart club outfits, the Attack, Gary Farr's T-Bones and the Mark Leeman Five. Very few groups stood for the original spirit of the underground. The overall atmosphere by the 'summer of '67' was one of exploitation, of cashing in on a rapidly expanding market for what was now being dubbed 'progressive' rock.

The underground and progressive music scene also encompassed the second British blues boom. The first, contemporaneous with the r&b upsurge of 1964–5, had never really taken off. The second, however, found a ready audience in the underground clubs and the expanding college/university circuit. Many of the leading blues exponents were refugees from the abortive first wave of groups – for example John Mayall, with a succession of different Blues Breakers, and Cream, featuring Eric Clapton, Ginger Baker and Jack Bruce. These two, aided by the newly arrived Jimi Hendrix, gave the blues movement its much-needed springboard. Hundreds of groups sprang up in 1967 and 1968; the best were Peter Green's Fleetwood Mac, Free, Jethro Tull, Taste and the Jeff Beck Group, featuring Rod Stewart. The second-division front-runners included the Groundhogs, Savoy Brown, Chicken Shack and Ainsley Dunbar's Retaliation.

The new progressive music – groups such as Yes, the Nice, Genesis and Led Zeppelin, all formed around this time – and the blues bands both required a new outlet for recording. Where British beat/r&b had happened in spite of a record business system dominated by four major companies – Decca, EMI, Pye and Philips – the new emphasis on esoteric albums, which the underground had instigated, called for a change in attitude from record companies which, perhaps, only a new type of label would be flexible enough to achieve.

Island became the prototype for this new breed of independent label. In 1967, Island was well disposed to break new ground: following the break-up of the Spencer Davis Group, which Island had managed, the new group Traffic, formed by Stevie Winwood, was signed by them as their first 'underground' band. Once underground/progressive music had come out into the open, Island was seen to be *the* British label, scooping many of its leading exponents: Fairport Convention, Spooky Tooth, Jethro Tull and Free in addition to Traffic. Island was attracting the best of the new blood, not only by a policy of offering the kind of artistic freedom that was wanted, but because they stood for the new order in a way that the old majors never could.

The majors' answer was to launch new progressive labels under their patronage – Decca with Deram, EMI with Harvest, Pye with Dawn and Philips with Vertigo, shifting appropriate artists from the parent label to the 'new' one. Thus, the Moody Blues and Ten Years After went to Deram, Pink Floyd to Harvest and the Bystanders, a pop cabaret group about to be released from their old contract with Pye, reappeared on Dawn as Man, one of our most enduring underground groups. The old associations with the parent label were never really shaken off; Vertigo had an impressive roster of artists, among them the leading new jazz-rock groups (yet another growing trend) Colosseum and Nucleus, but could never get the label on the right footing, as could the *genuine* independents that formed following Island's success, labels such as Chrysalis, Charisma and Virgin.

The arrival of these new labels was, to some extent, the final triumph of the British pop explosion. It marked the first real change in the music industry since the war. Sadly, though, the progressive era that the independents represented soon threw British pop/rock into a state of thorough confusion. Eventually it became clear that a new hierarchy had simply replaced the old one. The mixed fortunes of rock under its new masters – heavy metal, glitter rock, ponderous symphonic/opera rock, superstars and supergroups – the leading exponents of which had come through the sixties experience anyway, sent the British rock industry back into a coma as deep as the one in 1960. The new wave groups of recent years have roused it once again, but how long will it be before the pop cycle turns once again to engulf them as well?

British Beat : Albums

The Searchers

The Searchers File (PYE FILD 002)

Sweets For My Sweet/Sugar 'N' Spice/Ain't Gonna Kiss Ya/Farmer John/Love Potion No. 9/Alright/Needles And Pins/Saturday Night Out/Don't Throw Your Love Away/Some Other Guy/Saints And Searchers/Ain't That Just Like Me/Someday We're Gonna Love Again/No One Else Could Love Me/It's In Her Kiss/When You Walk In The Room/Sea Of Heartbreak/What Have They Done To The Rain?/This Feeling Inside/Goodbye My Love/Till I Met You/Each Time/He's Got No Love/When I Get Home/Take Me For What I'm Worth/Take It Or Leave It/Have You Ever Loved Somebody?/Popcorn, Double Feature/Western Union/Second Hand Dealer

Named after the great John Ford movie, the original Searchers were Mike Pender, lead guitar, John McNally, rhythm, Tony Jackson, bass, and Chris Curtis, drums. Formed in Liverpool in 1961, their first single, 'Sweets For My Sweet' gave them a chart-topper in the summer of 1963. For the next two years they ranked second only to the Beatles among Merseybeat groups. The Searchers could never be described as an outright rock group but before Tony Jackson quit (in early 1965) their singles and three fine albums (*Meet The Searchers* and *Sugar 'n' Spice* are particularly recommended) had considerable bite, belied by their trade-mark, light harmonies. Their musical style, more than any other group, demonstrates the importance of the rhythm guitar to the Mersey sound. Never able to write convincing original material they covered most of the Liverpool standards, drawing often from American boy-and-girl groups, but always bringing to their covers a unique sense of style. After Tony Jackson left (replaced by Frank Allen), Pender switched to lead voice but Jackson's harder nasal tones were sorely missed. The group have struggled on gamely since without ever disgracing their name. With Pender, McNally and Allen still in the group, they are still popular around the northern and European cabaret clubs.

The Beatles

Revolver (PARLOPHONE PCS 7009)

Taxman/Eleanor Rigby/I'm Only Sleeping/Love To You/Here, There And Everywhere/Yellow Submarine/She Said She Said/Good Day Sunshine/And Your Bird Can Sing/For No One/Dr Robert/I Want To Tell You/Got To Get You Into My Life/Tomorrow Never Knows.

Of all the albums the Beatles made, *Revolver* stands as the most timeless and unblemished. Their first album as a purely 'studio' group, it may have been less far reaching in its impact than *Sergeant Pepper*, but it has aged so much more gracefully. *Revolver* is perhaps the key album in contrasting the individual talents of Lennon and McCartney. The world-weary, introspective Lennon had already shown his hand on *Rubber Soul* ('Norwegian Wood', 'Nowhere Man', 'Girl' etc), but *Revolver* sees McCartney moving on from such cloying efforts as 'Michelle' to write fully-fledged songs like 'For No One', 'Eleanor Rigby' and 'Got To Get You Into My Life'; the last is almost an exercise in writing to order for the then soul boom. Lennon, meanwhile, turns in three of his best ever: 'I'm Only Sleeping', 'She Said She Said' and 'Tomorrow Never Knows'. Apart from the polarization of Lennon and McCartney's roles, the seeds of the Beatles' destruction are all sown in *Revolver*: George Harrison's emergence, his dubious fascination with Indian music and, particularly, the whole group's indulgence in drugs and things mystical, which gradually dissipated their collective force. Above all, though, *Revolver* marks the end of an era, the end of the joyous innocence and enthusiasm of the Beatles' first flush of success. The transformation was mirrored in British pop generally.

The Rolling Stones

The Rolling Stones (DECCA LK 4605)

Route 66/I Just Wanna Make Love To You/Honest I Do/I Need You/ Baby/Now I've Got A Witness/Little By Little/I'm A King Bee/Carol/ Tell Me/Can I Get A Witness/You Can Make It If You Try/Walking The Dog

That the Rolling Stones came into being deputizing for Alexis Korner's Blues Incorporated (while Korner played a BBC 'Jazz Club' session) in July 1962, and that Jagger, a member of Korner's group, commented in *Jazz News*, 'I hope people don't think it's rock 'n' roll,' is the perfect scene-setter for the British r&b boom, and the Stones' predominant role in it. Almost two years later, when this, their first album, was released, the music came across with a conviction that suggested the group were still set on spreading the word about r&b; they were still crusading rather than trying to become pop stars. The album reflects the main sources of the Stones' then repertoire – Chuck Berry, Bo Diddley, Jimmy Reed, Willie Dixon – and its success heralded the ready acceptance of r&b throughout Britain. At the same time, *The Rolling Stones* was the model for the most widespread basic style of British r&b, especially since the originals, certainly those on Chess, soon became easily available. As an album, this is arguably the finest debut by any group. Not just a bunch of white kids aping the masters – 'Route 66', 'Walking The Dog', 'I Just Wanna Make Love To You' and 'Carol' have an arrogant confidence that gives them the edge over the originals. An outstanding and crucial album.

The Rolling Stones

Rolled Gold (DECCA ROST 1/2)

Come On/I Wanna Be Your Man/Not Fade Away/Carol/It's All Over Now/Little Red Rooster/Time Is On My Side/The Last Time/(I Can't Get No) Satisfaction/Get Off Of My Cloud/19th Nervous Breakdown/

As Tears Go By/Under My Thumb/Lady Jane/Out Of Time/Paint It Black/Have You Seen Your Mother Baby Standing In The Shadows/ Let's Spend The Night Together/Ruby Tuesday/Yesterday's Papers/We Love You/She's A Rainbow/Jumpin' Jack Flash/Honky Tonk Women/ Sympathy For The Devil/Street Fighting Man/Midnight Rambler/ Gimme Shelter

The perfect Stones primer, this album gathers all the group's A-sides, together with choice album cuts, from their vintage recording years with Decca, 1963–9. *Rolled Gold* builds up a composite story not only of the Stones' eventful career but also of the pattern of British pop in the sixties. Unlike most of their peers, the Stones were able to stay the course, Mick Jagger and Keith Richard becoming first-rate song-writers. By way of an apprenticeship they made masterly arrangements of 'Not Fade Away' and 'It's All Over Now', perfect stop-gaps until they were able to create quality songs of their own. With 'Satisfaction' they proved the point beyond question. The fuzz tone guitar riff alone would have singled it out for attention, but Jagger's lyrics turn it into the ultimate, strung-out sixties blues. They never bettered it, although they came pretty close. Each phase of their evolving career is charted here: the social concern of *Aftermath*, the misguided flower-power era and their infamous drug busts, the intense, almost overpowering *Beggar's Banquet* ('Sympathy For The Devil' and 'Street Fighting Man'), the death of Brian Jones and the ability to drag themselves back with yet another classic single ('Honky Tonk Women') and album *(Let It Bleed)*. Years of success and excess, punctuated with fine music. The Stones remain one of the world's leading groups, but now concentrate essentially on spectacular live shows. Their best recorded work is here.

The Yardbirds

Five Live Yardbirds (COLUMBIA 33SX 1677)

Too Much Monkey Business/I Got Love If You Want It/Smokestack Lightning/Goodmorning Little Schoolgirl/Respectable/Five Long Years/ Pretty Girl/Louise/I'm A Man/Here 'Tis

Of all the groups to adopt the Rolling Stones' model for r&b, the Yardbirds were far and away the best. While their early singles lacked the presence and originality of the Stones' work, manager Giorgio Gomelsky fortunately decided to record them 'live' at the Marquee club in mid 1965 for their first album. It captures the group at its peak – Keith Relf, vocals, harmonica; Paul Samwell-Smith, bass; Chris Dreja, rhythm guitar; Jim McCarty, drums; and Eric Clapton guitar – a good few months before Clapton became disillusioned by the shift towards pop with 'For Your Love'. While the group went on to make a dazzling string of pop/psychedelic masterpieces ('Shapes Of Things', 'Over, Under, Sideways, Down', etc) after Jeff Beck had replaced Clapton, *Five Live Yardbirds* remains as much an ultimate statement of British r&b as the first Stones' album. Where the Yardbirds – at least the Stones' live equals – differed from them was in their extraordinary rhythmic power, which allowed Clapton full scope for his masterly lead guitar work – check out 'Five Long Years' or 'Louise', single-mindedly fresh playing that fills out each song with flair and precision. Alongside this, Relf's singing – hardly the typical Jaggeresque sneer – is almost flat, nasal and unusually pleasant in manner. It was an unlikely blend but, as *Five Live Yardbirds* shows, it fired on all cylinders

Georgie Fame and the Blue Flames

Rhythm and Blues at the Flamingo

(COLUMBIA 33SX 1599)

Night Train/Let The Good Times Roll/Eso Beso/Work Song/Parchment Farm/You Can't Sit Down/Humpty Dumpty/Shop Around/Baby, Please Don't Go

One of the forgotten masterpieces of British r&b; its rarity aside, this is partly due to the low credibility afforded to Fame these days. But in 1963, when this was recorded, the Flamingo sound was one of the staple r&b forms, largely invented by Fame and adopted by the likes of Zoot Money, Chris Farlowe and Ronnie Jones, among others. It wasn't purely a Flamingo/London phenomenon but was popular throughout the regions, in clubs like the Mojo, Sheffield, the Twisted Wheel, Manchester, or the A Go Go, Newcastle. Essentially, the

Flamingo was a black club; it opened when the other London r&b clubs closed and its 'all-niters' were generally exclusive to its own more mature crowd. The track listing indicates Fame's unique synthesis of r&b – a mixture of mellow jazz and rampant soul – three Mose Allison songs, James Brown, Rufus Thomas and West Indian and Latin curiosities. Strangely, Booker T's 'Green Onions' (On *Fame At Last*), another staple of the set, isn't included. The line-up, too, was significant; Fame dominated the sound with his Hammond organ, but the other key instruments were the tenor and baritone saxes and conga drums. The Flamingo sound was as distinct from the Blues Incorporated/Marquee style horn riffing as it was from the Stones' model rhythm & blues. It had little chart impact and within a few years had given way to an attempted approximation of the Stax sound; but, in its day, the Flamingo sound – heard here in its purest and most atmospheric form – was arguably the most totally original r&b style in Britain.

The Animals

The Animals (EMI STARLINE SRS 5006)

Story Of Bo Diddley/Bury My Body/Dimples/I've Been Around/I'm In Love Again/The Girl Can't Help It/I'm Mad Again/She Said Yeah/The Right Time/Memphis/Boom Boom/Around And Around

The Animals achieved one of the most successful and influentia variations of the three basic r&b models that grew up in London. The group hailed from Newcastle and evolved quite distinctly and separately. The basic difference was that, where the usual five-piece r&b groups relied heavily on rhythm guitar, the Animals had a piano/organist (Alan Price), plus, in Eric Burdon, a blues shouter rather than a singer. Price was also a deft arranger, particularly noticeable on his arrangements of 'Baby Let Me Take You Home' and 'House Of The Rising Sun' from Dylan's first album. *The Animals* was their debut album, released in the wake of the superb smash hit 'Rising Sun', and including most of the stock numbers from their set of the day. Along with a recently released, highly recommended, 'live' album from the Newcastle Club A Go Go (CHARLY CR 300016), this album captures the original, brash Animals at their strongest. 'Dimples', for example, has lovely rolling piano work from Price, where later recordings featured ubiquitous organ. Hilton Valentine, a much underrated guitarist (listen to 'I'm Mad Again'), gets more opportunity to solo than on later efforts. Also *The Animals* has Eric Burdon shouting the lyrics as if his life depended on it – true 'bottled soul'. Magnificent, raw r&b, a sound much blanketed, though still excellent, on their series of hits from 1964 to 1966 available on *The Most of the Animals.*

Them

The World of Them (DECCA PA86 – MONO VERSION)

Here Comes The Night/Baby Please Don't Go/I'm Gonna Dress In Black/Richard Cory/I Put A Spell On You/Bring 'Em On In/Gloria/Mystic Eyes/Turn On Your Love Light/It's All Over Now, Baby Blue/One Two Brown Eyes/Don't Start Crying Now

Van Morrison is apt to dismiss most of Them's recordings, claiming that the only true Them was heard at Belfast's Maritime Hotel long before they ever came to record. He clearly resents the fact that Them's sessions were augmented by or composed entirely of session players. Them had little wider influence but, whatever Morrison feels, they made some singularly stylish recordings. A curious group, they had the usual rebellious image (the angry young Them) but Van was the musician's singer, his stocky, ragged, tousle-haired image unlikely to win the group a massive following among the usual record buyers. However flawed, their two albums did contain many a special moment. *The World of Them* documents most of these: 'One Two Brown Eyes' and 'Don't Start Crying Now', their first single, pure, unsophisticated Them; and the superb control of 'Baby Please Don't Go' and its flip, 'Gloria', the later punk standard. Despite Decca's clear attempts to turn Them into another Animals, the essence of the group comes through in the energetic drive of 'Mystic Eyes', the interpretive, delicate 'It's All Over Now, Baby Blue' or the jazzy 'Bring 'Em On In', very suggestive of Van Morrison's later work. All these bear witness to the freshness and striking depth and range of Them's music; probably only Van Morrison knows what they might have achieved.

John Mayall with Eric Clapton

Blues Breakers (DECCA LK4804)

All Your Love/Hideaway/Little Girl/Another Man/Double Crossing Time/What'd I Say/Key To Love/Parchman Farm/Have You Heard/Ramblin' On My Mind/Steppin' Out/It Ain't Right

John Mayall had begun his self-styled blues crusade back in the early sixties in the North-west, but it was not until he based himself in London and had acquired the services of former Yardbirds guitarist, Eric Clapton, that he spread the word beyond a cult level. Mayall played harmonica and piano/organ and sang lead vocals, and Clapton, John McVie (bass) and Hughie Flint (drums) completed the Blues Breakers. For Clapton they were the ideal vehicle. Playing the same circuit as he had with the Yardbirds in the year before *Blues Breakers* was released, his performances were already something of a legend. The album showcased Clapton admirably, featuring his showstopping instrumentals 'Hideaway' and 'Steppin' Out', plus exquisite soloing on the Mayall originals 'Have You Heard', 'Double Crossing Time' and Otis Rush's 'All Your Love' that displayed a feeling and technique second to none among British guitarists. Mayall's performance was overshadowed. After Clapton left he found a more sympathetic guitarist in Peter Green. Their only album together, *A Hard Road*, remains Mayall's most convincing body of work. From this point on, musicians came and went with the seasons; Mick Taylor replaced Green, the rhythm section fluctuated, horns were added and then dropped. The father of British blues had stuck to his task, but once the blues boom had come and gone by the end of the sixties, he realized that there was little future in Britain. Now resident in Laurel Canyon, his undistinguished albums reflect a lack of true purpose in the seventies.

Cream

Disraeli Gears (RSO 2394129)

Strange Brew/Sunshine Of Your Love/World Of Pain/Dance The Night Away/Blue Condition/Tales Of Brave Ulysses/Swlabr/We're Going Wrong/Outside Woman Blues/Take It Back/Mother's Lament

The original 'supergroup'. Eric Clapton, his reputation as Britain's finest blues guitarist beyond question, teamed with two former members of the Graham Bond Organization, Jack Bruce and Ginger Baker, to form Cream in 1966. The pedigree was impeccable but the hurried debut album, *Fresh Cream*, was rather stilted ('I'm So Glad' excepted) and the group also clearly sought commercial success. By the time they came to record *Disraeli Gears*, however, these early inconsistencies had been ironed out. They resisted the temptation towards too many fashionable psychedelics, and cut a blues-based album entirely of original songs. Bruce wrote with poet Pete Brown – 'Sunshine Of Your Love' being the outstanding collaboration – while Clapton, writing with 'underground' artist Martin Sharp, came up with the album's highlight in 'Tales Of Brave Ulysses'. Inevitably, Cream's next album had to capture the group's live show, especially as there were already, in 1968, signs of the relationships becoming strained. *Wheels of Fire* was the result – a live and a studio album combined. The live album had considerable impact, each of the group doing their particular 'thing'. Cream can hardly be blamed for the fact that what they did brilliantly others took to the point of pure ennui and self-indulgence. Accordingly, Cream's reputation has been tarnished. *Disraeli Gears*, however, is the case for the defence.

The Who

Meaty, Beaty, Big and Bouncy (TRACK 2406 006)

I Can't Explain/The Kids Are Alright/Happy Jack/I Can See For Miles/Pictures Of Lily/My Generation/The Seeker/Anyway, Anyhow,

Anywhere/Pinball Wizard/Legal Matter/Boris The Spider/Magic Bus/ Substitute/I'm A Boy

Considering that the Who were originally fashioned, by managers Kit Lambert and Chris Stamp, to appeal to a particular audience, the group soon broke away impressively from the shackles of their mod image to produce some of the finest rock of the mid sixties. They were responsible for a series of minor classics built around 'mod' life-styles, culminating in 'My Generation', which managed to sum up the mods' tireless life both in Pete Townshend's lyrics and in the Who's thundering sound. There followed a flush of fine singles about a series of odd characters, youthful paranoias and obsessions, singles remarkable for their all-round originality. Through two albums, *A Quick One* and *Sell Out*, they continued to churn out adventurous and intriguing songs before all the strains were pulled together in the widely acclaimed rock opera, *Tommy*. A vastly imperfect work, it checked the Who's loss of contact with its audience. They became the darlings of the new order of serious rock critics and boosted their grass-roots popularity with their biggest hit in years, 'Pinball Wizard'. Like the Stones, the Who became an essentially live group in the seventies. They no longer made singles, but consistency in albums also eluded them. *Meaty, Beaty, Big and Bouncy* captures their most vital and exciting years, before *Tommy* became a millstone rather than a milestone and before 'superstar' status had sapped their life's blood.

The Kinks

The Kinks File (PYE FILD 001/2)

Long Tall Sally/You Still Want Me/You Really Got Me/All Day And All Of The Night/I've Got That Feeling/I Gotta Go Now/Things Are Getting Better/Tired Of Waiting For You/Everybody's Gonna Be Happy/ Set Me Free/See My Friends/A Well Respected Man/Till The End Of The Day/Dedicated Follower Of Fashion/Sunny Afternoon/Dead End Street/Mr Pleasant/Waterloo Sunset/Death Of A Clown/Autumn Almanac/Suzannah's Still Alive/Wonderboy/Lincoln County/Days/Hold My Hand/Plastic Man/Driving/Shangri-la/Victoria/Lola/Apeman

Unsung in their day, the Kinks went through a staggering number of seemingly unrelated phases during the sixties. Their early hits, from the primitive impact of 'You Really Got Me' in mid 1964 to 'Till The End Of The Day' at the close of 1965, were brash, proto-punk, three-chord epics that varied enough to include the brooding 'Tired Of Waiting For You' and the innovative, suggestive 'See My Friends'. Ray Davies then began widening the group's musical horizons (hardly difficult) and used the Kinks' lyrics to document the 'swinging sixties' as expertly as anyone in any medium in the period. Songs like 'Dedicated Follower Of Fashion' and 'Well Respected Man', and albums like *Something Else* and *Face to Face*, led to a handful of singles – 'Waterloo Sunset', 'Dead End Street', 'Autumn Almanac' – that were unsurpassed even in this highly creative period of British rock. By the end of 1968, however, the Kinks' singles' era was drawing to a close. Ray Davies, in any event, had turned to concept albums, *The Village Green Preservation Society* and *Arthur*, advance warning of his erratic work in the seventies. A remarkable group, the Kinks' firsts went virtually unnoticed. They were beholden to no one, always challenging and, arguably, Britain's finest singles group of the sixties. As if to serve a pleasant reminder, they topped the charts for the last time in 1970 with the ambiguous, risqué 'Lola'.

The Troggs

Vintage Years

(SIRE SASH 3714–2: IMPORT)

Wild Thing/With A Girl Like You/Lost Girl/Give It To Me/Say Darlin'/I Want You/Gonna Make You/I Can't Control Myself/From Home/Girl In Black/Jingle Jangle/6–5–4–3–2–1/Hi Hi Hazel/I Can Only Give You Everything/Love Is All Around/Any Way That You Want Me/Hip Hip Hooray/Cousin Jane/Night Of The Long Grass/You Can Cry If You Want To/Come Now/Surprise Surprise/Lover/The Raver/Purple Shades/Maybe The Madman/Off The Record/Feels Like A Woman

Somewhat surprisingly perhaps, the Troggs are still playing today and with undaunted enthusiasm. Singer Reg Presley, drummer Ronnie Bond (both still in the group), guitarist Chris Britton and bassist Pete Staples achieved a world-wide smash for the Andover group in mid

1966 with their suggestive, Kinks-like version of Chip Taylor's 'Wild Thing'. Highlighted by Presley's leering vocal, it was to set the pattern for a series of hits that either followed the formula exactly or slowed down the tempo to create some of the finest beat ballads in pop history – 'Love Is All Around' and 'Any Way That You Want Me' in particular. It was the Troggs' anti-progressive approach which singled them out in the experimental/transitional phase that British pop was going through. Today the Troggs have new-found credibility as the only British group to approximate the *Nuggets*-era punk that was rife in the States at the time (see p. 269). The notes to *Trogglodynamite* more than substantiate this: 'The deadly deceptive lull before an electric storm – Trogophony: tomorrow's sounds detonated on today's disc.' The Troggs were fun when all around were becoming serious and mystical. They could also turn their hand to other genres. Listen to the bubble-gum rocker 'Hip Hip Hooray', their psychedelic spoof 'Purple Shades' or the heavy metal tour-de-force 'Feel Like A Woman', that would have shaken even Black Sabbath fanatics. Today's sounds yesterday.

Pink Floyd

A Nice Pair: The Piper at the Gates of Dawn/A Saucerful of Secrets

(HARVEST SHDW 403)

Astronomy Dominé/Lucifer Sam/Matilda Mother/Flaming/Pow R Toc H/Take Up Thy Stethoscope And Walk/Interstellar Overdrive/The Gnome/Chapter 24/The Scarecrow/Bike/Let There Be More Light/Remember A Day/Set The Controls For The Heart Of The Sun/Corporal Clegg/A Saucerful Of Secrets/See-Saw/Jugband Blues

Originally playing r&b-based music, Pink Floyd first began playing improvised passages and making feedback experiments during the 'Spontaneous Underground' regular afternoon gigs at the Marquee in 1966. They evolved to become one of Britain's first psychedelic groups through appearances at the London Free School's Sound/Light Workshop in Notting Hill in October that year. Within months they had set up their hippie management company, Blackhill, had a regular light show and had become the house band at the new 'underground' club, UFO. Along with groups such as Soft Machine, Tomorrow and the Crazy World of Arthur Brown, they represented a parallel movement to that in San Francisco. No leading underground event in 1967 would have been complete without Pink Floyd, and their status was unaffected by their achieving a Top Five hit with 'See Emily Play' that summer. By now performing only their own material, almost exclusively written by guitarist Syd Barrett, they recorded their debut album, *Piper*. It revealed Barrett to be a master of charmingly simple songs, while on 'Astronomy Dominé' and 'Interstellar Overdrive' they unveiled the space rock epics that had grown out of their on-stage improvisations. Barrett, however, left in April 1968, following a nervous breakdown. Dave Gilmour replaced him as guitarist, with bassist Roger Waters assuming the creative mantle within the group. Unable to write lyrics to order, Pink Floyd concentrated on evocative music, particularly space rock. This set the seal on their future development: largely extended musical, improvisational albums and increasingly rare but spectacular live performances.

Traffic

Best of Traffic (ISLAND ILPS 9112)

Paper Sun/Heaven Is In Your Mind/No Face, No Name, No Number/Coloured Rain/Smiling Phases/Hole In My Shoe/Medicated Goo/Forty Thousand Headmen/Feelin' Alright/Shanghai Noodle Factory/Dear Mr Fantasy

Traffic were one of the first new groups to be formed in the wake of the 'underground' movement. Steve Winwood left the Spencer Davis Group within only months of their two finest singles, 'Gimme Some Lovin'' and 'I'm A Man', to form Traffic with fellow Birmingham area musicians Chris Wood (saxes, flutes), Dave Mason (guitar) and Jim Capaldi (drums). The four, in what became almost a commonplace, retired to a country cottage to 'get it together'. The resulting musical activity, which included two characteristically engaging hit singles, 'Paper Sun', with its giveaway, summer-of-love sitar runs, and the trite, dreamy 'Hole In My Shoe', culminated in a very schizoid debut album, *Dear Mr Fantasy*. Mason's naïve, wistful songs conflicted with the rest's jazzier, r&b/soul approach throughout the album. The highlights were Winwood's singing and guitar/organ playing and Wood's reed work. Mason departed at the end of that idyllic year but returned in 1968, writing songs with more muscle, including 'Feelin' Alright', for Traffic's eponymous second album. Mason left once again – joining and leaving at regular intervals throughout Traffic's history. After his third farewell, the group called it a day, offering *Last Exit* as a patchy, premature, valedictory album. They regrouped again, of course, in 1970, but *Best of Traffic* charts their first phase as one of the underground's most creative and pleasing groups.

Family

Music in a Doll's House (REPRISE K 44057)

The Chase/Mellowing Grey/Never Like This/Winter/Old Songs New Songs/Variation On A Theme Of The Breeze/Hey Mr Policeman/See Through Windows/Variation On A Theme Of Me My Friend/Peace Of Mind/Voyage/The Breeze/3 X Time

Formed from a nucleus of Leicester and Nottingham groups in 1967, Family were one of the first provincial groups to make an impact on London's underground scene. With a line-up of Roger Chapman, vocals, 'Charlie' Whitney, guitars, Rob Townshend, drums (the three constant members up to their disbandment in 1973), Rick Grech, bass and violin, and Jim King, various saxes and flute, the group had a combination of instruments ready-made for experimentation. That they did it with such undoubted style and aplomb and continued to make thoughtful, exciting music is a testament to their skills, particularly those of the writing team Chapman and Whitney. *Music in a Doll's House* was recorded and released in 1968; in places it sounds anachronistic and over-produced today with its feedback violins and backwards-played mellotrons but, by the standards of its day, no other album so aptly displays the sense of crazed invention that was rife. Family's music holds together through a blend of intelligent lyrics, keen arrangements and the presence and power of Roger Chapman's frenetic, vibrato singing. Family never really moved into the top league. They were erratic, invariably extreme in live performance and suffered too many personnel changes over the years to fully establish themselves. At their best, though, on *Doll's House* or the 1971 album *Fearless*, they were without equal.

Various Artists

The Roots of British Rock

(SIRE SASH 3711/2: IMPORT)

Singin' The Blues (Tommy Steele)/Rock Island Line (Lonnie Donegan)/ What Do You Want To Make Those Eyes At Me For (Emile Ford and the Checkmates)/Freight Train (Chas McDevitt)/Does Your Chewing Gum Lose Its Flavour On The Bedpost Overnight? (Lonnie Donegan)/ Rainbow (Russ Hamilton)/I Remember You (Frank Ifield)/He's Got The Whole World In His Hands (Laurie London)/Stranger On The Shore (Acker Bilk)/Sailor (Petula Clark)/Look For A Star (Gary Mills)/ Midnight In Moscow (Kenny Ball)/Wimoweh (Karl Denver Trio)/ Walkin' Back To Happiness (Helen Shapiro)/What Do You Want (Adam Faith)/Petite Fleur (Chris Barber)/Move It (Cliff Richard)/ Apache (The Shadows)/Halfway To Paradise (Billy Fury)/Tell Laura I Love Her (Ricky Valance)/Well I Ask You (Eden Kane)/Diamonds (Jet Harris and Tony Meehan)/Only Sixteen (Craig Douglas)/Living Doll (Cliff Richard)/Shakin' All Over (Johnny Kidd and the Pirates)/ Picture Of You (Joe Brown)/Bad Boy (Marty Wilde)/Tribute To Buddy Holly (Mike Berry)/Silver Threads And Golden Needles (The Springfields)/You Don't Have To Be A Baby To Cry (The Caravelles)/Telstar (The Tornadoes)

British rock & roll may have lacked spirit and a true identity, but it was not without its significance or the occasional unexpected gem. This album conveniently covers the different strains of pre-Beatles pop. Skiffle was of untold importance in the scheme of things, though it was intrinsically short-lived; the chasm between Lonnie Donegan's seminal 1956 hit 'Rock Island Line' and the 1959 'Chewing Gum' speaks volumes. Skiffle's close cousin, trad, equally ephemeral, is also represented at its best (Barber) and worst (Ball and Bilk). In between, skiffle had given many of our rock & rollers a start: Tommy Steele,

Adam Faith and, of course, Cliff Richard, who can be heard at his most rampant (the brilliant 'Move It') and minus the sting ('Living Doll'). Even singing big ballads, Billy Fury stands head and shoulders above the other Larry Parnes-managed performers, Joe Brown and Marty Wilde. The Shadows provide the link between the two eras; more sixties musicians must have begun life playing Shadows' hits than any other way. Their hardly-close rivals, the Tornadoes, offer a timely bridge: 'Telstar' was still in the charts when 'Love Me Do' first entered. The British rock & roll revolution was about to be unleashed. Before 1963, only isolated examples – 'Shakin' All Over' or 'Tribute To Buddy Holly' – suggested that it was possible; they were the glimmer of light at the end of a long tunnel.

Various Artists

Hard Up Heroes (DECCA DPA 3009/10)

Some Other Guy (The Big Three)/Give Her My Regards (Steve Marriott)/I Got My Mojo Working (Alexis Korner and Cyril Davies)/My Baby Left Me (Dave Berry)/Everything's Alright (The Mojos)/Long Tall Shorty (Graham Bond Organization)/You Came Along (The Warriors)/Tobacco Road (The Nashville Teens)/Da Doo Ron Ron (The Andrew Loog Oldham Orchestra)/The Uncle Willie (Zoot Money)/So Much In Love (The Mighty Avengers)/I'll Cry Instead (Joe Cocker)/I Go Ape (The Rockin' Vickers)/Now We're Thru (The Poets)/Good Morning Little Schoolgirl (Rod Stewart)/Tell Her No (The Zombies)/Leaving Here (The Birds)/Watcha Gonna Do About It (The Small Faces)/Have You Heard (John Mayall's Blues Breakers)/(Do I Figure) In Your Life (Honeybus)/The London Boys (David Bowie)/The Story Of Them, Parts I and II (Them)/The First Cut Is The Deepest (Cat Stevens)/Beggin' (Timebox)

Spanning 1963–8, this selection is drawn entirely from the Decca vaults, an almost bottomless source of choice cuts from one of the four major British companies of the sixties. The result is a fascinating mixture of classic singles, valuable period pieces and obscurities from then unknowns who have since found fame and fortune. The latter group dominates and many of the tracks (from Joe Cocker, the Warriors with

Jon Anderson, and Steve Marriott, for example) are purely of curiosity interest today. Others (from Rod Stewart or the Birds, featuring Ron Wood) are of much less dubious value. A handful of undisputed classics stand out – the Mojos, the Nashville Teens, Honeybus, the Big Three – all quite timeless. The period pieces range from two r&b classics, 'I Got My Mojo Working' and 'Long Tall Shorty', to Them's paean to the Maritime Hotel, Belfast, to the haunting Bowie track – a story of pill-poppin' mods, the spiritual ancestor of 'All The Young Dudes', as the intelligently annotated track listings point out. This is a valuable and lovingly compiled album (by *NME* writers Roy Carr and Charles Shaar Murray), complete with useful photos and thumb-nail sketches of each artist.

Various Artists

Mersey Beat '62–'64 (UNITED ARTISTS USD 305/6)

Let's Stomp (Faron's Flamingos)/Fortune Teller (The Merseybeats)/ Farmer John (The Searchers)/Peanut Butter (The Big Three)/Who Shot Sam (Sonny Webb and the Cascades)/Everybody Loves A Lover (The Undertakers)/The One To Cry (The Escorts)/Someday (Mark Peters and the Silhouettes)/Stupidity (Kingsize Taylor and the Dominos)/ Lies (Johnny Sandon and the Remo Four)/Thumbin' A Ride (Earl Preston and the TTs)/Tricky Dickie (Danny Seyton and the Sabres)/ Some Other Guy (The Big Three)/I Can Tell (Rory Storm and the Hurricanes)/I Know (Beryl Marsden)/I Ain't Mad At You (Howie Casey and the Seniors)/Shake Sherry (Faron's Flamingos)/Skinny Minnie (Lee Curtis and the All Stars)/Money (The Shakers)/You've Got Everything (Sonny Webb and the Cascades)/Peter Gunn Locomotion (Freddie Starr and the Midnighters)/Really Mystified (The Merseybeats)/Be My Girl (The Dennisons)/All Around The World (Earl Preston and the TTs)/Everything's Alright (The Mojos)/Dizzie Miss Lizzie (The Escorts)/Do You Love Me (Faron's Flamingos)/ Twist And Shout (The Searchers)/I'm With You (The Big Three)/ Beechwood 4–5789 (Ian and the Zodiacs)/Walking The Dog (The Dennisons)/(Do The) Mashed Potatoes (The Undertakers)/Dr Feelgood (Rory Storm and the Hurricanes)/Let's Stomp (Lee Curtis and the All Stars)

The majority of Liverpool groups didn't achieve commercial success, often because their sound was too raw and raunchy to be widely palatable, even though it conformed to the basic Liverpool style. There *was* undoubtedly a recognizable Merseybeat style, nowhere better defined than by Greg Shaw in the essential 1973 issue of *Who Put the Bomp* magazine: '(It) was defined by close vocal harmonies, pounding drums and, above all, a crashing, ringing, torrent of chords from the rhythm guitar highlighted with cymbal taps . . .' Despite some variation, this album, featuring mostly second-division Liverpool groups, adheres to the norm. Most of the tracks are covers, many typically obscure – Liverpool was always a source for Americana, including records, items brought in by the so-called 'Cunard Yanks' – and they are usually drawn from singles or from the invaluable *This is Merseybeat*, a two-volume set released on Oriole in 1963. Above all else, *Mersey Beat '62–'64* illustrates the limitations of Merseybeat. Like skiffle, trad and nascent British punk of recent years, it was a naturally ephemeral form, having little scope but providing an important apprenticeship, since neither sophisticated equipment nor brilliant musicianship were required. That said, this album is brimming with bona fide classics: 'Dizzie Miss Lizzie', 'Some Other Guy', 'Everything's Alright' and 'Mashed Potatoes' among them.

Various Artists

The Beat Merchants (UNITED ARTISTS UDM 101/2)

Road Runner (Wayne Fontana and the Mindbenders)/I Can Tell (The Zephyrs)/Yes I Do (Pete Maclaine and the Clan)/Shake, Shake, Shake (Tony Rivers and the Castaways)/All I Want Is You (The Escorts)/You Really Got A Hold On Me (Cliff Bennett and the Rebel Rousers)/I Just Don't Understand (The Cresters)/Dr Feelgood (Gerry Levene and the Avengers)/Poison Ivy (The Paramounts)/Summertime Blues (Dave Curtiss and the Tremors)/What'd I Say (The Big Three)/My Babe (The Pirates)/Let's Make It Pretty Baby (The Soul Agents)/See If She Cares (Faron's Flamingos)/Baby Jean (The Country Gentlemen)/No Other Guy (Mike Sheridan and the Nightriders)/That's What I Want (The Marauders)/Got My Mojo Working (The Sheffields)/Roll Over Beethoven (Pat Wayne with the Beachcombers)/Money (Bern Elliott and the Fenmen)/Sick and Tired (The Searchers)/Oh Yeah (The Others)/ Baby What's Wrong (The Downliners Sect)/I Like It Like That (The Farinas)/I Still Want You (Mickey Finn and the Blue Men)/Boom Boom (Blues By Five)/I'm Looking For A Woman (Jimmy Powell and the Five Dimensions)/Things Will Never Be The Same (The Four Just Men)/Back In The USA (Brian Howard and the Silhouettes)/Memphis Tennessee (Dave Berry and the Cruisers)/Talking About You (The Redcaps)/Bad Time (The Roulettes)/Last Night (The Merseybeats)/ Look At Me (The Whirlwinds)/That's My Girl (The Addicts)/Don't You Care (The Interns)/Que Sera Sera (Earl Royce and the Olympics)/ Juliet (The Four Pennies)/Forever (The Mojos)/Too Much Monkey Business (Keith Powell and the Valets)/Watch Your Step (Earl Preston and the TTs)/Casting My Spell (The Pirates)

A worthy companion to the *Mersey Beat* album, this album comes close to being a British *Nuggets* in exploring the overlaps and divergencies of the thousands of emerging groups between 1963 and 1965. As with *Mersey Beat*, few commercially successful groups figure, but the album is liberally sprinkled with singles that might, indeed should, have happened: listen to the Marauders' offering or Dave Curtiss's tremendous rendering of 'Summertime Blues'. Most of the young hopefuls here found themselves back in their day-jobs once the boom was over, though some stuck to it. Graham Gouldman and Eric Stewart of 10cc can be heard with the Whirlwinds and the Mindbenders respectively; the precursors of Family and Procul Harum are here as the Farinas and the Paramounts. These two, from Leicester and Southend, remind us that British Beat was not just a Liverpool/London phenomenon. Both areas are well represented, including the *Big Three at the Cavern* EP and an early Searchers' track recorded at the Star Club, Hamburg. London's scene is paraded by, among others, the Zephyrs, Cliff Bennett, the Downliners Sect and the Pirates. Brumbeat, never anything recognizable although Birmingham was an active beat centre, is chronicled by the excellent Redcaps, Mike Sheridan, Keith Powell and Jimmy Powell. There are a handful of absolutely vintage tracks here: for verification, check out the Others, the Beat Merchants or Brian Howard's stunning 'Back In The USA'. No album better unveils British beat in its original form and in transition, once the Merseybeat imitators had given way to those who fancied themselves able to play r&b.

British Beat: Singles

The Beatles: *She Loves You* (1963)

The definitive early Beatles single; nothing epitomizes Beatlemania as readily as the 'Yeah Yeah Yeah' hook.

The Swinging Blue Jeans: *Hippy Hippy Shake* (1963)

The essence of Merseybeat: an obscure song, absolutely transformed by the strident rhythm and raw energy of the one-take Blue Jeans version.

The Dave Clark Five: *Glad All Over* (1963)

Characteristic DC5 pile-driver; Clark's production gave the group the fullest possible sound with deliberate emphasis on the thumping rhythm track.

The Zombies: *She's Not There* (1964)

The only British chart hit from the thinking man's beat group. Superb natural timing and pacing on a highly sophisticated debut single.

Unit 4+2: *Concrete And Clay* (1965)

Classic one-hit-wonder group who produced this striking folk-beat single. They appeared to have everything going for them – except an image.

The Animals: *House Of The Rising Sun* (1964)

The first folk-rock single and the first hit to defy the three-minute rule.

Manfred Mann: *Pretty Flamingo* (1966)

Their last hit with Paul Jones in the middle, and their most endearing single; Jack Bruce played bass on this one.

The Easybeats: *Friday On My Mind* (1966)

Shel Talmy produced this classic teenage weekend song for the Aussie-based Easybeats. It's distinguished by some superb rhythm playing and singing.

Chris Farlowe: *Out Of Time* (1966)

It took a Jagger/Richard song and a Jagger production to earn the popular club performer his only hit. Music to clear the throat to.

The Yardbirds: *Shapes Of Things* (1966)

Prime British psychedelic single featuring a consummate guitar solo from Jeff Beck.

The Hollies: *King Midas In Reverse* (1967)

The Hollies' finest original single and one of the best British flower-power efforts but scarcely a hit. No wonder Graham Nash left . . .

The Small Faces: *All Or Nothing* (1966)

Always following leaders, this gave them their only Number 1; easily the most worthy of their string of hits.

The Creation: *Painter Man* (1966)

Pop-art rock of the first water; Shel Talmy produced this for his own Planet label.

The Spencer Davis Group: *Gimme Some Lovin'* (1966)

Relying too heavily on Steve Winwood's mature voice and musicianship, they rarely came up with the goods to do justice to his all-round talent. When they did . . .

Procul Harum: *A Whiter Shade Of Pale* (1967)

No single better conjures up the spirit of '67 – mysterious, hallucinogenic lyrics and a brooding organ, based on a Bach cantata. Magic.

Jimi Hendrix: *Hey Joe* (1967)

The impact of hearing Jimi Hendrix for the first time was only eclipsed by seeing him perform this on TV for the first time.

The Beatles: *Strawberry Fields Forever* (1967)

British acid rock in classic form – a totally different animal to the American model.

Arthur Brown: *Fire* (1967)

The most memorable underground hit; a tour-de-force performance from Arthur Brown, screaming and gyrating, matched by Vincent Crane's powerful organ work.

MICK HOUGHTON

California Sun

Throughout the fifties, the record industry on the West Coast of America was at once both peculiarly diverse and constricted; centred in Los Angeles, where it was overshadowed by the movie industry, it presented an amorphous mass of small labels and small recording studios, but lacked direction. By 1965, however, LA's record industry had completed its long apprenticeship and had advanced to a point where it could offer a serious challenge to New York's supremacy in the industry. To some extent encouraged by the emergence of LA, San Francisco also flourished in the mid sixties, only to flounder again before the decade was out. Between them, though, LA and San Francisco, despite the latter's decline, had established beyond question the West Coast as a thriving catchment area for rock music.

LA's rock community had traditionally taken the form of a series of interrelated groups of writers, musicians, performers and entrepreneurs, the most enduring of which centred around a bunch of middle-class high-school kids: Herb Alpert, Lou Adler, Terry Melcher, Jan and Dean and the Beach Boys. Crystallizing around this nucleus of people, the LA music industry finally secured an identity. Two factors were influential in this: on the one hand, the proximity of the long-established movie industry led to a preoccupation with professionalism and perfection in production; on the other, the almost idyllic nature of the California climate resulted in a devotion to recreational pursuits that gave rise to surfing and hot rod music and general 'Fun Fun Fun'. A clique grew up around the Beach Boys, Jan and Dean, Terry Melcher, Roger Christian, Lou Adler, Gary Usher, Steve Barri, P. F. Sloan, Bruce Johnstone and others, while behind them lay yet another set of people, accomplished session musicians. These, who included Leon Russell, Glen Campbell, Larry Knechtel, Joe Osborne, Hal Blaine, Jim Gordon, David Gates and Van Dyke Parks, not only played on a good many of the hits to come out of LA in the sixties, but, later, often emerged as successful front men in their own right. David Gates's amazing commercial triumph with Bread, or Glen Campbell's with 'countrypolitan' music, epitomizes this process.

Surfing put LA well and truly on the map, but with Dylan and protest music rising in importance in 1965, it was the Byrds who were to boost the next phase in LA's growth with their folk-rock adaptation of 'Mr Tambourine Man'. Ironically, Roger McGuinn was the only Byrd who played on the 'Tambourine' session (though the vocals were provided by the group), and the Byrds remained aloof from the post-Dylan protest circle. They did, however, help spawn a local club scene – notably Ciro's, the Crescendo, the Kaleidoscope and Sunset Strip clubs such as the Whiskey – from whence sprang groups like the Doors, Love, the Leaves, the Seeds, and the Standells.

The LA garage bands stood in sharp contrast to the polished LA vocal groups. The latter perfected immaculate harmonies – often utilizing four- and five-part arrangements – plus, of course, slick instrumental backing. Among the leading groups were the Mamas and the Papas, Spanky and Our Gang, the Turtles, the Association and Harpers Bizarre. As a sign of LA's impact on the East Coast, the New York Kama Sutra label was launched in 1965 with a deliberately Californian 'good time' sound, and featuring groups such as the Lovin' Spoonful, the Tradewinds, Innocence and the San Francisco group Sopwith Camel. New York had acknowledged the threat of LA in the most flattering manner – by imitation.

Lou Adler's career effectively encapsulates almost all the major trends of California pop/rock. As early as 1959 he'd been manager of Jan and Dean, working for several small labels over the next few years before, in 1964, forming Dunhill Productions. He employed Steve Barri and P. F. Sloan, writers of hundreds of surfing/protest era classics and themselves performers. Together, they were the Fantastic Baggys, while Sloan was perhaps the definitive LA protest singer. Adler later brought together and produced The Mamas and the Papas, and when, in 1966, he sold Dunhill to ABC, his newly formed label Ode scored immediately with Scott McKenzie's 'San Francisco' anthem. He further spread the word about California pop by co-organizing the Monterey Pop Festival in 1967, where many of San Francisco's leading groups played for the first time outside the city. Later, in 1970, he reunited with Carole King, who, under Adler's tutelage, helped establish the next major trend in LA rock – the singer/song-writer.

By 1965, with LA's share of the music industry consolidating, in San Francisco, 450 miles to the north, the first stirrings of the 'Frisco scene were taking place. Within two years San Francisco would be dubbed 'Liverpool USA' but, tragically, the seeds of the scene's destruction had already been sown by then. The pre-boom 'Frisco scene hinged around a handful of local labels. Most only managed local hits – Fantasy, for example, with the Golliwogs, later to become Creedence Clearwater Revival; but Autumn managed several Top Forty successes, notably by the Beau Brummells, one of the earliest 'English Invasion' style groups in America. Autumn involved two figures better known in other spheres: Tom Donahue, who owned the label, was a pioneer of 'underground' radio, while Autumn's A&R production chief was Sly Stewart, later Sly of the Family Stone.

The new strain of 'Frisco groups was, however, beginning to appear by the summer of 1965, and had little to do with labels such as Autumn and Fantasy. The acknowledged pioneers of the 'Frisco scene were the Charlatans; the place where it all began, though, was in Nevada, at the Red Dog Saloon. All the different facets of the 'Frisco scene were there in their infancy: a rock & roll band, a crude light show, the first psychedelic dance poster and plenty of LSD. Other groups were already coming together, all very different musically. Grace Slick's Great Society, Big Brother and the Holding Company (sans Janis Joplin), Jefferson Airplane and the Warlocks, soon to become the Grateful Dead. It was a tight-knit scene; many of the individuals knew each other from playing the folk circuit, others studied art and design together at college. This helped forge another key element of the local scene: the creation of posters and elaborate slide/light shows.

If the scene began at the Red Dog Saloon, it evolved fully at dances in San Francisco itself. These, initially, were promoted by the Family Dog, fronted by Chet Helms; beginning with dances at the Longshoreman's Hall, the Family Dog soon found a permanent home at the Avalon Ballroom, while another of the new breed of promoters, Bill Graham, provided competition at the Fillmore. Dancing was a vital aspect of 'Frisco music; it was only in the later sixties that music became a concert phenomenon. In 1965 music was for dancing and free expression. Invariably having consumed large doses of acid, then still legal, the local community of hippies would dance wildly to music that, typically, was loud and improvisational.

The scene was at its true peak in 1966. New groups were forming (Quicksilver Messenger Service, Moby Grape, Country Joe and the Fish) while musicians were flooding in to play the 'Frisco ballrooms. The Sir Douglas Quintet, 13th Floor Elevators, Steve Miller (who remained there) travelled from Texas; Love, the Leaves and Kaleidoscope came north from LA and the Lovin' Spoonful, Blues Project and Paul Butterfield's Blues Band arrived from the East Coast. But, at this stage, the scene was still local; anyone drawn there was drawn by word of mouth alone. Publicity was scant but both the record industry and the media soon heard about the scene on the grapevine; the rot was about to set in. The halcyon 'summer of '67' would actually see the demise of the San Francisco scene proper.

By 1967 most of the original groups had signed major deals; sadly the Charlatans missed out but the Airplane, the Dead and Big Brother all became household names. Second-generation groups were swelling the scene at an alarming rate, but it was the intervention of the media which killed the scene more than anything else. The 'hippie' community supplied irresistible media fodder and, once exposed, the 'love generation' was ripe for exploitation by businessmen–merchandizers and record company people alike.

The local scene had lost its inner cohesion as its once idealistic founders, one by one, set their sights on new horizons. Bill Graham, once a member of the Mime Troupe, for example, had become a big-time promoter. By 1969, San Francisco, having helped spawn the underground cult in Europe, particularly London, and in other American cities, had become just another underground music centre, and a dying one at that.

The music industry in the city had expanded, of course – especially the importance of major studios like Wally Heider's, Columbia or Alembic (formerly Pacific High); San Francisco was on the map as a rock centre, but it was no longer a distinctive and creative one. Ironically, in the later sixties a number of international groups did emerge – Creedence Clearwater Revival, Santana, Sly and the Family Stone – but they had little in common with the crazy days of 1965–6. Similarly, in the bars and clubs, the scene had little to link it with the glorious past, apart from the presence of a handful of survivors from groups such as Big Brother, Moby Grape, Quicksilver and the Youngbloods, still trucking after all these years. Three of the original spirits have seen out the years – the Grateful Dead, now almost an institution, the Jefferson Airplane/Starship and Steve Miller – but, at least in the case of the last two named, they have kept abreast of the times by adopting a strictly Los Angeles approach.

Despite that great flurry of activity in the mid sixties San Francisco today is back where it was fifteen years earlier, making little impact on the musical scene outside the city. LA, meanwhile, had continued to build on its sixties platform. Two new trends appeared in the seventies – country rock and singer/song-writers. They flourished and, to some extent, have now fused to produce hi-fi/FM radio-orientated rock that, with disco music, now dominates the US music industry.

Country music became the dominant new influence in LA from 1968 onwards and, typically, it was in the hands of a small, cross-bred group of people. After Dylan had offered his seal of approval (*Nashville Skyline*), two groups, the Byrds and Buffalo Springfield, virtually spawned the whole country-rock movement. Spinning off into the Flying Burrito Bros., Dillard and Clark's Expedition, Mannassas, the Eagles, Poco, Loggins and Messina and Firefall – not to mention Crosby, Stills, Nash and Young, who, while hardly playing country rock, helped foster that LA country-rock devotion to harmony singing – there are few major groups which do not stem from their family tree. Country rock even influenced San Francisco's musicians; it certainly gave the Grateful Dead a direction which bore fruit in their most satisfying studio albums, *Workingman's Dead* and *American Beauty*, as well as producing the enjoyable spin-off group, the New Riders of the Purple Sage. Courtesy of Creedence Clearwater's John Fogerty, San Francisco also contributed another of the country-rock genre's greatest albums, *Blue Ridge Rangers*.

Amidst the roll-call of players descending from the Byrds/Springfield axis, none made sure country rock would spread more effectively than the Eagles. Their decisive commercial success ensured that country rock would be widely adopted by their LA peers. Their influence has become all-encompassing and with one or two notable exceptions – Little Feat and Steely Dan spring readily to mind – LA groups have become alarmingly bland, uninspiring and complacent.

The other main trend, the singer/song-writer boom, soon fell prey to the same malady. Led by Carole King, James Taylor, Joni Mitchell and the individuals within Crosby, Stills, Nash and Young, the singer/song-writers took a firm grip on the LA recording scene. Along with many of the prime movers in country rock, they'd cut regular solo albums, aided and abetted by one another and with old 'Frisco pals from the Dead and the Airplane often lending a hand. A steady flow of female accompanists emerged to swell the list: Linda Ronstadt, Emmylou Harris, Maria Muldaur, Bonnie Raitt and, more recently, Nicolette Larson.

A few broke free from this soporific world: Neil Young, Joni Mitchell and Jackson Browne stand apart as three of the most talented artists in rock. Sadly, the LA process of sucking the lifeblood from an artist has seen even Jackson Browne looming dangerously on the edge of disaster, after mingling too much with the Eagles and achieving Top Forty success. If he does succumb, his protégé, Warren Zevon, looks best-placed to replace him in that triumvirate. Others have remained aloof from the hip circle: Randy Newman, Van Dyke Parks and, until his death in 1975, Tim Buckley, must have cringed at the thought of being labelled singer/song-writers.

The two strains have now come together in what has been dubbed Hip Easy Listening – album music geared to endless hi-fi/FM radio consumption. The most successful exponents include the Eagles, Jefferson Starship, Fleetwood Mac (three fifths English but fully-fledged Californians nonetheless), Linda Ronstadt, Fire-fall and, increasingly, Jackson Browne. The music is intrinsically LA – perfectly played (indeed, a new clique of session-players, including David Lindley, Lee Sklar, Russ Kunkel and Danny Kootch, has formed around these soft rockers), perfectly sung, perfectly produced, and insidious. The lyrical themes, passed on from the singer/song-writers, concern adult love; Fleetwood Mac's *Rumours*, with its measured, unchallenging but skilful performance, and gently shifting moods and rhythms, is the definitive example of this growing genre.

The Los Angeles music scene, then, is ostensibly the same as in 1965; as clique-ridden and incestuous as ever, it is still chiefly concerned with recreational pursuits, though now sex and drugs have replaced kissin' and surfin'. The sun, needless to say, shines as warmly and brightly as ever.

Together with New York, Los Angeles remains at the heart of American rock music. Although there are still creative and original artists associated with the city (for example Ry Cooder, Joni Mitchell, Tom Waits and Neil Young) its primary importance is as the main influence on the all-pervasive 'easy-listening rock': at the start of a new decade, this is still proving one of the most commercially potent of contemporary styles.

California Sun : Albums

Various Artists

Golden Summer

(UNITED ARTISTS UA LA627H2: IMPORT)

Surfin' (The Beach Boys)/Surfer's Stomp (The Marketts)/Hawaii Five-O (The Ventures)/Summer Means Fun (The Fantastic Baggys)/Surf City (Jan and Dean)/Wipe Out (The Surfaris)/Honolulu Lulu (Jan and Dean)/Balboa Blue (The Marketts)/Underwater (The Frogmen)/ Muscle Beach Party (Frankie Avalon)/Surfin' Safari (The Beach Boys)/ Sidewalk Surfin' (Jan and Dean)/Surfer Joe (The Surfaris)/Let's Go Trippin' (Dick Dale and the Del-Tones)/Surfin' Bird (The Trashmen)/ Pipeline (The Ventures)/Ride The Wild Surf (Jan and Dean)/Surfer Girl (The Beach Boys)/New York Is A Lonely Town (The Tradewinds)/ Lonely Surfer (Jack Nitzsche)/Beach Party (Annette Funicello)/Let's Go (Pony) (The Routers)

Surf music began in 1961 as an extension of the gritty rock, sax and guitar instrumentals of Duane Eddy, Johnny and the Hurricanes etc, the chief inspiration being Dick Dale and the Del-Tones. 'King of the surf guitar' Dale's 'Let's Go Trippin'', with its staccato guitar runs, conveyed the elation of surfin' itself. A spate of imitations followed; the Chantays' 'Pipeline', covered on this album by the Ventures, and 'Wipe Out' were perhaps the best. But it was Brian Wilson and the Beach Boys who sparked the real craze by adding lyrics: 'Surfin'' was their first regional hit, 'Surfin' Safari' breaking nationally. The Beach Boys readily acknowledged Jan and Dean's pioneering singles of the late fifties; they already had the California-style falsetto lead and doo-wop-derived harmonies down pat and were soon fed with a succession of inventive surfin' and, later, hot-rod songs by a small clique of writers/producers, including Brian Wilson, Jan Berry himself, P. F. Sloan, Steve Barri, Roger Christian, Terry Melcher and Gary Usher. Many of the vintage tracks of the 'golden era' – 1962–5 – were theirs, 'Surf City', 'Summer Means Fun' and 'Ride The Wild Surf' among them. Surf music spread rapidly to the most unlikely places; the Trashmen hailed from the Mid-west, the Tradewinds from New York. By 1966 the surfing era had passed once the simple pleasures of beaches, girls, cars and parties gave way to more serious issues. Put simply, the surfing generation grew up.

The Beach Boys

Pet Sounds (CAPITOL ST 2458)

Wouldn't It Be Nice/You Still Believe In Me/That's Not Me/Don't Talk (Put Your Head On My Shoulder)/I'm Waiting For The Day/Let's Go Away For A While/Sloop John B/God Only Knows/I Know There's An Answer/Here Today/I Just Wasn't Made For These Times/Pet Sounds/Caroline No

An almost faultless album, *Pet Sounds* was the culmination of a growing maturity in the Beach Boys' music that was already evident from songs such as 'California Girls', 'Help Me Rhonda' and the neglected masterpiece 'Don't Worry Baby'. Brian Wilson was no longer simply documenting the Californian surfing/dragster culture but, retired from touring since 1965, was exploring new possibilities in pop music and sound techniques. Aside from assimilating the production methods of Phil Spector, Wilson's particular flair for melody was enhanced by his use of unusual combinations of musical instruments. While others, the Byrds and the Beatles, Wilson's declared rivals, were experimenting with backwards tapes and electronic trickery, he was dabbling in pure acoustic sound. The fullest fruition of Brian Wilson's ideas comes on *Pet Sounds*, a timeless album, though one that is flawed lyrically in places. At best ('Caroline No', 'Here Today') it's quite breathtaking. It's tragic that *Pet Sounds* sold poorly and was overshadowed for critics by the Beatles' *Revolver*; this spurred Wilson on to his ill-advised link with Van Dyke Parks, the abortive *Smile* and the overrated

'Good Vibrations'. Ironically, after this enigmatic period had set the Beach Boys back several years, eventual critical acclaim came with albums that were vastly inferior to *Pet Sounds.*

The Lovin' Spoonful

The Lovin' Spoonful File (PYE FILD 009)

Do You Believe In Magic?/My Gal (Poor Gal)/Blues In The Bottle/Fishin' Blues/On The Road Again/You Baby/Did You Ever Have To Make Up Your Mind/Younger Girl/Daydream/It's Not Time Now/You Didn't Have To Be So Nice/Jug Band Music/Bald Headed Lena/Didn't Want To Have To Do It/Butchie's Tune/Pow/Summer In The City/Nashville Cats/Rain On The Roof/Coconut Grove/Lovin' You/Darlin' Be Home Soon/You're A Big Boy Now/She Is Still A Mystery/Younger Generation/Money/Six O'Clock/Never Goin' Back/As Long As You're Here/Priscilla Millionaira/The Room Nobody Lives In/She's A Lady

Although not from California, the Lovin' Spoonful offered one of the most popular versions of folk rock, and also had considerable influence on early West Coast groups, notably Jefferson Airplane. Nevertheless, it was their Greenwich Village folk/blues background that defined their rock & roll/jug band hybrid, a style which hinged on the superior musicianship of John Sebastian, Zal Yanovsky, Steve Boone and Joe Butler over their West Coast peers. Sebastian's delightful songs were the key, however: endearing, superbly crafted songs conveying any number of themes. Accordingly, Spoonful albums combined adolescent love songs ('Younger Girl', 'You Didn't Have To Be So Nice'), songs of graceful tranquillity ('Coconut Grove', 'Daydream'), and totally original gems like 'Nashville Cats', Sebastian's paean to country music, or 'Summer In The City', tense and uneasy; not least is that marvellous celebration of pop music, 'Do You Believe In Magic'. Sadly, following their third album, *Hums*, the group began to disintegrate. Two patchy sound-track albums and an uninspired fourth album with Jerry Yester replacing Yanovsky were capped by the awful *Revelation – Revolution*, recorded after Sebastian had left the group to pursue what has become an intermittently successful, often embarrassing, solo career.

The Byrds

Mr Tambourine Man (CBS 62571)

Mr Tambourine Man/I'll Feel A Whole Lot Better/Spanish Harlem Incident/You Won't Have To Cry/Here Without You/The Bells Of Rhymney/All I Really Wanna Do/I Knew I'd Want You/It's No Use/Don't Doubt Yourself Babe/Chimes Of Freedom/We'll Meet Again

This seminal folk-rock album alone would have been a worthy claim to fame for the Byrds. Yet with virtually every album up to their sixth, *Sweetheart of the Rodeo*, in 1968, the Byrds opened up new doors, shifting with ease from folk rock through experimental acid and space rock to country rock, which they adhered to, in one form or another, until their demise in 1972. Each of the original Byrds lived through the early sixties folk boom until, as legend has it, Roger McGuinn, inspired by the film *A Hard Day's Night*, had the notion of forming an electric group. Teaming up with fellow folkies Gene Clark and David Crosby, they later added Chris Hillman, a former bluegrass musician, and Michael Clarke, on bass and drums, neither of whom had played their chosen instruments before. At manager Jim Dickson's request they recorded Dylan's 'Mr Tambourine Man', and the rest, as they say, is history. In fact, only McGuinn played and sang on the monumental single, but the others did supply the three-part harmonies that set the Byrds apart from the characteristic surfing groups as much as McGuinn's ringing lead voice and jangling twelve-string. If McGuinn stole most of the honours, it is to be remembered that Gene Clark sang most of the leads on the album and wrote the group's original material. It is Clark's measured writing that turns this into a classic album rather than a collection of fillers for the hits that open each side of the album.

The Byrds

Younger than Yesterday (CBS 62988)

So You Wanna Be A Rock 'n' Roll Star/Have You Seen Her Face/CTA 102/Renaissance Fair/Time Between/Everybody's Been Burned/

Thoughts And Words/Mind Gardens/My Back Pages/The Girl With No Name/Why

When the Byrds recorded their third album *Fifth Dimension* their chief song-writer, Gene Clark, had already left the group, and the others had turned to experimentation with jazz forms and electronics by way of compensation. *Eight Miles High* is the finest expression of this new pursuit, but the whole album is important in that it offered a basic style which many of LA's emerging garage bands adopted. Within a year, on *Younger Than Yesterday*, the significance of Clark's loss was further reduced by the emergence of the rest of the group as song-writers. With hindsight, it's clear that the *5D* album influenced the Beatles on *Revolver*, but nowhere near as much as *Revolver* inspired the Byrds while recording *Younger than Yesterday* (listen to 'CTA 102' or 'Thoughts And Words'). A flawed album (Crosby's 'Mind Gardens' is utterly embarrassing), the highlights are the sardonic 'So You Wanna Be A Rock 'n' Roll Star', Dylan's 'My Back Pages' and two beauties from Crosby, the delicate 'Renaissance Fair' and the haunting 'Everybody's Been Burned', which set the pattern for many of his later songs with CSN. Most encouraging, though, is Chris Hillman's emergence. His bass playing is exemplary throughout, but it's his nascent country-rock songs, complete with guitar work by future Byrd Clarence White, that point the way forward. Overshadowed by the Beatles' *Sergeant Pepper*, *Younger than Yesterday* is far more impressive than the acclaimed *Notorious Byrds Bros.*, the album which saw Crosby's departure prior to the group's complete adoption of country rock.

The Flying Burrito Bros.

The Gilded Palace of Sin (A&M AMLS 931)

Christine's Tune/Sin City/Do Right Woman/Dark End Of The Street/ My Uncle/Wheels/Juanita/Hot Burrito No. 1/Hot Burrito No. 2/Do You Know How It Feels/Hippie Boy

This group was formed in 1968 by Gram Parsons and Chris Hillman, who as members of the Byrds had been the chief instigators of the Byrds' ambitious country album *Sweetheart of the Rodeo*. The Burritos were completed by bassist Chris Ethridge and steel guitarist Sneaky Pete; original Byrds drummer Mike Clarke joined after *The Gilded Palace of Sin* was recorded. Unlike *Sweetheart*, the Burritos' debut was mostly composed of original songs by Parsons and Hillman. Their quality was beyond reproach, particularly two achingly beautiful love songs, sung emotively by Parsons in his own cracked, vulnerable manner, 'Hot Burrito' Numbers 1 and 2, and the remarkable 'Sin City', which managed to convey traditional country values in a highly modern context. It was all part of Parsons' vision of 'cosmic' country, something he'd already tried with the pioneering International Submarine Band, and which went beyond a mere marriage of country and rock. He left after the disappointing *Burrito Deluxe* in 1969, to continue exploring that vision on two exceptional solo albums made before his tragic death in 1973. The Burritos rode on with a never-ending supply of new blood; the key recruits were Bernie Leadon, Rick Roberts, Al Perkins and Byron Berline. The surprisingly good farewell album, the live *Last of the Red Hot Burritos*, documents the group's torrid history.

The Eagles

Desperado (ASYLUM K 53008)

Doolin-Dalton/Twenty One/Out Of Control/Tequila Sunrise/Desperado/ Certain Kind Of Fool/Outlaw Man/Saturday Night/Bitter Creek/ Doolin-Dalton (reprise)/Desperado (reprise)

Where commercial success eluded the later Byrds, Burritos and Poco, it came almost immediately for the Eagles, although they were playing music which was directly descended from these forerunners. In fact, two of the founder-members, Bernie Leadon and Randy Meisner, played in the last-named bands; the other two members were Glenn Frey and Don Henley, equally well entrenched in country-rock backgrounds. A single from the group's debut album *Eagles*, 'Take It Easy', became a huge US hit. It seemed a trifle unwarranted, especially as *Eagles* was a highly derivative album. *Desperado*, their second, released in 1973, more than compensated for the first. Cleverly developing the theme of the gunslinger/outlaw as rock & roll star, the album's strength lies in the pacing and structure of the highly individual songs, and the emphasis on each member's distinctive lead voice as well as on the matchless harmonies. Where *Eagles* seemed prematurely weary, *Desperado* has tremendous vitality and emotion. This has gradually fallen away on subsequent albums, which have seen the departure of Leadon and Meisner and the addition of guitarists Don Felder, Joe Walsh of the James Gang and Timothy B. Schmit from Poco. The group's career has been wisely handled; they are now superstars but their bland, soulless music has come to epitomize that much-used term 'laid-back', and is aimed at the widest possible audience via FM radio.

Buffalo Springfield

Again (ATLANTIC K588 094)

Mr Soul/A Child's Claim To Fame/Everydays/Expecting To Fly/Bluebird/Hung Upside Down/Sad Memory/Good Time Boy/Rock & Roll Woman/Broken Arrow

Few groups can have been afforded the same degree of legendary status as Buffalo Springfield, despite releasing only three albums, of which only *Again* was fully realized. The essence of the group was a highly charged chemistry that emanated from the three guitarists and song-writers, Steve Stills, Ritchie Furay and Neil Young. Their first album saw them out on a limb, ignoring many of the stock folk-rock tendencies of their contemporaries. But it was a typical debut; too many rough edges, too much outside interference, which meant, in particular, that Young was unable to sing lead on most of his own songs. By the time they recorded *Again* in late 1967, the three personalities emerge strongly but there *is* still a definite Springfield sound: a unique fusion of electric and acoustic instruments and styles, precisely arranged interplay between the guitars (notably on 'Bluebird'), highly individual singing and harmony work and the continual ability to surprise. Kicking off with the hard rock of Young's 'Mr Soul', they lead into Furay's country pop; the jazzy electronic piano of 'Everydays' is juxtaposed with Young's savage fuzz guitar, while on 'Hung Upside Down', Stills and Young embark on a sizzling guitar duel. There are also two unforgettable tracks from Young: his breathtaking collaboration with Jack Nitzsche on 'Expecting To Fly' and the enigmatic 'Broken Arrow', an intriguing series of musical threads. Already, by this album, the group's vital chemistry was proving too volatile. A third, pieced-together album, *Last Time Around*, was posthumous and erratic.

Crosby, Stills, Nash and Young

4 Way Street (ATLANTIC K60003)

On The Way Home/Teach Your Children/Triad/The Lee Shore/Chicago/Right Between The Eyes/Cowgirl In The Sand/Don't Let It Bring You Down/49 Bye-Byes/Love The One You're With/Pre Road Downs/Long Time Gone/Southern Man/Ohio/Carry On/Find The Cost Of Freedom

With their almost too perfect, predominantly acoustic debut album, *Crosby, Stills and Nash*, the group made an immediate impact both sides of the Atlantic, bringing about a new awareness of what could be done quietly and melodically, with thoughtfully arranged harmonies, at a time when 'heavy metal' was the norm. But their flawless studio sound lacked muscle in live performances until Neil Young, Stills's sparring partner from Buffalo Springfield, was brought in. *Déjà Vu*, the foursome's first album, was patchy, Young's material eclipsing everyone else's. Young was also responsible for their most memorable song, the emotionally charged 'Ohio', recorded after the Kent State killings. Such fired performances were usually reserved for live performances, though, and their set, around 1970, is captured on *4 Way Street*. On the first two sides they play acoustically, Young and Crosby coming across particularly well. The electric sides contain two magical performances of longish versions of Young's 'Southern Man' and Stills's 'Carry On'. Crosby reveals what an underrated rhythm guitarist he is, while Young and Stills battle it out as of old. CSNY succeeded, where perhaps only the Doors and Jefferson Airplane had before, in drawing together LA studio precision and electrifying 'Frisco-style live performances. With the release of the album, the four went their prophesied separate ways, CSN reuniting in 1977 to produce an unimpressive album.

Love

Forever Changes (ELEKTRA K42015)

Alone Again Or/A House Is Not A Motel/Andmoreagain/The Daily Planet/Old Man/The Red Telephone/Maybe The People Would Be The Times Or Between Clark And Hilldale/Live And Let Live/The Good Humor Man He Sees Everything Like This/Bummer In The Summer/You Set The Scene

The first rock band to sign to Elektra, in 1966, Love paved the way for others, notably the Doors, who helped establish Elektra as a leading contemporary label. Love's first album was in the typical LA punk style but, by *Da Capo*, their second, they had developed fast, the album fulfilling the promise of singer/guitarist/composer Arthur Lee. Apart from a brave but flawed long track that took up a whole side, there were six songs of startling originality on the other. One, 'Seven And Seven Is' gave them a US hit; the high point, however, was the acoustic, Spanish-tinged 'The Castle'. It gave a clear indication that Love were capable of something very special – and that something was *Forever Changes*. This album saw the fullest exposition of Lee's warped vision of the world in a literate, poetic, philosophic body of lyrics. Musically, too, *Forever Changes* was decidedly ambitious. Driven by a light but powerful rhythm, the sweet orchestrations contrasted sharply with Lee's stark lyrics and John Echols's savage guitar solos. Love's other writer, rhythm guitarist Brian McClean, contributed the album's best known cut, 'Alone Again Or'. Love's wider influence was minimal; they were purely a cult group. The group broke up after an abortive fourth album, Lee resurfacing with new versions of Love every so often and moving closer to r&b.

The Doors

The Doors (ELEKTRA K 42012)

Break On Through/Soul Kitchen/The Crystal Ship/Twentieth Century Fox/Alabama Song/Light My Fire/Back Door Man/I Looked At You/End Of The Night/Take It As It Comes/The End

There can be few debut albums as impressive as *The Doors*, which sounds as forceful today as it did in 1967. The Doors were one of the few underground groups of this era to reach a mass audience, achieving six hit singles in America. And, unlike the bulk of LA groups, they had a magnificent presence live, touring frequently and controversially due to singer Jim Morrison's overtly sexual manner of performance. Morrison's image, a mixture of Presley and early James Dean that smacked of rebellion, was all the more potent because he was, at the same time, highly articulate. Morrison wrote all the Doors' lyrics, and the ones on this album are particularly accomplished. The highlight is 'Light My Fire', which in edited form gave the Doors a Number One hit. Such a strong group performance is rare; aside from Morrison, Ray Manzerek's pervasive organ playing, John Densmore's calculated drumming and Robbie Krieger's guitar playing – particularly his precisely timed solo – are an immaculate combination. The whole album has the same power: it is virtually a single boastful, sexual threat from Morrison, culminating in the dramatic, Freudian 'The End'; but their preoccupations are equally apparent in their choice of Willie Dixon's 'Back Door Man'. The Doors never made a wholly bad album, their last, *L A Woman* (1970), being one of the best. Once described by Morrison as 'erotic politicians', the group split up after Morrison's death in 1971, but not before it had left an indelible mark on the sixties music, one that still stands as an example to others.

The Mothers of Invention

Freak Out

(VERVE SELECT 2683 004)

Hungry Freaks Daddy/I Ain't Got No Heart/Who Are The Brain Police?/Go Cry On Somebody Else's Shoulder/Motherly Love/How Could I Be Such A Fool?/Wowie Zowie/You Didn't Try To Call Me/Any Way The Wind Blows/I'm Not Satisfied/You're Probably Wondering Why I'm Here?/Trouble Every Day/Help, I'm A Rock/The Return Of The Son Of Monster Magnet

In 1970, Frank Zappa disbanded his four-year-old Mothers of Invention, arrogantly claiming that audiences had 'not properly assimilated the recorded work of the group'. Thereafter his work became more widely palatable and accessible. *Freak Out*, however, the debut album from the original group in 1966, in common with all the Mothers' sixties albums, explains why the group was branded, in Zappa's favourite phrase, as having 'no commercial potential'. Much of *Freak Out* hasn't stood the test of time but it was unique in its day. The album mixes parodies of fifties and sixties pop forms and outrageous social satire of the kind that dominated the Mothers' following albums (*Absolutely Free* and *We're Only in It for the Money*), but the songs are unexpectedly and abruptly interrupted by avant-garde electronic and classical sequences, and advanced jazz rock that is anything but clichéd. These now familiar Zappa trade-marks might have led one to conclude that he didn't take himself seriously. Whether he does today is arguable but, between *Freak Out* and *Burnt Weenie Sandwich* (1969), Zappa was piecing together a very complex jigsaw-puzzle; it's this fascinating pot-pourri which has rightly earned him his reputation as a leading figure in contemporary rock.

Jefferson Airplane

After Bathing at Baxter's (RCA SF 7926)

The Ballad Of You And Me And Pooneil/A Small Package Of Value Will Come To You Shortly/Young Girl Sunday Blues/Martha/Wild Tyme/The Last Wall Of The Castle/Rejoyce/Watch Her Ride/Spare Chaynge/Two Heads/Won't You Try/Saturday Afternoon

Jefferson Airplane were quick to appreciate the need to distinguish themselves in the studio as well as in the ballrooms. With one folksy album under their belt, they were well prepared when they came to record *Surrealistic Pillow*, especially as they'd since acquired the services of Grace Slick as singer/writer. It was two of her songs, 'White Rabbit' and 'Somebody To Love', which launched the group nationally but, more importantly, her soaring voice blended perfectly with those of Marty Balin and Paul Kantner to give the Airplane their three-strong vocal mark of distinction. Strangely, though, instead of consolidating their commercial platform, they recorded *After Bathing at Baxter's*, an album of staggeringly ambitious artistic merit that effectively meant commercial suicide for the group. The almost pretty melodies are set against an atonal rhythm line much of the time, while, throughout, Jorma Kaukonen's guitar tone is constantly unnerving, intermittently savage. Sample the 'Saturday Afternoon'/'Won't You Try' sequence or the violent 'Last Wall Of The Castle'. *Baxters'* was advance warning of the group's disintegration, as Marty Balin began to take more of a back-seat role. The group became increasingly political in outlook, recording battle cries for the young American left (*Volunteers*); Balin left at this point while the others involved themselves in various spin-off projects. Kaukonen and Casady formed Hot Tuna while Slick and Kantner concentrated on solo projects that would ultimately evolve into the immensely popular, but invariably sterile, Jefferson Starship.

The Grateful Dead

Live Dead (WARNER BROS. K66002)

Dark Star/St Stephen/The Eleven/Lovelight/Death Don't Have No Mercy/Feedback/We Bid You Goodnight

Like a good many of the early 'Frisco groups, the Grateful Dead's origins lay in folk music, and they gradually evolved into an electric group by 1965. This coincided with their involvement with Ken Kesey's Pranksters and the notorious acid (LSD) tests, where their blues-based music began to take on its more meandering/experimental shape. Soon the Dead became the focal point of a growing family of musicians, poets, sound- and light-show operatives, wives, friends, children and others; the family moved to 710 Ashbury where the myth that surrounded it took shape. Heavily in debt (they mostly played for free), the group reluctantly signed with Warner Bros. in 1967. Through three ragged, esoteric albums that bear witness to the Dead's anarchic, multi-directional evolution (*Anthem of the Sun* epitomizes acid rock), the group amassed further debts, as none of the albums sold well. For their fourth album they decided simply to capture the essence of their live performances. *Live Dead* is an unmitigated triumph. The first three sides are one continuous expanse of music, totally integrated, as the group execute masterful rhythm changes with disdainful ease. The tapes were well chosen with no patchy, aimless passages (which can occur in Dead performances), while the core of their sound,

Jerry Garcia's highly personalized lead guitar and Phil Lesh's fluid, melodic bass lines, is gripping throughout. The turning-point for the Dead, the album halted their plunge into debt. They also began to tour widely, making much-needed visits to Europe. Most significantly, though, they finally learnt how to make disciplined studio albums, with two stylish country-rock efforts, *Workingman's Dead* and *American Beauty.*

Moby Grape

Moby Grape (CBS S 63090)

Hey Grandma/Mr Blues/Fall On You/8.05/Come In The Morning/ Omaha/Naked, If I Want To/Someday/Ain't No Use/Sitting By The Window/Changes/Lazy Me/Indifference

While 'Frisco music was typically undisciplined, essentially a live form that was difficult to convey to those who didn't relate to the narrow city scene, Moby Grape produced a debut album that was quite universal in its appeal: thirteen snappy songs, rather than the usual rambling attempts to simulate a live show. Moby Grape were a five-piece, each member contributing to the songs, with a complex acoustic/electric three-guitar sound that was ahead of its time. Each member of the group had a recognizable lead voice, though bassist Bob Mosley usually took the honours, while the whole group was capable of enterprising harmony work. '8.05' clearly foreshadows Crosby, Stills and Nash. In Jerry Miller and Peter Lewis they had two accomplished lead guitarists able to handle a multiplicity of styles, fashionable psychedelic, blues, folk, and the economical 'funk' style of guitar-playing pioneered by Stax-label musician Steve Cropper. But it was all to no avail. Columbia indulged in the worst kind of promotional overkill, releasing five simultaneous singles from the album, and the group lost credibility, both in 'Frisco and the wider world, neither of which was able to stomach the hype. The damaging promotion was repeated for the follow-up, *Wow*, less consistent but occasionally quite brilliant. Part of the hype (commonplace today) was a free 'superjam' album (another first) involving Al Kooper and Mike Bloomfield. The group became disillusioned. Founder and rhythm guitarist Skip Spence left and three later albums and attempts to pick up the pieces were mostly distressing failures. But for outside interference . . .

Quicksilver Messenger Service

Happy Trails (CAPITOL E-ST 120)

Who Do You Love/Mona/Calvary/Happy Trails

Formed in 1965, Quicksilver were one of the leading Bay area groups although, by choosing to remain aloof from record companies until 1968, they missed out on any real financial reward. No album better illustrates the 'Frisco sound in its purest form than the mostly live *Happy Trails*. Two tracks, 'Who Do You Love' and 'Mona', are classic rock guitar work-outs but, more than that, can be seen as the quintessence of the 'Frisco sound. The key to Quicksilver in their heyday lay in the twin lead guitars of Gary Duncan and John Cippolina. 'Who Do You Love', which purists will consider a travesty alongside the concise Ronnie Hawkins version of Bo Diddley's original, is the ultimate 'Frisco guitar statement. Set against the reliable rhythm of Dave Frieberg's bass and Greg Ellmore's drums, Duncan and Cippolina trade off one another. Cippolina's characteristic growling and snarling guitar, frequently sliding into alternately fierce and melodic wah-wah and feedback, complements perfectly Duncan's more regular, rhythmic, jagged approach. The partnership was soon broken, though, when in 1969 Duncan left to join Dino Valenti, who was to have been in the original Quicksilver line-up but was otherwise detained on a drugs charge. British session pianist Nicky Hopkins came in for the uneven *Shady Grove*, after which Duncan and Valenti returned. A series of albums, usually with variations on the above line-ups, failed to rekindle the old magic.

Country Joe and the Fish

Electric Music for the Mind and Body

(VANGUARD VSD 79244)

Flying High/Not So Sweet Martha Lorraine/Death Sound/Porpoise Mouth/Section 43/Superbird/Sad And Lonely Times/Love/Bass Strings/ The Masked Marauder/Grace

Part of the distinction between Country Joe and the Fish and the other leading 'Frisco groups lay in their Berkeley origins. As a result, they were politically motivated from the start. Country Joe McDonald and guitarist Barry Melton had been together in a rallying jug band which grew to become the Fish in 1965. They recorded two EP's, 'magazines in record form', one of which included the original version of Joe's 'I Feel Like I'm Fixing To Die Rag'. The most accomplished version of the Fish, which recorded *Electric Music* in 1967 and the two subsequent albums which include their finest work, saw the group completed by David Cohen (guitar/organ), Bruce Barthol (bass/harmonica) and Chicken Hirsch (drums). *Electric Music* was surprisingly low on the expected political satire (only 'Superbird') but was an eclectic mixture nonetheless. Joe's poetic love songs, 'Grace', about Grace Slick, and the beautifully erotic 'Porpoise Mouth', stood in pleasing contrast to the acid rock of 'Bass Strings' and 'Death Sound', and Barry Melton's weaker soul outings. Instrumentally, however, Melton's lyrical, fluid guitar runs characterized the Fish sound, although Cohen's reedy organ was often used effectively, notably on the dreamy instrumental 'Section 43'. The Fish's finest hour came on 'Eastern Jam', on *I Feel Like I'm Fixing to Die*, their second, equally excellent, album. Country Joe will probably be best remembered for the infamous 'Fish' cheer, performed at Woodstock with a later, poorer incarnation of the Fish. There are much finer moments to savour, however.

Big Brother and the Holding Company

Cheap Thrills (CBS 63392)

Combination Of The Two/I Need A Man To Love/Summertime/Piece Of My Heart/Turtle Blues/Oh Sweet Mary/Ball And Chain

Originally titled *Sex, Dope and Cheap Thrills* (Columbia wouldn't buy the full title) this album is best remembered for capturing Janis Joplin in her most joyously rampant form, though the crucial contribution of the group has often been overlooked. They were one of the most popular Bay Area outfits from 1965 onwards; Janis, who moved to San Francisco from Texas, joined in mid 1966, giving them the extra dimension they'd previously lacked. Big Brother was a deafeningly loud (only a few decibels below the notorious Blue Cheer) hard rock outfit with a classic twin-guitar sound provided by Sam Andrews and James Gurley. Neither were stylish but they compensated with their enormous enthusiasm; while Janis was with them, she shared that vital urge, though once she had become a household name (largely through this album and the Monterey Pop Festival of 1967), she seemed to lose it. At her best, she could sing the blues like few white singers and, on later recordings, 'Kosmik Blues' and the posthumous 'Pearl', she showed greater vocal control, but the thrill was gone. The special talent she once had is quite clear throughout much of *Cheap Thrills*, but particularly on the tremendously powerful 'Ball And Chain' and the moving 'Piece Of My Heart'. Janis died of a heroin overdose in October 1970. The group limped along without her – she had left them, anyway, two years earlier – making a couple of indifferent albums.

The Steve Miller Band

Sailor (CAPITOL ST 2984)

Song For Our Ancestors/Dear Mary/My Friend/Living In The USA/Quicksilver Girl/Lucky Man/Gangster Of Love/You're So Fine/Overdrive/Dime-A-Dance Romance

An extraordinary number of Texas musicians and groups found their way to San Francisco during its heyday. The Sir Douglas Quintet and the 13th Floor Elevators made regular, influential visits; others, such as Mother Earth and Janis Joplin, remained there. The original four-piece Steve Miller Blues Band included three refugees from a once flourishing scene in Wisconsin, Texas – Miller himself, Tim Davis and Curley Cooke. When Cooke left he was replaced by another of the Wisconsin fraternity, Boz Scaggs. Completed by Lonnie Turner and Jim Peterman, they recorded two excellent albums for Capitol. A tighter, more disciplined group than most of the native 'Frisco outfits, the Steve Miller Band were also more at ease in the studio. They cut their debut album in England, *Children of the Future* – memorable for an extended suite and some good blues playing – but their early reputation rests largely on *Sailor* (1968), a superb album that has little in common with the 'Frisco output of the day. *Sailor* contains a striking range of styles: the atmospheric instrumental 'Song For Our Ancestors' and the McCartneyesque 'Dear Mary' show an intuitive sense of good contemporary pop, while much of the rest is either very bluesy, including Miller's adopted (from Johnny 'Guitar' Watson) theme song, 'Gangster Of Love', or peerless hard-driving rock ('Living In The USA', 'Overdrive'). The resulting album is closer to vintage Beatles than to 'Frisco. After *Sailor*, Scaggs and Peterman left and Miller has soldiered on gamely ever since. Through a string of variable albums, Steve Miller creditably plugged away until the eighth, *The Joker* (1974), gave him the popular break-through. Today he's a regular chart contender but the music lacks the old bite. His old friend Boz Scaggs enjoys a similar popularity and suffers from the same malady.

Santana

Santana's Greatest Hits (CBS 69081)

Evil Ways/Jin-Go-Lo-Ba/Hope You're Feeling Better/Samba Pa Ti/Persuasion/Black Magic Woman/Oye Como Va/Everything's Coming Our Way/Se A Cabo/Everybody's Everything

By the end of 1968, the third generation 'Frisco groups were still emerging fast even though the scene was past its peak. The Santana

Blues Band was one such, though within two years they'd established themselves on an international footing that was the envy of the earlier generation groups. This was the result of a conscious effort by founder Carlos Santana, who'd moved to the city from Mexico a year earlier, to distinguish his group from the pack. When he added Mike Carrabello (congas) and Jose Chepito (percussion), he immediately struck a winning formula - Latin rock. The power of the group, however, on their debut album *Santana*, was essentially that of any first-rate 'Frisco ballroom group - plus that Latin ingredient. The *Woodstock* film made them overnight superstars - a spectacularly filmed segment that, for once, captured a 'Frisco group to advantage. The timing was perfect; interestingly, noted San Francisco entrepreneur Bill Graham got them onto the Woodstock bill. He'd promoted their early gigs and later managed the group. To their credit, Santana had considerable flair. They produced an appealing second album, *Abraxas*, slicker and more authentic than the first due to the addition of further Latin musicians. They are still a heavy-selling, major concert act, though much changed in personnel, but they have never surpassed *Abraxas*. This is perhaps because Carlos Santana is a limited player; his technique is based on a pleasant, pure tone and an ability to sustain feedback that seems heavily inspired by Britain's Peter Green. Their version of 'Black Magic Woman' would appear to substantiate this.

California Sun: Singles

The Rivieras: *California Sun* (1964)

Euphoric 'California' anthem from the Florida-based Rivieras; a cunning mixture of surfer pop lyrics and the brash pre-punk style.

Jan and Dean: *Dead Man's Curve* (1964)

A classic on two counts, a hot-rod song and death disc combined; it acquired a dubious significance for Jan Berry two years later, when he barely survived a car crash.

The Beach Boys: *Don't Worry Baby* (1964)

Brian Wilson's most forgotten masterpiece, the quintessential early Beach Boy ballad; early confirmation of his production genius.

The Beach Boys: *California Girls* (1965)

Brian Wilson's tribute to the local girls on the beach. Peerless pop, complex in structure but made to sound so simple.

Barry McGuire: *Eve Of Destruction* (1965)

The archetypal protest song from the former New Christy Minstrel; written by P. F. Sloan.

The Beau Brummels: *Laugh Laugh* (1964)

An early answer to the English invasion. The group pre-dated the San Francisco boom with hits like this – produced by Sly Stewart, later leader of the Family Stone.

Sonny and Cher: *I Got You Babe* (1965)

Utterly simple, infectious song, indebted to Phil Spector, that sold as much on the oddball image of the duo as on the song's obvious charms.

The Turtles: *Happy Together* (1967)

Still reminiscent of the surfing sound, one of a string of breezy, impeccably produced/arranged hits; a natural in '67.

The Mamas and the Papas: *California Dreamin'* (1966)

Quality folk rock with both East and West Coast influences – distinctively sung, played and arranged. A timely anthem written by group member John Phillips.

Scott McKenzie: *San Francisco* (1967)

The ultimate hippie, flower-power hymn.

Jefferson Airplane: *White Rabbit* (1967)

Lovely single. Cleverly contrived, ambiguous enough to avoid being banned but clearly celebrating the new drug culture.

The Byrds: *Eight Miles High* (1966)

Courageously inventive single: it seems to hold together by a mere thread yet packs a devastatingly powerful punch.

The Youngbloods: *Get Together* (1967)

Much recorded summer-of-love song, written by Chester Powers (a.k.a. Dino Valenti), which was ideally suited to Jesse Colin Young's relaxed style.

The Association: *Along Comes Mary* (1966)

The underrated harmony group fell somewhere between straight pop and the new West Coast music; there's still speculation about whether this was a 'drug' song.

The Seeds: *Pushin' Too Hard* (1966)

The LA punk group's first hit; raw and simple with characteristic bubbling piano, fuzzy guitar and quirky vocals from arch-weirdo Sky Saxon.

The Standells: *Sometimes Good Guys Don't Wear White* (1966)

The most enduring of the LA garage bands, this is easily their finest punk protest epic.

Harpers Bizarre: *59th Street Bridge Song (Feelin' Groovy)* (1967)

Brilliant soft-rock arrangement of the Paul Simon song; their five-part harmonies were rivalled only by Spanky and Our Gang in the field of sophisticated pop.

DAVE LAING

Dylan and After

Some years ago an American magazine featured a poster of Bob Dylan with his 'roots and branches'; those musicians who had influenced him, and those whom he had influenced in his turn. The 'roots' were the great figures of blues, folk music and rock & roll, while among the 'branches' was a wide variety of singers and groups. They ranged from earnest protest singers like Donovan through rock bands like the Byrds to bizarrely clad pop stars, Sonny and Cher. But the most important effect Bob Dylan has had on the growth of rock music has been to provide a model for a new type of artist, often called the singer/song-writer.

Before Dylan and the Beatles, it was unusual for pop or rock singers to write their own material. And those who did came up with lyrics of a conventional nature, invariably about love. Dylan changed all that, at first through his protest songs and later in the dense, image-packed observations set to rock accompaniments. After Dylan it was possible to be more ambitious and more imaginative in writing songs.

Dylan's own career, since he made his first album in 1961, has been varied and often unpredictable. Although there is only space for three of his records in this chapter, at least six more might easily have been chosen. His second album, *The Freewheelin' Bob Dylan* (1963) included such famous early songs as 'Blowin' In The Wind' and 'Don't Think Twice, It's All Right', while *Bringing It All Back Home* (1965) was the first album made by Dylan with rock musicians on some tracks, including 'Maggie's Farm' and 'Subterranean Homesick Blues'. Also essential is *Blonde on Blonde* (1966), a double album on which the surreal poetry of *Highway 61 Revisited* is taken to the extreme.

By this time, the pressures of success and stardom were beginning to tell, and a serious motorcycle crash led Dylan to spend nearly two years out of public view, during which time he recorded some songs known as 'the Basement Tapes', which were not officially released until 1975. These tracks are a strange mixture of off-beat humour, surreal word-play and ideas and images from the common stock of folk and traditional music. More of those ideas and images occur on *John Wesley Harding* (1968), but transformed by Dylan's quizzical view of things. With a relaxed accompaniment from Nashville sessionmen, it is Dylan's most mellow album.

During the 1970s, Dylan's output became less prolific and somewhat erratic. While the many commentators on Dylan's career have stressed the various changes in direction he has made, it is equally true that certain elements recur time and again in his music, most notably the forms and motifs of the blues and white folk traditions.

Bob Dylan was at first part of a group of young folk-singers living in New York's Greenwich Village, composing their own love songs and topical songs on the political events of the day. They included Phil Ochs, Tom Paxton and Patrick Sky. But Dylan was the most adventurous of them and the first to influence the approach of new writers. In England, Donovan wore a corduroy cap like his hero, and wrote simple but pleasant tunes, while Paul Simon spent a long time touring clubs in Britain until he had his first folk-rock hit, 'The Sound Of Silence'.

Twenty or thirty years earlier, both Paul Simon and Donovan would probably have turned to writing poetry as a form of artistic expression. But by the 1960s, mainly due to Dylan, song-writing and music was the most obvious medium for young people with the urge to express their thoughts and feelings. In fact, some of the singer/song-writers were actually poets as well. The most successful example was Leonard Cohen, a fashionable figure in the later 1960s and author of a few very good songs, notably 'Suzanne' and 'Hey, That's No Way To Say Goodbye'. There were many other poetic singers of the period, of whom the best were probably the young Californian Tim Buckley and Tim Hardin, a Greenwich Village song-writer who composed 'If I Were A Carpenter' and 'A Reason To Believe'.

Among the musicians who came after Dylan there were a significant number of women singers. In the pop music of the time, the roles allotted to women were very limited. They were expected to dress and perform according to a formula and most of the songs they were given to sing were uninspiring. In the folk scene, however, things were more easy-going. Women played instruments and sang alongside men in clubs and at concerts. Among those who became well-known were Carolyn Hester, Joan Baez and Judy Collins, who was particularly adept at finding new material by aspiring singer/song-writers. The outstanding women song-writers included the teenage Janis Ian, whose 'Society's Child' was a precocious protest song, and Joni Mitchell, the most gifted of them all.

Several songs from her early albums have become contemporary standards: 'Both Sides Now', 'The Circle Game', 'Chelsea Morning'.

By the time of *Blue* (1971), however, Joni had found a very individual singing style and on later records she found complex and unusual musical arrangements to match. Her most satisfying albums date from the early and mid 1970s (*For the Roses, Court and Spark, The Hissing of Summer Lawns*); some of the later material tended to become over-elaborate and to lack the poise and directness of those three records.

Carly Simon was another singer/song-writer who started out in folk, although she did not start recording until after the arrival of a new breed of musicians, unconnected with the folk world. The first of them was another woman, Carole King. During the 1960s she had worked in the 'song factory' of the Brill Building in New York, writing hit songs like 'Take Good Care Of My Baby' and 'The Locomotion'. In 1970, however, she released a solo album singing more personal songs, and her next album, *Tapestry* (1971), went on to sell over ten million copies, rivalling the success of Simon and Garfunkel's *Bridge over Troubled Water*. Paul Simon went on to join the new singer/song-writers as a solo artist, producing songs that were often more complex and enigmatic than Carole King's.

At the other end of the spectrum from Paul Simon was James Taylor, the simplicity of whose songs brought much criticism from commentators committed to the dynamism of 1960s rock. Like Carole King he made one very good album followed by a series of less interesting ones, but he also opened the way for a string of 'sensitive' singer/song-writers of whom Jackson Browne is one of the most successful.

Many of these newer singer/song-writers occupy a middle ground between rock music itself and middle-of-the-road music (MOR). Two very popular singers who come into this category are Neil Diamond and John Denver, both of whom have written some fine songs, although too much of their output is marred by a tendency towards pop clichés (in the case of Diamond) or sentimentality (Denver).

One final strand which deserves a mention in any survey of singer/song-writers in America is made up of those musicians who, like Bob Dylan, have attached themselves to some aspect of their American musical heritage. Don Maclean, whose record 'American Pie' was one of the best singles of the 1970s, plays banjo and learned a great deal from Pete Seeger. Arlo Guthrie is Woody's son, and his best albums, *Hobo's Lullabye* and *Last of the Brooklyn Cowboys*, show him carrying on the family tradition by combining modern themes with folk and country music.

Singer/song-writers have played a much less important part in British rock over the last ten years, mainly because there has been a far smaller audience for this kind of music than exists in America. The first to make their mark came out of the folk clubs and onto the concert platform. Donovan, Ralph McTell, Roy Harper and Al Stewart all took that route. Others, like Harvey Andrews and the much underrated Pete Atkin, had difficulty finding an audience, since their music could be categorized neither as 'folk' nor 'rock', something which counted in their favour artistically, but not commercially. The richest source of new song-writing has turned out to be the electric folk movement, with Richard Thompson as the major figure. The late Sandy Denny also contributed some good songs, of which 'Who Knows Where The Time Goes' is the best known, and Maddy Prior, formerly of Steeleye Span, began a promising solo career singing only her own compositions. Two other women, with contrasting styles, are among the best of the newer singer/song-writers in Britain: Joan Armatrading and Kate Bush. Armatrading leans on the soul balladry of Nina Simone while Kate Bush owes a debt to Joni Mitchell, to which she adds her own very theatrical approach to song-writing and performing.

Dylan and After: Albums

Bob Dylan

The Times They are A-changin' (CBS 62251)

The Times They Are A-Changin'/Ballad Of Hollis Brown/With God On Our Side/One Too Many Mornings/North Country Blues/Only A Pawn In Their Game/Boots Of Spanish Leather/When The Ship Comes In/The Lonesome Death Of Hattie Carroll/Restless Farewell

Come gather round people
Wherever you roam
And admit that the waters
Around you have grown.

The opening lines of the title song introduce an album which clinched Dylan's reputation as the spokesman, prophet and guru of a generation of activists and students. Released in 1964, it was his third album and contained nothing but original compositions, most of which are concerned with social comment and protest.

The title track, 'With God On Our Side', and 'When The Ship Comes In' became anthems of the protest movement and are sung with the confidence of the truly committed, backed up by the relentless guitar strumming that is the only accompaniment. But the album is more varied than that. Often overlooked are a group of songs which portray the contemporary lives of Woody Guthrie's people, the lower-class whites of America. There is the terse 'Hollis Brown' and the panoramic 'North Country Blues', while 'Pawn In Their Game' is a song of unusual political subtlety and compassion.

Among the other 'non-political' songs, 'Boots Of Spanish Leather' is cast in the mould of the traditional ballad, with a mysterious and enigmatic conclusion.

Bob Dylan

Highway 61 Revisited (CBS 62572)

Like A Rolling Stone/Tombstone Blues/It Takes A Lot To Laugh, It Takes A Train To Cry/From A Buick 6/Ballad Of A Thin Man/Queen Jane Approximately/Desolation Row/Highway 61 Revisited/Just Like Tom Thumb's Blues

'Something is happening but you don't know what it is' sings Dylan on this 1965 album. The comment was certainly true as regards his hard-core folk following, since *Highway 61 Revisited* is fully involved in electric music and surreal lyrics.

But, as the title hints, Dylan had not entirely abandoned the past. Several of the songs do indeed re-visit musical forms, people and places, including Highway 61 itself, the road north from Mississippi, made famous in the country blues. In Dylan's song, however, the highway is peopled with biblical characters, Western gamblers and hustlers. In a more sombre mood, the famous 'Desolation Row' mixes together a variety of historical and literary characters who drift across a bleak landscape of pessimism and decay. 'Tombstone Blues' is a faster series of wisecracks at the expense of the established order of things, featuring figures as diverse as Jack the Ripper and John the Baptist.

The sound which accompanies the words is more assured than on earlier records. It is dominated by Al Kooper's piano and organ playing, the lush phrasing of which sets the very different moods of 'Queen Jane' and 'Like A Rolling Stone', two of the more personal lyrics on the album.

Bob Dylan

Blood on the Tracks (CBS 69097)

Tangled Up In Blue/Simple Twist Of Fate/You're A Big Girl Now/ Idiot Wind/You're Gonna Make Me Lonesome When You Go/Meet Me In The Morning/Lily, Rosemary And The Jack Of Hearts/If You See Her, Say Hello/Shelter From The Storm/Buckets Of Rain

This is Dylan's finest album of the 1970s. It does not necessarily 'sum up' the decade, as perhaps *The Times They are A-Changin'* did for the political questions of the sixties. But appearing in 1974, when Nixon ruled America and rock was besotted with glam, glitter and apocalyptic imagery announcing the imminent end of everything, Dylan offered another viewpoint on the situation.

It is, first of all, an album which recognizes its connections with the past, with history. It contains a blues ('Meet Me In The Morning'), a narrative ballad ('Lily, Rosemary And The Jack Of Hearts') and a re-working of an early Dylan theme ('If You See Her, Say Hello'). The same is true of the lyrics of the two strongest songs, 'Tangled Up In Blue' and 'Idiot Wind'. The first traces a career and love affair of a singer who's 'still on the road', while 'Idiot Wind', beginning apparently as a personal attack on someone 'planting stories in the press', grows over its seven minutes into a deeper, general definition of a corrupting wind 'Blowin' like a circle around my skull/From the Grand Coulee Dam to the Capitol'. The shorter, less ambitious love songs, like 'You're A Big Girl Now' and 'If You See Her', are equally successful miniatures, to be put beside these full-sized portraits.

Phil Ochs

Chords of Fame (A&M SP 4599)

I Ain't Marchin' Anymore/One More Parade/Draft Dodger Rag/Here's To The State Of Richard Nixon/The Bells/Bound For Glory/Too Many Martyrs/There But For Fortune/I'm Going To Say It Now/Santo

Domingo/Changes/Is There Anybody Here?/Love Me, I'm A Liberal/When I'm Gone/Outside Of A Small Circle Of Friends/Pleasures Of The Harbour/Tape From California/Chords Of Fame/Crucifixion/The War Is Over/Jim Dean Of Indiana/Power And The Glory/Flower Lady/No More Songs

One of the best features of this memorial double album to Phil Ochs, who died in 1977, is the exhaustive sleeve-note by Ed Sanders, who describes the man as 'a clear-voiced singer, a true chronicler of the age, and a shaper of beautiful melodies'.

In the 1960s, Ochs was the most prolific of topical song-writers and one who was not afraid to criticize the short-comings of those on 'his' side, in songs like 'Love Me, I'm A Liberal' and 'Outside Of A Small Circle Of Friends'. The latter has a delightfully ironic use of a honky-tonk piano behind lines like 'Look outside the window, there's a woman being stabbed'. The point about the apathy of those who 'don't want to get involved' is forcibly made.

Ochs has been unfavourably compared to Bob Dylan, and his longer, electric songs are often uneven. But his melodic gifts are unusual among his contemporaries, and more than make up for any other deficiences on 'Pleasures Of The Harbour', 'Changes' and 'There But For Fortune', which in Joan Baez's version was Ochs' only hit. A prolific writer in the 1960s, his output was more erratic in the uncertain political climate of the 1970s, although 'Here's To The State Of Richard Nixon' is a magnificently scornful attack.

Judy Collins

So Early in the Spring (ELEKTRA K62019)

Pretty Polly/So Early, Early In The Spring/Pretty Saro/Golden Apples Of The Sun/Bonnie Ship The Diamond/Farewell To Tarwathie/The Hostage/La Colombe/Coal Tattoo/Carry It On/Bread and Roses/Marat-Sade/Special Delivery/The Lovin' Of The Game/Both Sides Now/Marieke/Send In The Clowns/Bird On The Wire/Since You've Asked/Born To The Breed/My Father/Holly Ann/Houses/Secret Gardens

Subtitled *The First 15 Years*, this double album is drawn from a dozen records made between 1961 and 1976. Its four sides are chosen to illustrate the varying types of material associated with Judy Collins: traditional folk songs, songs of social comment, material by contemporary writers and six of her own compositions.

The last are worth emphasizing, since Judy Collins's reputation has stressed her success as an interpreter of other people's songs, notably new or unknown writers. Leonard Cohen ('Bird On The Wire') and Joni Mitchell ('Both Sides Now') were among the singer/song-writers whom Judy Collins helped to bring to public notice, and the dramatic 'Marat-Sade', from the Peter Weiss play, was the highlight of her pioneering 1967 album *In My Life*.

What was impressive there and throughout her subsequent work was the variety of material she brought together within an album: folk, popular ballads ('Send In The Clowns') and political comment, as well as her own songs – about her father, sister, son, lover – which exhibit the clear-eyed intelligence and emotional subtlety that make Judy Collins one of the great, mature singers of the era.

Simon and Garfunkel

Greatest Hits (CBS 69003)

Mrs Robinson/For Emily, Whenever I May Find Her/The Boxer/The 59th Street Bridge Song (Feelin' Groovy)/The Sound Of Silence/I Am A Rock/Scarborough Fair/Canticle/Homeward Bound/Bridge Over Troubled Water/America/Kathy's Song/El Condor Pasa (If I Could)/Bookends/Cecilia

A selection from the duo's five albums, which includes nearly all of their many American hits. Unfortunately, the songs aren't placed in chronological order, for to follow Paul Simon's song-writing through from 'I Am A Rock' to 'El Condor Pasa' is to hear the growth of one of the major song-writers of the age.

The earliest songs are very consciously 'poetic', and opinions will vary as to their effectiveness, although 'Kathy's Song' and 'The Sound Of Silence' have a quiet intensity lacking in 'For Emily'. 'America' and 'Homeward Bound' represent a step forward, with the more exact nature of Simon's observation: 'Every day's an endless stream/Of cigarettes and magazines'. In 'America' the focus shifts from a Greyhound bus at night to the immensity of America as a place and an ideal.

With the exception of 'Bridge Over Troubled Water' and 'El Condor Pasa' (both based on non-rock styles – gospel and South American Indian), the later Simon and Garfunkel songs are clever and intricate. But their phenomenal success was also due to their sound, with Art Garfunkel's classically pure voice predominating. As one critic put it, 'the restless generation had its own Everly Brothers'.

Paul Simon

Greatest Hits Etc (CBS 10007)

Slip Slidin' Away/Stranded In A Limousine/Still Crazy After All These Years/Have A Good Time/Duncan/Me And Julio Down By The Schoolyard/Something So Right/Kodachrome/I Do It For Your Love/50 Ways To Leave Your Lover/American Tune/Mother And Child Reunion/Loves Me Like A Rock/Take Me To The Mardi Gras

Simon and Garfunkel split up in 1970. By 1977, when this selection was released, Paul Simon had made only three further studio albums, but each was among the best few records of its year. The first of them included the jaunty word-play of 'Me And Julio' as well as the haunting 'Mother And Child Reunion', whose reggae backing showed that Simon's interest in a wide range of musics had not diminished.

The explorations continued on the *There Goes Rhymin' Simon* album (1973), which included the powerful gospel song 'Loves Me Like A Rock' and 'Mardi Gras', with its nod towards the creole jazz of New Orleans. There was also 'American Tune', Paul Simon's most ambitious song, and conceivably his best. It vividly evokes the mood of young Americans in the period of Vietnam and Nixon, when the American Dream became a nightmare.

A similar melancholy dominates the third album, *Still Crazy after All These Years* (1975), making the wit of the title track and '50 Ways To Leave Your Lover' even sharper. Paul Simon's stature as a writer rests on his success in pinning down the emotional shifts in his generation over the past fifteen years.

Joni Mitchell

For the Roses (ASYLUM SYLA 8753)

Banquet/Cold Blue Steel And Sweet Fire/Barangrill/Lesson In Survival/ Let The Wind Carry Me/For The Roses/See You Sometime/Electricity/ You Turn Me On I'm A Radio/Blonde In The Bleachers/Woman Of Heart And Mind/Judgement Of The Moon And Stars (Ludwig's Tune)

Blue (1971) found Joni Mitchell moving away from an acoustic to a rock accompaniment. Her next album, *For the Roses*, took a greater musical leap towards a loose, jazzy approach where the line of the music follows the individual patterns of her words and voice.

The themes which inspire Joni Mitchell's best work have remained remarkably consistent. Her love songs are always restless, questioning herself and her relationships. According to one commentator, they probe the conflict 'between romantic love and the liberation of women'. In Mitchell's songs, things are never that abstract, but aspects of that conflict between heart and mind appear in 'Lesson In Survival', 'See You Sometime' and 'Woman Of Heart And Mind': 'I'm looking for affection and respect/A little passion/And you want stimulation – nothing more.'

The other theme which flows through the album is the paradox of the creative artist working in an industry, brilliantly dissected in the title track: 'In some office sits a poet/And he trembles as he sings/And he asks some guy/To circulate his soul around.' Unlike many others who have taken similar themes, Joni Mitchell is emotionally involved but without self-pity.

Carole King

Tapestry (EPIC EPC 82308)

I Feel The Earth Move/So Far Away/It's Too Late/Home Again/ Beautiful/Way Over Yonder/You've Got A Friend/Where You Lead/

Will You Love Me Tomorrow/Smackwater Jack/Tapestry/(You Make Me Feel Like A) Natural Woman

'Her voice is just ragged enough, just imperfect enough to provide the proper ring of understanding, warmth and authenticity to such songs as "You've Got A Friend".' One critic's description of Carole King's low-key approach, which formed a bridge between the conventional pop romanticism of her earlier work and the starker self-analysis of a Leonard Cohen or James Taylor.

To prove the point, *Tapestry* contains restrained and moving readings of two of the older songs, the teenage lament 'Will You Love Me Tomorrow' and 'Natural Woman', with its atmospheric opening lines: 'Looking out on the morning rain/I used to feel so uninspired.' That note of honesty and self-awareness permeates the whole album with a maturity that had been rare in rock music before *Tapestry* was released in 1971.

The two most complete tracks are songs of separation and loss. 'It's Too Late' conveys the pain of owning up to the fact that a relationship has died, and 'So Far Away' asks the question, 'Doesn't anybody stay in one place anymore?' The album owes its mood largely to the sparse backing track, in which Carole King's meditative, soul-inspired piano lines predominate.

James Taylor

Sweet Baby James (WARNER BROS. WS 1843)

Sweet Baby James/Lo And Behold/Sunny Skies/Steamroller/Country Road/Oh Susannah/Fire And Rain/Blossom/Anywhere Like Heaven/Oh Baby Don't You Loose Your Lip On Me/Suite For 20G

On its appearance in 1970, this album was greeted as a sign of a new mood among young Americans. It was low-key, even sombre, and the pessimism which seemed to haunt even the cheerful songs like 'Oh Susannah' and the satirical 'Steamroller' was seen as part of a reaction against the feverish activism of the 1960s.

'Fire And Rain', the most famous and the most intense of James Taylor's songs, was mostly responsible for that image. Taylor himself described the song, which concerns the feeling of loss at a friend's death, as 'just a hard-time song, a blues without being in a blues form'.

But despite the gloominess of its themes, *Sweet Baby James* is a very attractive album to listen to. The arrangements of Taylor's neat melodies are in a 'semi-acoustic' format, with Danny Kootch's guitar and Carole King's piano to the fore. Combined with Taylor's casual, lightweight voice, the music gives the album a dream-like quality, as if it were a set of counter-culture lullabies. The tension between that quality and many of the lyrics, with their expression of fear and insecurity, is one of the enduring qualities of the album, and one which is seldom found in Taylor's later work.

Gordon Lightfoot

Summer Side of Life (REPRISE K44132)

10 Degrees and Getting Colder/Miguel/Go My Way/Summer Side Of Life/Cotton Jenny/Talking In Your Sleep/Nous Vivons Ensemble/Same Old Loverman/Redwood Hill/Love and Maple Syrup/Cabaret

After Joni Mitchell, Lightfoot is the best-known Canadian songwriter, though his approach is very different from hers. He belongs to the borderland between folk and country music, where cowboy songs meet the tunes of Woody Guthrie and the highway travellers. This album, made in Nashville in 1971, opens with a song about a musician on the road and a cowboy ballad ('Miguel'). In contrast, 'Cotton Jenny' is a love song enhanced by a few deft touches which paint in the routine of a mill-hand, and 'Nous Vivons Ensemble' is a bi-lingual piece about the co-existence of French and English in Canada. The remainder of the tracks are love songs, of which 'Talking In Your Sleep' is the best, with its full-blown romantic sadness.

It's also a good example of Gordon Lightfoot's singing style, which blends with the mainly acoustic backing tracks on all his records. Here, a battery of finger-picked guitars provide an ever-changing background to the effortless flow which is characteristic of Gordon Lightfoot's best music.

Country Joe McDonald

Paris Sessions (VANGUARD VSD 79328)

Fantasy/Movieola/I'm So Tired/Moving/I Don't Know Why/Zombies In A House Of Madness/Sexist Pig/Colorado Town/Coulene Anne/St Tropez

The career of Joe McDonald in itself encapsulates the exploits of a whole generation of Californian musicians. From folk-singer to leader of the psychedelic Country Joe and the Fish, he went on to explore his roots with a Woody Guthrie and a country music album. *Paris Sessions*, made in 1973, contains probably his best songs of social comment, aimed mainly at media manipulation and sexism. 'Fantasy' is an attack on the image of women in television, while 'Movieola' is a very funny comment on the cinema of sexual violence.

'I'm So Tired' was described by Joe McDonald himself as a 'new kind of love song about two people who work', and is the most moving song on the album. In contrast are the hard-rocking pro-feminist songs, 'Sexist Pig' and 'Coulene Anne'. The first ridicules the 'macho' male image ('He's a fool who thinks his tool/Is the revolution') and the second the tale of a battered wife who fights back. The music is by McDonald's All-Star Band, which included three women. The group disbanded soon after this album, which still stands alone as an effective and entertaining album of political songs.

Steve Goodman

Words We Can Dance To (ASYLUM K 53038)

Roving Cowboy/Tossin' And Turnin'/Unemployed/Between The Lines/Old Fashioned/Can't Go Back/Banana Republics/Death Of A Salesman/That's What Friends Are For/The Story Of Love

The album's title comes from 'Banana Republics', a song with sweet, Latin accompaniment about expatriate Americans 'hustling the senoritas/As they dance beneath the stars'. This bitter-sweet mixture in individual songs is one of the most attractive features of Steve Goodman's music. A Chicago-based singer/song-writer, he is very much at home with all kinds of American music, from the cowboy ballad style of 'Roving Cowboy' and the rock & roll revivalism of 'Tossin' And Turnin'' to the lush Broadway ballad, 'That's What Friends Are For'.

But he is also part of the tradition of social comment that derives from the folk scene. 'Unemployed' is a contemporary lament on that situation, but done with a jaunty Dixieland jazz backing. And 'Death Of A Salesman' goes along at a breakneck pace, with a different instrument taking the brief solo at the end of each verse. The story, told in traditional ballad style, is a familiar modern one of the lecherous salesman and the young girl, but this time the salesman gets his come-uppance. The verve and enthusiasm of Steve Goodman's singing here is typical of the album as a whole.

Bonnie Raitt

Taking My Time (WARNER BROS. K 46261)

You've Been In Love Too Long/I Gave My Love A Candle/Let Me In/Everybody's Cryin' Mercy/Cry Like A Rainstorm/Wah She Go Do/I Feel The Same/I Thought I Was A Child/Write Me A Few Of Your Lines/Kokomo Blues/Guilty

Like Judy Collins, Bonnie Raitt is an interpreter of contemporary songs, but a member of a new generation which includes Maria Muldaur, Linda Ronstadt and Emmylou Harris. Her own roots are in the blues and this, her second album, includes blues songs by Mose Allison and Fred McDowell, on which she plays bottleneck guitar.

Bonnie Raitt's voice has the strength of a Janis Joplin but it is combined with the poise and confidence of a Joni Mitchell. The combination is irresistible, especially when the album contains the sly, funny, feminist 'Wah She Go Do' (a calypso-style West Indian song) as well as soul-baring love songs like 'Cry Like A Rainstorm' and 'I Gave My Love A Candle'. And, as more than one reviewer has pointed out, in 'Wah She Go Do' and 'You've Been In Love Too Long' Raitt is addressing other women not as fellow-sufferers but from a positive, initiative-taking point of view.

Released in 1973, the album also offered something different musically. Among those playing on it are members of Little Feat, and the overall sound shares in the mellow blues-rock atmosphere of that band's best recordings.

Donovan

Sunshine Superman (PYE NPL 18181)

Sunshine Superman/Legend Of A Girl Child Linda/The Observation/Guinevere/Celeste/Writer In The Sun/Season Of The Witch/Hampstead Incident/Sand And Foam/Young Girl Blues/Three Kingfishers/Bert's Blues

Starting out unpromisingly as a blatant Dylan and Guthrie imitator, Donovan surprised many with this album, whose songs caught the spirit and the feeling of the early underground era in a coherent and melodic way. He was greatly aided by producer Mickie Most, and by John Cameron's arrangements, which used strings, harpsichord and jazz soloists.

But it is the unerring ability of the songs themselves to avoid the pitfalls of whimsy and hippie mindlessness which remains the most impressive aspect of *Sunshine Superman.* The title song and 'Season Of The Witch' use a hypnotic riff and rock rhythms to convey the euphoria and the paranoia of flower-power. 'Linda' and 'Guinevere' manage to evoke the imagery of fairy-tale and of Arthurian legend with a psychological insight and relevance to contemporary impulses; they go beyond nostalgia.

Each song has its particular virtues, although several, of which 'Hampstead Incident' is the most notable, are concerned with visionary experiences, drug-induced or otherwise. At another, more moving level is 'Young Girl Blues', an unvarnished portrait of a lonely bedsit dweller, the other side of 'Swinging London'.

Kate and Anna McGarrigle

Kate and Anna McGarrigle

(WARNER BROS. K 56218)

Kiss And Say Goodbye/My Town/Blues In D/Heart Like A Wheel/ Foolish You/(Talk To Me Of) Mendocino/Complainte Pour Ste-Catherine/Tell My Sister/Swimming Song/Jigsaw Puzzle Of Life/Go Leave/Travelling On For Jesus

Specialists in unfashionable close harmonies and poignant songs of love lost or past, the McGarrigle sisters first made an impact when other women singers recorded their material, especially Anna's 'Heart Like A Wheel'. This record was released in 1976 and its freshness and distance from the rock mainstream won them an instant following.

There is a special McGarrigle tone, which comes from the strange tension between the intensity of the emotions described in the lyrics and the quality of the singing voices. The formal, slightly archaic harmonies often betray, behind the reticence, a hint of barely controlled feeling. 'Heart Like A Wheel', for instance, describes a desolate state of mind with a vocal line whose lack of histrionics heightens the emotional impact.

Kate and Anna's style comes from the white folk and popular ballad tradition which they absorbed while growing up in Quebec. The album includes a traditional gospel song as well as one sung in French. They are accompanied by a small folk band, with various combinations of piano, fiddle and guitar joining the rhythm section. None of the sisters' later records has quite the directness and individuality of this one.

Randy Newman

Sail Away

(REPRISE K 44185)

Sail Away/It's Lonely At The Top/He Gives Us All His Love/Last Night I Had A Dream/Simon Smith And His Amazing Dancing Bear/

Old Man/Political Science/Burn On Big River/Memo To My Son/ Dayton Ohio – 1903/You Can Leave Your Hat On/God's Song

The title track begins, 'In America you'll get food to eat/Won't have to run through the jungle/And scuff up your feet.' It's sung in Newman's lazy, bluesy drawl, which lulls the listeners so that it's a while before they realize that this is the song of a slaver, praising the American Way of Life to his African slaves. This is Randy Newman's characteristic approach to taboo topics. It's not directly satirical, but instead it presents the logic of the subject-matter itself in such a way as to show up its absurdity.

'God's Song' is the other main example on *Sail Away*. This is sung by God himself, who concludes: 'You all must be crazy to put your faith in me/That's why I love mankind.'

Other Randy Newman songs are less weighty curiosities. 'Simon Smith' is a cheerful and tuneful tale of a boy and a performing bear which was actually a pop hit for Alan Price, while 'Lonely At The Top' is a lightweight satire on the plight of the unhappy star. Probably the best-liked track on the album is 'Political Science' which deals with the American dislike of foreigners and their ingratitude towards the USA. The solution is simple: 'They all hate us anyhow/So let's drop the big one now.'

Ralph McTell

Not Till Tomorrow (REPRISE K44210)

Zimmerman Blues/First Song/When I Was A Cowboy/Nettle Wine/ Sylvia/Birdman/Barges/Standing Down In New York/Another Rain Has Fallen/This Time Of Night/Gypsy

In 'Sylvia', a song to the poet Sylvia Plath, Ralph McTell sings: 'It seems there's one or two who can say it for the few/And maybe just a few who can say it for the many.' McTell is one of that 'few' himself, a song-writer who sketches in situations that are often familiar to his audience, rather than exotic or fantastic. *Not Till Tomorrow*, released in 1972, contains songs about childhood, gypsies, the media image of the cowboy, living in the country and the end of a love affair. This last,

'First Song', has an extra dimension, since it is both about how memory changes the meaning of events and how time can change the meaning of a song.

McTell is one of the short story writers of popular music, and many of his best songs conjure up a particular person, scene or moment in time. 'Zimmerman Blues' is untypical because it deals with the persona of a successful artist, and the problems that success brings (Zimmerman being Dylan's real name). Ralph McTell himself has always avoided that kind of fame and reputation, remaining very much a craftsman among song-writers and guitarists, with whom he is renowned for his skill at ragtime playing.

Alan Price

Between Today and Yesterday

(WARNER BROS. K 56032)

Left Over People/Away Away/Between Today And Yesterday/In Times Like These/Under The Sun/Jarrow Song/City Lights/Look At My Face/Angel Eyes/You're Telling Me/Dream Of Delight/Between Today And Yesterday

The song that links side one ('Yesterday') and side two of this album is 'Jarrow Song', a Top Ten hit in 1974. This epic track describes the hard times of the 1930s when the unemployed of Alan Price's home town marched to London in protest. Brass band and rock guitar combine to provide the crescendos of sound. The song's coda refers to Price's own situation in the present time and asks, 'Where do I stand/ Either side or none?'

The album as a whole is intended to show the two aspects of Price's own thinking: his concern for his roots in the past of industrial Tyneside, and his own role as a rootless musician in the London entertainment world. The first side contains some of the finest songs Price has written in a career going back to his days with the Animals. 'Left Over People' is a cry of pity and outrage whose emotional power is underlined by Derek Wadsworth's orchestration, which uses a jazz big band. A contrasting song is 'In Times Like These', which takes the form of the classic sing-along pub song.

Although *Between Today and Yesterday* has its flaws, it remains almost the only attempt by a British musician to use rock music in a search for his own cultural roots, rather than for American ones.

Richard and Linda Thompson

I Want to See the Bright Lights Tonight

(ISLAND ILPS 9266)

When I Get To The Border/Calvary Cross/Withered And Died/I Want To See The Bright Lights Tonight/Down Where The Drunkards Roll/We'll Sing Hallelujah/Has He Got A Friend For Me/The Little Beggar Girl/The End Of The Rainbow/The Great Valerio

Richard Thompson was formerly the guitarist with Fairport Convention and all his songs are filled with the imagery and colours of traditional folk songs: 'A man is like a rusty wheel', 'I'll be your light till Doomsday', 'I've only sad stories to tell to this town'. That last line, from 'Withered And Died', almost sums up Thompson's approach to songwriting. He takes a gloomy but all too accurate view of life's possibilities, and even the songs containing some optimism, like 'When I Get To The Border' and the title track, seem tinged with sadness.

'Bright Lights' itself is sung by Linda Thompson, whose clear, flawless voice is the perfect vehicle for Richard's metaphorical lyrics. As well as a writer and a suitably mournful singer, Richard Thompson is a master guitarist. On various songs, his playing ranges from heavy-rock chords to the intricacies of a more folk-influenced approach. He is a thoughtful player who pays attention to what he omits as well as to what he puts in. The short solo which concludes 'The End Of The Rainbow' distils the Thompson pessimism into a brief series of notes.

Dylan and After: Singles

Bob Dylan: *Like A Rolling Stone* (1965)

A record which shifted the centre of gravity of the hit single, with its swirling organ sounds and hustling, vehement lyrics.

Simon and Garfunkel: *The Sounds Of Silence* (1965)

Originally acoustic track, but dubbed with electric backing to turn it into folk rock. The lyrics are a perfect summation of teenage alienation.

Barry McGuire: *Eve Of Destruction* (1965)

The identikit protest song, written to order by P. F. Sloan, with outrageous rhymes and curious, growling vocals.

Tim Hardin: *Reason To Believe* (1966)

Rod Stewart did a memorable version of this classic love song, but the original recording is more restrained and more moving.

Tim Buckley: *Morning Glory* (1967)

'There is no name yet for the places he and his voice can go . . . always managing to be wildly passionate and pure at the same time.' (Lillian Roxon)

Alan Price: *Don't Stop The Carnival* (1968)

Showing the positive influence of Randy Newman, the record combines Caribbean rhythms with a sketch of West Indian life in Britain.

Michael Nesmith: *Joanne* (1970)

Pedal-steel guitar pervades one of the finest songs by an intriguing but overlooked writer who was once a Monkee.

Neil Diamond: *I Am . . . I Said* (1971)

The most personal song of a talented pop hit writer, pinpointing the feeling of isolation in being 'lost between two shores', New York and Los Angeles.

Dory Previn: *The Lady With The Braid* (1971)

A perfectly controlled performance which subtly unfolds to show the need and the loneliness masked by the sophistication of the 'swinging singles' era.

Buffy Saint-Marie: *Soldier Blue* (1971)

The theme song from a movie whose power in portraying the genocide of the American Indians matched the passion of Buffy's singing.

Carly Simon: *Anticipation* (1971)

One of her early hits, lacking the hard-bitten quality of the records of a few years later.

Arlo Guthrie: *City Of New Orleans* (1972)

An evocative Steve Goodman song, using a train journey as a metaphor for a reflection on the character of America.

Don Maclean: *American Pie* (1972)

The brilliant, lengthy tour-de-force, in which Maclean presents the history of rock music and of a generation.

Rick Nelson: *Garden Party* (1972)

A neat and enjoyable song about the fans who won't free a singer/song-writer from his past as a rock & roll star.

Danny O'Keefe: *Goodtime Charlie's Got The Blues* (1972)

A deceptively simple lyric, using traditional images, which also captures the confused mood as the Vietnam War drew to its close.

Neil Young: *Heart Of Gold* (1972)

His only Number 1 hit, a stark love song uniting Young's mournful voice with unexpected images.

Jim Croce: *I Got A Name* (1973)

Croce had several hits based on a melodic approach to acoustic music and reflecting a blue-collar street-level attitude, as in this song.

John Denver: *Rocky Mountain High* (1973)

A clear, unsentimental picture of life in the Rockies and the threats to it. By far his best song.

Harry Chapin: *W.O.L.D.* (1974)

A tale of an ageing disc-jockey told with compassion by a very popular American artist.

Janis Ian: *At Seventeen* (1975)

A beautifully performed, low-key song of experience – a contrast to her earlier precocious protest material.

Gerry Rafferty: *Baker Street* (1978)

A fine comeback single from one of Britain's best, charting the common city emotion of wanting to 'get away from it all' with accuracy and sympathy.

NICK KIMBERLEY

Reggae

Jamaica is a poor island, trying to find a place for itself in the Third World. Reggae expresses many of the contradictions of the island's situation; but it also exists as an escape route from the real world, like any other pop music. Most attempts to provide a context for the music have failed to take into account its real history, opting instead for a romanticized view of reggae as a revolutionary force. Certainly reggae has positioned itself in society in a unique, sometimes revolutionary, sometimes reactionary way; but no sense can be made of its social role without an accurate idea of its internal history as another pop music.

Reggae's roots go back to the early fifties, when the musical diet (calypso, its local variant, mento, and church music) no longer satisfied Jamaican audiences. Radio's alternative was bland pop, so people turned instead to the dance-halls, which, at a time when there were no record-pressing plants on the island, thrived on American rhythm and blues records. The increasingly sophisticated Kingston dancers insisted on Smiley Lewis, Amos Milburn and Roscoe Gordon, and sound-system operators struggled to stay ahead of the game. The best sounds (Sir Coxsone the Downbeat, Duke Reid the Trojan, V Rocket and later Prince Buster) almost literally fought over the best, most exclusive American records: Contacts were established in the States, boats docking in Kingston Harbour were plundered, and rivalry often boiled over: Buster had his head broken by a brick-wielding gang of Duke Reid's men, and such confrontations were not uncommon. For the most important occasions, opposing systems would play out against each other, the audience deciding whether Coxsone had dropped V Rocket, or vice versa. Eventually, there simply weren't enough records to go round, and the far-sighted (notably Coxsone Dodd and Duke Reid) saw that staying ahead would mean making their own music in the studios of radio station RJR, which were duly invaded by local musicians able to imitate r&b. The results were cut as acetates at Richard Khourys's Federal plant (opened in 1958), and then played at dances to an ecstatic reception: as far as the dancers knew, they were hearing new American records.

This response established a market for home produce, and when Khourys opened his Federal Recording Studios, quickly followed by Coxsone's Studio One at Brentford Road, Jamaica had a nascent music industry all its own. Records like Theophilus Beckford's 'Easy Stepping' or 'Pink Lane Shuffle' by Duke Reid's Group (1960), after proving popular on the dance-floor over a period of weeks, months or even years, would eventually be issued to the public. The sound was a primitive tribute to the rolling r&b of New Orleans: the nearly-boogie piano carried the rhythm with the drums, while sax, trombone or sometimes a vocal would provide the lead, supported by a guitar plucked on the beat. But the demand was for freshness, and musicians as talented as Don Drummond (trombone), Tommy McCook and Roland Alphonso (saxes), and Richard Ace (piano) were innovators as well as copyists, so something less derivative inevitably evolved. Prince Buster suggests that musicians adopted the rhythms of Pocomania, a local Afro-Christian cult of possession; certainly there's a manic, almost possessed raucousness to new music of 1961, christened 'ska'. The best records retained the r&b feel, emphasizing the offbeat; instrumentals predominated, and the Skatalites, including the soloists listed above, were the best band, working mainly with Dodd and Reid. Their 'Treasure Island', a typical ska vehicle, issued here in 1964 under the name of Don Drummond and Drumbago, defines the music's potential: the beat is established by drums, bass and guitar; the horns join in with a simple tune, followed by sax and trombone solos against furious riffing from the ensemble. The solos betrayed a familiarity not only with the r&b of Fats Domino, but also with the hard bop of fifties jazz. Another Skatalites tune, 'Ball Of Fire', moves along in similar fashion, with the addition of a novel percussion instrument: the human voice. Ska's most endearing trait was to use an obviously well-lubricated throat, clucking and sputtering along with the band, and it's possibly this scat vocalizing which gave ska its onomatopoeic name.

Prince Buster incorporated this trick into his declamatory style, the mid-sixties ska archetype, on 'Al Capone', 'Dance Cleopatra', etc. Buster moved from DJ to producer to performer with ease; his records observed every aspect of Kingston life, from his wife's lasciviousness to the street-roaming of local youths, the rude boys. The rudies invested ska with the first suggestion of 'rebel music', although responses to their hooliganism were predictably confused: Buster's 'Judge Dread', representing outraged law and order, sentences Emmanuel Zachariah Zachypum, George Grabanflee and cohorts to 400 years imprisonment. For the defence, young Bob Marley's Wailers offered 'Jailhouse': 'Can't fight against the youth now . . . we're gonna rule this land.' The outlaw rudies provided obvious heroes for youth fighting the tyranny of unemployment, poverty and exploitation; and Buster, sensing that he'd backed the wrong horse, granted freedom to his prisoners with 'Judge Dread Dance The Pardon', on condition they guarantee 'no more looting, no more shooting, no more bum-showing'. These records also usher in a new era: ska's reign from 1961 to 1966, when its r&b roots were becoming dated, was terminated with the arrival of rock steady.

Still with an eye on black America, Kingston now took to the more melodic soul music of Curtis Mayfield, Joe Tex, and Sam Cooke, and local talent had to adapt accordingly. The call was for tuneful vocals, more emphatic bass and a slower rhythm, accurately labelled 'rock steady'. 'Hold Them' by Roy Shirley inaugurated the sedate sound; immediately Coxsone covered 'Hold Them' with Ken Boothe, and the race was on. Ska's brashness was replaced by delicate singers like Slim Smith and Pat Kelly; Dodd and Reid still dominated, with the Duke's Treasure Isle studios and label perhaps just ahead. Slim Smith's Coxsone-produced 'Born To Love You' (1967) displays all the rock steady virtues: guitar states the melody while the ponderous bass underpins the drumming, and Slim's mildly hysterical vocal perfectly catches the poignancy of the Isley Brothers' tune, despite fumbling the words. Love songs saw the music through its brief heyday, and broader issues took second place. By 1968, love alone wouldn't do. Something more committed, more frenetic, was needed, and musicians and producers stepped forward to provide.

Using rock steady bass, while harking back to the chugging ska rhythms, the 1968 sound was known as 'reggae', a word allegedly coined by the Maytals in 'Do The Reggae'. The music was popular with Britain's rudies, the skinheads, and reggae's early days saw London's best attempts at an imitation of the real thing; Laurel Aitken's 'Woppi King' (1969) is an excellent example. Back in Kingston, instrumentals by the Upsetters and the Dynamites embody the effervescent reggae beat, but sound flaccid now. By contrast, Burning Spear's 1969 vocal 'Door Peeper' maintains its sombre power, reflecting young Jamaica's growing preoccupation with Rastafarianism, still reggae's overriding ideology. Briefly, Rastas see themselves as Africans exiled and captive in Babylon, which represents all forms of oppression from baton-happy police to money-grabbing producers. Haile Selassie is the godhead, and the cult's adoption of dreadlocks, and ganja as a sacrament, is overwhelmingly attractive to Jamaican youth. It is also attractive to European youth, so that 1966's rudie, Bob Marley, a rebel in 1971 with 'Screw Face', had by 1973 become absorbed into rock music with the *Catch a Fire* album. Simultaneously, the youth market allowed younger producers like Lee Perry and Niney to challenge the supremacy of Dodd and Reid. Reid had played his ace back in 1969, taking young U Roy into Treasure Isle to cut the records which best defined reggae's latest hero, the 'toaster'.

The sixties sound systems had spawned a new star, the DJ, who talked and shouted over the records, encouraging and berating his audience. Some, like the legendary Count Machuki, never recorded; others (Sir Lord Comic and especially King Stitt) successfully recreated their act on record. U Roy had been Stitt's deputy at Downbeat, but, fed up with playing second fiddle, he left to join King Tubbys' system. Displaying his unique patter, called 'toasting', Roy had little success with his first records, but at Treasure Isle the sparks began to fly. 'Wake The Town', 'Rule The Nation' and 'Wear You To The Ball' occupied the top three positions in the JA charts in 1969, giving producers one more bandwagon to jump on. Scores of DJs, on hundreds of records, still try to steal Roy's thunder, but few have bettered their teacher: only the best – Dennis Alcapone, I Roy and Big Youth – stand the comparison. Artistically, most of the others struggle, although often with some financial reward; ten years after the event, U Brown still pays obvious homage to the master, and reaches the lucrative African market. U Roy's trick was to string together nonsense catch-phrases, bouncing ideas off the rhythm track; others, especially Big Youth and I Roy, use the DJ mode for their political and religious, basically Rastafarian, beliefs.

The cult also gave birth to another sound-system convention: various DJs relied for their success on custom-pressed acetates of familiar rhythms, with which they could win support; these 'dubs' offered remixed versions of vocal hits, with voice mostly removed and drum and bass brought forward. Audiences clamoured for their favourite dub cuts from their favourite DJs, and producers saw in drum and bass versions a cheap way to increase sales, with a version on the B-side of their records. The Hippy Boys 'Voodoo', the drum and bass flip to Little Roy's 'Hard Fighter' (1971), is a good early example, produced by Matador Daley. As techniques improved, more elaborate horns, organ, echo or equalizer versions followed, while for Herman Chin-Loy's Aquarius label, a shy young session-man turned out versions using a melodica, a child's toy halfway between harmonica and piano: Augustus Pablo made a virtue of the melodica's limitations on countless records like 'East Of The River Nile' and 'Bells Of Death'. Again, Herman capitalized on dub's popularity with the first completely dub album: *Aquarius Dub* was the first of many, and if it sounds uncomplicated by today's standards, the quality of the music makes it a classic nonetheless.

These then are contemporary reggae's major issues: DJs, dub and the flirtation with Rasta. This short essay cannot cover every twist and turn of reggae eccentricity: the flying cymbal sound, for example, proposed by Bunnie Lee as a concession to New York disco tastes ('None Shall Escape The Judgment' by Johnnie Clarke is a fine 1973 example). Then there's Sly Dunbar's fussy 'rockers' drumming, pioneered on the Diamonds' 1975 hit, 'Right Time', and eventually parodied by every drummer in Kingston, including Sly himself. These, and every other trick used by reggae, are designed to take the music forward while reaching a larger audience. With white record companies controlling so much, reggae approaches 1980 in amiable chaos, on the knife-edge of political and artistic disaster. A lot of real (and some minimal) talent is trying to make a lot of real money, and only time will tell if the music has already passed its peak, or whether it can pull itself back from the abyss of pop culture. Meanwhile, Jamaican history progresses, and reggae continues to be used by those shaping that history, both as an instrument for change and as a sop offered instead of real change.

Reggae albums are often quickly deleted, especially in England. Many vital examples of the music never see the light of day here, so this list includes several Jamaican imports (marked JA after the label). In addition, Kingston labels have generally dispensed with catalogue numbers, so those are only given where available. Most reggae shops now carry a selection of import albums, but in the event of any problems, the most comprehensive mail-order service (including lists) is offered by Dub Vendor, 18 St Johns Avenue, London SW15.

Reggae : Albums

The Skatalites

Best of the Skatalites (STUDIO ONE JA)

Air Raid Shelter/Below Zero/Road Block/Black Sunday/Don't Slam The Door/Spread Satin/Fidel Castro/Jr Jive/Always On Sunday/ Phoenix City/Scambalena/Beard Man Ska

The Skatalites were by no means the only ska band: Baba Brooks Band, the Soul Brothers and Clue J and the Blues Blasters all made many classic records. This album demonstrates why the Skatalites were number one; the quality of the individual musicianship from Drummond, Alphonso, McCook and Co. is impeccable throughout, and the exuberance of 'Jr Jive' and 'Always On Sunday' ensured hyperactive dancing. When released as singles, some tracks were credited to the various soloists ('Phoenix City' was a small UK hit for Roland Alphonso), but it's the collective effort which counts. Don Drummond's preoccupation with Rasta is reflected in the title of 'Beardman Ska' (beardman=dreadlocked Rastafarian): Drummond died young, in a mental institution, and so never lived to see the music he helped build grow into reggae. Other Skatalites like McCook, Jackie Mittoo (keyboards), Alphonso and Jah Jerry (guitar) still appear on reggae sessions, and McCook in particular has an important part to play.

Prince Buster

Fabulous Greatest Hits (FAB MS 1)

Earthquake/Texas Hold-Up/Freezing Up Orange Street/Free Love/Julie/Take It Easy/Judge Dread/Too Hot/Ghost Dance/Ten Commandments/Al Capone/Barrister Pardon

Not all the tracks here have stood the tests of time – 'Julie' is a painful love ballad – but most are interesting at least, and some are peerless examples of Buster's casual lunacy. 'Texas Hold Up' is a ska celebration of the Kennedy assassination, while 'Ten Commandments' is the best example of vinyl misogyny: Buster warns his woman 'thou shalt not commit adultery, or the world will not hold me guilty if I commit murder'. The two parts of the Judge Dread saga already mentioned are here, but a third is unfortunately omitted; 'Ghost Dance' is an eerie letter to Buster's friend 'down there in boneyard'; and 'Al Capone' is the most famous record ska produced. As a whole, the album demonstrates how ska from 1964 to 1966 grew into rock steady; if only Prince Buster saw fit to engage himself in contemporary reggae, instead of dismissing it as a debased form of the music he loved, the future of JA music would look much more solid.

Various Artists

Hottest Hits (VIRGIN FRONT LINE FL 1034)

Those Guys (The Sensations)/Come On Little Girl (The Melodians)/Loving Pauper (Dobby Dobson)/Midnight Hour (The Silvertones)/Heartaches (Vic Taylor)/Cry Tough (Alton and the Flames)/Queen Majesty (The Techniques)/Right Track (Phyllis Dillon and Hopeton)/I'll Never Fall In Love (The Sensations)/The Tide Is High (The Paragons)/Things You Say You Love (The Jamaicans)/It's Raining (The Three Tops)

The late Duke Reid's rock steady productions showed off the very best in the music: Dobby Dobson's 'Loving Pauper', for example, is a well-constructed song, perfectly sung over a concentrated but tuneful rhythm. The violin on the Paragons' 'The Tide Is High' is an imaginative foil to John Holt's lead vocal, and Alton Ellis's 'Cry Tough' neatly straddles ska and rock steady. The best track is the Techniques' 'Queen Majesty', with Pat Kelly singing lead, a superb example of 1968 reggae with rock steady harmonies; like many of these songs, it is still being produced in versions ten years later, when the lessons of rock steady production are being learned again. Sonia Pottinger, who acquired the Treasure Isle catalogue when Reid died, has not tried to update the mixing of these tracks, although it's worth noting her (largely successful) attempts to dub up the Treasure Isle sound on three albums: *Treasure Dub*, 1 and 2, and *Pleasure Dub*. *Hottest Hits* offers the perfect selection of rock steady and early reggae up to 1969.

Slim Smith

Early Days (TOTAL SOUNDS JA)

Give Me Some More/Build My World Around You/Let Me Go, Girl/My Woman's Love/Love And Affection/Version Of Love/Watch This Sound/Out Of Love/If It Don't Work Out/Please Don't Go/Girl Of My Dreams/I'm Lost/3 Times 7/Keep That Light

There aren't many voices like Slim's, who recorded for Buster as Dakota Jim before working with the Techniques, then the Uniques, and finally under his own name. Most of these tracks are from his time with the Uniques, singing rock steady and reggae. There's also a ska/r&b tune ('3 Times 7') and an almost-calypso ('My Woman's Love', originally recorded by Curtis Mayfield, Slim's vocal mentor). 'Version Of Love' stands out, as Slim, encouraged by Martin Riley of the Uniques, shows us just how much rock steady owed to the best American soul music. On Buffalo Springfield's 'Watch This Sound', his garbled reading of the lyric completely changes the sense of the song, but it's still infinitely better than the original, thanks to Slim's voice. His suicide in 1973 has never been clearly explained, but it certainly deprived reggae of its most expressive singer.

The Heptones

The Heptones on Top (STUDIO ONE JA)

Equal Rights/Pure Sorrow/Heptones Gonna Fight/I Hold The Handle/ My Baby Is Gone/Soul Power/Take Me Darling/We Are In The Mood/ Sea Of Love/Pretty Looks Isn't All/Party Time/I Love You

The liner note says this is a rock steady album, which it is; but the Heptones were beginning to define the style of vocal group singing which still dominates reggae. Lead singer Leroy Sibbles (who left the group in 1978) also worked at Studio One as an arranger and session bass-player, and here shows his all-round ability with soulful vocals and articulate song-writing. There is a mixture of love songs and sufferer's protest songs, with Coxsone's rhythms again providing the perfect backing. Several of the songs were revived in the late seventies, when reggae plundered Studio One archives as if they were public property (to be fair, Coxsone isn't above playing the same game), but the original usually came out on top. 'Pretty Looks Isn't All' and 'I Hold The Handle' ('. . . you've got the blade/don't try to fight it babe, you'll need first aid') are clever lyrics well-performed, and are the outstanding tracks. Phil Phillips's 'Sea Of Love' and Solomon Burke's 'Take Me' both adapt well to the JA rhythm, and all twelve tracks show us Kingston harmonies at their best; many of the rhythms turn up on Studio One dub albums.

Burning Spear

Studio One Presents Burning Spear (STUDIO ONE JA)

Ethiopians Live It Out/We Are Free/Fire Down Below/Creation Rebel/ Don't Mess With Jill/Down By The Riverside/Door Peep Shall Not Enter/Pick Up The Pieces/Get Ready/Journey/Them A Come/He Prayed

Winston 'Burning Spear' Rodney's 1969 recording of 'Door Peeper' is reggae's best record; the Rasta lyric ('chant down Babylon . . .') is one of the first of its kind, and Spear's brooding vocal is matched by the rhythm: Clement 'Coxsone' Dodd knew how to use horns over the easy reggae beat. Several other tracks here ('Ethiopians Live It Out' and 'Creation Rebel') are in the same class, and even a silly 'Don't Mess With Jill' is delivered with dignity. Although two other members provide harmonies, it's undoubtedly Rodney's personality and ability which permeate the album, and only Coxsone could have provided, in 1969–70, the right setting for his ideas. Ten years later, Spear was still using some of these tunes (and those on the companion *Rocking Time* album, almost as good) as the basis for his self-produced music. The sleeve is a typical Studio One lesson in how to undersell your product.

The Wailers

African Herbsman (TROJAN TRLS 62)

Lively Up Yourself/Small Axe/Duppy Conqueror/Trench Town Rock/African Herbsman/Keep On Moving/Fussing And Fighting/Stand Alone/All In One/Don't Rock The Boat/Put It On/Sun Is Shining/Kaya/Riding High/Brain Washing/400 Years

Bob Marley's Wailers are reggae's (and Rasta's) First Ambassadors; their Island albums are usually cited as quintessential JA music, but their best work came earlier. With Upsetter Lee Perry, they cut many rebel tunes from 1969 to 1971, and on this album Marley is seen at his peak on 'Lively Up Yourself' and 'Duppy Conqueror'. It's true to say that Upsetter taught Marley how to express himself in the studio, and Bob went away to apply the lessons on his own Tuff Gong label, on which he released 'Screw Face', the Wailers' best record, unfortunately not included here. Like all JA groups, the Wailers enjoy recutting old hits: 'Put It On' was originally recorded at Studio One, and several of the other songs here have reappeared in Marley's more messianic latter days. The *African Herbsman* set shows us the Wailers with urchin roots still showing, and the young Lee Perry perfectly captures a true rebel sound (although 'Lively Up Yourself' and 'Trench Town Rock' are both Marley-produced, and very much in the Upsetter style). Marley sings lead on all tracks except 'Riding High' and 'Brain

Washing', which feature Bunny Livingstone, and '400 Years', a Peter Tosh song.

Burning Spear

Marcus Garvey (ISLAND ILPS 9377)

Marcus Garvey/Slavery Days/The Invasion/Live Good/Give Me/Old Marcus Garvey/Tradition/Jordan River/Red, Gold And Green/Resting Place

When the 'Marcus Garvey' single came out in 1974, it had almost as galvanic an effect as 'Door Peeper' had had five years earlier. Spear had been off the scene for three years, suddenly re-emerging with Jack Ruby as producer, and with a record at once threatening and optimistic. Spear continued to urge youth to locate themselves in JA history with 'Slavery Days', which is perhaps even better than 'Garvey', and titles like 'Tradition' and 'The Invasion' give an idea of the overall tone. Jack Ruby's production was perfect for the mid-seventies sound, but he eventually proved to have his eye too much on the white market, and Winston Rodney left to become his own producer; the later *Dry and Heavy* and *Marcus' Children* albums are masterpieces too, but the *Marcus Garvey* set earns its place here because it defines Spear music for the seventies, enabling the man to carry on under his own banner later.

Mighty Diamonds

Right Time (VIRGIN V 2052)

Right Time/Why Me Black Brother Why/Shame And Pride/Gnashing Of Teeth/Them Never Love Poor Marcus/I Need A Roof/Go Seek Your Rights/Have Mercy/Natural Natty/Africa

Joe Joe Hookim's Well Charge and Channel One labels had a reputation as important small labels when, in 1975, Joe Joe took the Diamonds in, cut 'Right Time' and 'Back Weh' with his usual studio musicians, and set reggae's pace for the next three years. The Diamonds openly acknowledged a debt to rock steady vocal groups, and the elaborate drumming of Sly Dunbar caused a sensation, proving so dynamic that he became the first session-man superstar; he eventually allowed his style to develop into 'rockers' drumming, which still dominates every Kingston studio. On top of that, the Diamonds' two massive hits, and several smaller ones almost as good, persuaded Virgin Records to sign them as one of their first acts, following Island's success with the Wailers – a first step towards the white-owned labels' domination of reggae. The *Right Time* album unfortunately doesn't include 'Back Weh', but 'I Need A Roof', 'Have Mercy' and 'Shame And Pride' are adequate substitutes. The high harmonies of the Diamonds are faultless throughout, and the session-men put together Channel One music which wasn't yet as stereotyped as it became in 1976–7.

Gregory Isaacs

Extra Classic (CONFLICT COLP 2002)

Mr Cop/Rasta Business/Black Against Black/Extra Classic/My Religion/Promise/Dread Locks Love Affair/Loving Pauper/Something Nice/Warriors/Jailer Jailer/Once Ago

Isaacs' career has taken him to almost every producer and studio on the island (but never Studio One, surprisingly). He's not only prolific, he's also very erratic, but this album offers twelve good examples of his style of singing: even when he's singing 'Rasta Business' he sounds as if he's been hurt by love. 'Mr Cop' and 'Black Against Black' are strong pleas for blacks to work together against iniquity, while 'Loving Pauper' is the best version of the tune after Dobby Dobson's original. The songs here cover the period 1973–7; as usual, some classics ('Look Before You Leap', 'Way Of Life') have been omitted. Nevertheless, what's left gives an idea of the Isaacs talent at work for various producers, including himself; I suspect Gregory isn't quite as vulnerable as he sounds, though.

U Roy

Version Galore (VIRGIN FRONT LINE FL 1018)

Your Ace From Space/On The Beach/Version Galore/True Confession/ The Tide Is High/Things You Love/The Same Song/Happy Go Lucky Girl/Rock Away/Wear You To The Ball/Don't Stay Away/Hot Pop

Reissues aren't common in reggae, so Virgin (who were at the same time issuing U Roy's inferior 1978 music) did well to see the demand for this piece of DJ history. Only one of U Roy's chart-topping trio is here, but there isn't a single bad track. As suggested, much of the strength of 'Your Ace From Space', 'Version Galore', etc, lies in the original rhythm which Roy toasts: John Holt's Paragons supply many classics here, including 'Wear You To The Ball' and 'The Tide Is High'; every track shows Duke Reid's masterful technique, and Roy's infectious babble fits like a glove, even at the hectic ska pace of 'True Confession': 'extraordinary musical shower every hour on the hour' sums it up. 'Wear You To The Ball' is the best here: the wedding of John Holt's sentimental singing and Roy's effervescent toast ('chicka-bow, chicka-bow, chicka-bow-wow-wow' and 'did you hear what the man say baby? Said be your best 'cos this gonna be your musical test') show us the new musical idiom in full flower.

I Roy

Presenting I Roy (TROJAN TRLS 63)

Red, Gold And Green/Pusher Man/Black Man Time/Smile Like An Angel/Peace/Coxsone Affair/Screw Face/First Cut Is The Deepest/ Melinda/Tourism Is My Business/Tripe Girl/Cow Town Skank

I Roy's pace was more relaxed than U Roy's, while his message was more political: 'Black Man Time', a toast to 'Slaving' by Lloyd Parks, is perhaps too familiar now, but still demonstrates a thoughtful man's toast, as chartered accountant I Roy preaches against begging, suggesting that, instead, youth enrols in Jamaica's literacy programme.

I Roy set the style for the DJ who feeds off everyday life, though he did so with more consideration than most of his followers. Again, the rhythms assembled by producer Gussie Clarke are part and parcel of the quality: the Heptones' 'Tripe Girl' ('... girls of your type should be selling tripe') is just one of several remakes of Coxsone or Duke Reid hits which bring out the best in I Roy. 'Coxsone Affair' is a tribute to the London-based sound system of Lloydie Coxsone, not Dodd; while 'Melinda' tells of an abortive flirtation with a girl 'totally put together like Eve, Salome, Florence Nightingale, Cleopatra'. Roy's moralizing always had humour: another track, not included here, warned of the dangers of gonorrhoea or 'Clapper's Tail'.

Big Youth

Screaming Target (TROJAN TRLS 61)

Screaming Target/Pride And Joy Rock/Be Careful/Tippertone Rock/ One Of These Fine Days/Screaming Target Version 2/The Killer/ Solomon A Gunday/Honesty/I Am Alright/Lee A Low/Concrete Jungle

Screaming Target is Youth's first album, and while it's true that most of his best singles came later, this is the best long-playing sampler of his talents. Gussie Clarke is the producer again, and he captures the young man's fresh style perfectly, with help from backing tracks featuring Gregory Isaacs at his best, as well as another version of the 'Slaving' rhythm used by I Roy. Gussie himself was still a teenager, and obviously had a clearer idea than most about how Youth should sound. Even more than I Roy, who somehow always managed to look a gent, Big Youth captured all the stark eccentricity of ghetto life, whether talking about what was showing at the cinema ('Screaming Target'), or advising his brethren how to cope with life.

Herman Chin-Loy

Aquarius Dub (AQUARIUS AQ 001 JA)

Jah Rock/Rumbo Malt/I Man/Oily/Rest You Self/Jumping Jack/ Heavy Duty/Jah Jah Dub/Nyah Time/Jungle Rock

Herman is another low-profile producer who, especially in the early seventies, quietly shaped reggae's future; his 1972 dub experiment, the dub album, made room for a new idiom which saw some of JA's most creative work. *Aquarius* is a simple drum-and-bass affair for the most part, with an occasional dash of horns, keyboards and vocals. The simplicity allows the quality of Herman's reggae skeleton to show through, and this album compares favourably with the more excessive dubs that followed. On the other hand, although it's a classic, it will probably sound better *after* you've heard the full dub scope of the following albums.

Clement 'Coxsone' Dodd

Dub Store Special (STUDIO ONE JA)

Queen Of The Rub/Mo Jo Papa/Message From A Dub/Follow This Dub/ Idle Burg/Musical Science/Hanging On The Wall/Love Land/This Race/ Darker Black/Dub Creation/Life

The dozen or so Studio One dub albums are a mini-history of reggae, and all of them deserve a place in the discerning reggae collection. Dodd has a vast backlog of tapes to call on, covering the best in reggae and rock steady (because of ska's more primitive recording techniques, it rarely makes good dub fodder), and his music has always relied heavily on melody – so the elementary drum-and-bass sound on 'Dub Store' is filled out with horn riffs, vocal snatches, whatever is necessary to provide a link with the original tune. Titles on dub albums rarely coincide with those on the original, so here we have 'Hanging On The Wall' (sax version of Freddy McKay's 'Picture On The Wall'),

'Queen Of The Rub' (drum and bass version of the Eternals' 'Queen Of The Minstrels') and 'Life' (trombone version of John Holt's 'Sad News'), all showing us the range of Studio One music. With dub, it helps to be familiar with the original cut, but when the music itself is this good, it can easily stand alone.

Joe Gibbs (producer)

African Dub Almighty, Chapter 1

(LIGHTNING LIP 10)

African Dub/Universal Dub/Midnight Movie/Ghetto Skank/Lime Key Rock/Lovers' Serenade/Treasure Dub/Schooling The Beat/Campus Rock/Half Ounce/Worrier/East Africa

There are three African dub albums (Chapters 1, 2 and 3); the last, issued in 1977, coincided with the tastes of the English punk market, relying heavily on electronic trickery with little good music to support it. Chapter 2 from 1975 is a classic blend of inventive electronics and good music, but doesn't quite match the first in the series. Joe Gibbs (Joel Gibson) emerged as an important producer in 1966 with 'Hold Them', Roy Shirley's pivotal rock steady record, and he is always abreast of developments. *African Dub Almighty, Chapter 1* appeared in 1973, and is definitely of its time, demonstrating again the importance of Duke Reid and Coxsone tunes: 'Universal Dub' is a recut of John Holt's Studio One hit, 'My Heart Is Gone', for example. But Joe Gibbs's music stands on its own two feet, or at least it did in 1973; Gibbs's other dub album from that year, *Dub Serial*, is also worth a place in your collection.

Joe Joe Hookim

Vital Dub

(VIRGIN V 2055)

Roof Top Dub/Ital Step/Fence Dub/Ishens Dub/Total Dub/Merciful Dub/Cell Block 11/Killer Dub/Blacka Black Dub

By 1976, dub had become a very sophisticated medium, employing the whole range of studio techniques, often with little to show for it. 'Vital Dub' shows how to combine the best of both worlds: echo and equalizer are tastefully applied, in the manner pioneered at the mixing board of King Tubbys, and many of Joe Joe's best rhythms are on display, including several from the Diamonds' *Right Time* album, which is a useful companion set, worth-while in its own right. Yet again, Hookim draws liberally on the Studio One catalogue: 'Fence Dub' is an effective update of Coxsone's 'In Cold Blood' rhythm, originally used at Channel One for Middle Youth's 'Fence Skank'. If this genealogy seems academic, it should be remembered that reggae musicians always prefer to update an old rhythm when they can, and the music's ingenuity only shows through if you know the source. Nevertheless, the driving rockers music of 'Vital Dub' perfectly combines drum and bass, horns, keyboards and occasional vocals to make one of the last great dub albums before the engineer completely ruled the studio.

Augustus Pablo (producer)

King Tubbys Meets Rockers Uptown

(YARD MUSIC JA)

Keep On Dubbing/Stop Them Jah/Young Generation Dub/Each One Dub/555 Dub Street/Satta/Braces Tower Dub/King Tubbys Meets Rockers Uptown/Corner Crew Dub/Say So/Skanking Dub/Frozen Dub

Originally issued in America in 1976, this album appeared on Pablo's own label in 1977, with one extra track, 'Satta'. King Tubbys is a master engineer, while Pablo is perhaps the most imaginative producer of the late seventies. His own keyboard work here takes second place to the dubbing arts, and Tubbys mixes extra class into every track. The rhythms are drawn from Pablo's Rockers and Hot Stuff labels: 'Keep On Dubbing' is from Jacob Miller's 'Keep On Knocking', and there are also versions of Pablo's own 'Black Gunn' and 'Pablo Satta' (the track listing is inaccurate, which is not unusual). Tubbys' echo and equalizer effects ensure that everything sounds as modern as it should, and Pablo's debt to Jackie Mittoo, the Studio One organist, gives us plenty of good tunes, so this is the perfect overall dub album.

Augustus Pablo

This Is Augustus Pablo (KAYA JA)

Dub Organizer/Please Sunrise/Point Blank/Arabian Rock/Pretty Baby/Pablo In Dub/Skateland Rock/Dread Eye/Too Late/Assignment No. 1/Jah Rock/Lovers Mood

Pablo's instrumental abilities are on display here; producer Clive Chin capitalized on the man's 1973 popularity with the melodica, although we also hear him on piano, organ and clarinet. The unfussy reggae rhythm of the day suited the stark melodica sound, and Pablo's simple tunes are wholly appropriate. Dub techniques are sparingly used throughout, but this is an instrumental album, not strictly speaking a dub (drum and bass do not enter the proceedings). Only reggae could make an album featuring such rudimentary melodica solos, and then have the nerve to label it 'rebel rock'; but it's true that Pablo, particularly in 1972–3, embodied the spirit of Kingston street music, before Rastafarianism completely took over. There is no attempt to sell this album to a nebulous pop/white audience, and the music is that much stronger for it.

Jackie Mittoo

Macka Fat (STUDIO ONE JA)

Henry The Great/Good Feeling/Macka Fat/Lazy Bones/Fancy Pants/Something Else/Happy People/Purple Heart/Whoa Whoa/Division One/Ghetto Organ/Dad Is Home

Jackie Mittoo played piano and organ for the Skatalites while he was still at school, and for most of the other bands Dodd dreamt up for his Studio One sessions (Underground Vegetable, New Establishment, etc). When the reggae rhythm surfaced in 1968, Mittoo's organ was the perfect solo instrument, and so he made a number of solo albums, *Macka Fat* being the best. To ears accustomed to the organ in a rock context, Mittoo may sound a little too close to Reginald Dixon at the Blackpool Tower, but he nevertheless made some important records, not least because Coxsone always used his best rhythms at Mittoo sessions. If easy listening weren't a term of abuse, this music would deserve the name; it's simply Mittoo relaxing over some of the best rhythm tracks Jamaica has produced, with no iconoclastic overtones: remember that reggae, and especially ska and rock steady, were as much 'adult' music as they were 'youth' music, and if elder statesmen like Dodd and Duke Reid hadn't prepared the ground for reggae, then the music as we know it today simply wouldn't have existed. These men never allowed Rasta rhetoric to stand in the way of good music, and particularly now, when the future of reggae is doubtful, a straightforward musical album like *Macka Fat* may help to save its life.

Reggae: Singles

Baba Brooks Band: *Guns Fever* (1966, prod. Duke Reid)

Ska chaos at its best: gunfight sound effects, 'schookascicka' vocal hiccoughs, frantic rhythm, and a torrid horn section. All human life is here, somewhere.

Keith and Tex: *Stop That Train* (1968, prod. Derrick Harriott)

On *The Harder They Come* sound-track, Scotty toasted this as 'Draw Your Brakes', and both versions are brilliant. Harriott was a master of the cool approach to rock steady, both as singer and producer.

The Paragons: *So Close To You* (1968, prod. Duke Reid)

John Holt's best sentimental singing, the doowopping Paragons, a pretty organ and a subtle but solid rhythm attest to the Duke's rock steady primacy.

Carlton and the Shoes: *Love Me Forever/Happy Land* (1968, prod. C. S. Dodd)

As rock steady becomes reggae, the Shoes step forward as a seminal close harmony group. 'Happy Land' is a close relation to 'Satta Massa Gana' (see below), while 'Forever' has been recorded in countless versions.

The Eternals: *Queen Of The Minstrels/Stars* (1968, prod. C. S. Dodd)

Two of Dodd's favourite rhythms for dubbing; Cornell Campbell's fragile lead vocal was at its best on these early tracks, and the tuneful fills from the band show why these tracks dub up so well.

The Abyssinians: *Satta Massa Gana* (1969, prod. Bernard Collins)

Singer Collins took the Shoes' song and made a Rasta hymn and anthem from it. Ahead of its time in 1969, it took two years to become a hit, and still sounds modern today.

King Stitt: *Lee Van Cleef* (1970, prod. Clancy Eccles)

Deformed since birth, Stitt paraded his ugliness, on stage and record: here he issues a challenge to Clint Eastwood, over Eccles's chugging rhythm: 'This is the days of wrath, Eastwood; *I* am the Ugly One . . . DIE!'

Peter Tosh: *Here Comes The Judge* (1970, prod. Joel Gibson)

Over Gibbs' version of the 'Satta' rhythm, Tosh gives us his only classic: as a Buster-style Judge, he sentences white imperialists to be hanged by their tongues.

The Royals: *Pick Up The Pieces* (1970, prod. C. S. Dodd)

Very much in the Abyssinians' mould, lead Roy Cousins employs his lisp to good effect. Classic sufferers' music.

Dennis Brown: *If I Follow My Heart* (1972, prod. C. S. Dodd)

A mere lad of sixteen or so, Dennis handled this song of confused love like a veteran. Openly acknowledging his debt to Studio One, Brown, still in his early twenties, is one of the most talented singers and producers in JA.

Dennis Alcapone: *My Voice Is Insured For Half A Million* (1973, prod. Duke Reid)

Dennis's bragging toast to the Techniques' 'Queen Majesty' shows him at his best. Six years later, the fickle audience wouldn't give twopence for Alcapone's superior toasting.

Niney the Observer: *Ital Correction* (1973, prod. Niney)

Over the heaviest of heavy rhythms, Niney lectures on the re-appropriations of black JA vocabulary after its annexation by white exploiters. Much more fun than it sounds.

Big Youth and U Roy: *Battle Of The Giants* (1974, prod. Big Youth)

Although both artists are covered in the main text, this recorded confrontation is just too good to omit, and a rare chance to see Roy's old-style toasting mash up (well, almost) Youth's newer style.

Prince Jazzbo: *Step Forward Youth* (1974, prod. Prince Jazzbo)

Jazzbo was the most vituperatively racialist DJ, and here sulkily advises his brethren to rise up against Babylon, the Catholic Church, and capitalism. Another anthem for youth.

Dr Alimantado: *Best Dressed Chicken In Town* (1974, prod. Dr Alimantado)

An update of ska lunacy using electronics, a strong sound-system rhythm, and just about every trick in the DJs handbook; the Doctor was making good records long before the punk market discovered him, but not for long afterwards.

Desmond Young: *Warning* (1975, prod. Jimmy Rodway)

Desmond appeals to God over a rhythm as good as reggae ever produced, and one toasted by both Big Youth and I Roy.

Bunny Livingstone: *Battering Down Sentence* (1975, prod. B. Livingstone)

Bunny isn't very prolific, but at his best can equal Marley. In fact, despite his diffidence, he often seems to be the most talented Wailer, although he now only rarely associates himself with the group.

Johonny C. Brown: *Dance Good* (1975, prod. Glen Brown)

Johonny is a thinly disguised Glen Brown, who apparently never bothered to learn the finer points of the melodica. A grand eccentric in the studio, Glen concentrated on making this the perfect dance record, so melodica virtuosity was superfluous.

Pablo Moses: *I Man A Grasshopper* (1975, prod. Geoffrey Chung)

Chung's deft hand makes the record, with the biting guitar counter-pointing the jaunty rhythm, over which young Pablo preaches toleration for the ganja smoker.

Freddie MacGregor: *I Man A Rasta* (1976, prod. C. S. Dodd)

Over a dense rhythm, Freddie denounces capitalism in favour of revolution. After more than twenty years in the business, Coxsone could be forgiven for occasionally resting on his laurels, but here in 1976, and later with Prince Lincoln, he showed he still had something to teach the youngsters.

IAN BIRCH

Punk

As the newspapers never tired of telling us, something happened to British kids in 1976–7. Fleet Street, subscribing to the 'ten-year cycle' theory of adolescent upheaval, wasted gallons of ink, not on ripped-up cinema seats (1956–7 with Elvis and the Teds) nor on kaftans and 'meditation' (1966–7 with the Beatles and flower-power): this time it was be-leathered teens with multi-dyed hair terrorizing old ladies with razor-blades, in time to the loud and angry sound of the Sex Pistols, who set spanking new standards in bad taste and became society's latest whipping-boys. The Rolling Stones might never have existed.

We can spare ourselves yet another earnest discussion on the sociological cause and effect of youthful rebellion, and go straight to the lyrics of the songs that came out of this regeneration of musical energy.

All human dissatisfaction was there: poverty and the dole queue, petty crime, high-rise living, street violence and BOREDOM (relieved where possible by the cheap and fast drug amphetamine sulphate). The collective attitude seemed to waver between mind-crunching nihilism and resignation to an early self-administered death – not in itself new, but taken to new extremes of artlessness. Sniffing glue, surely the tackiest of highs became the title of the most famous of all the many fanzines that sprang up with the music, a significant indication that the audience for the 'new' sound was closely involved and identified with the bands themselves.

The idea was that *anyone* with a modicum or even minimum of musical talent could form a band, and that by keeping everything close to home, not only the recording and pressing of the disc, but publicity and distribution as well, one could by-pass the major record companies, which now epitomized the big-star élitism of a dollar-conscious rock scene that had become hopelessly out of touch with the fan-in-the-street. That, at least, was the idea; and no one can deny that in the hot summer of '76 there was a certain something in the air.

But this outbreak of do-it-yourself spontaneity, which was soon producing a dozen new British independent record labels a week, far from being a real innovation, was more an overdue realization of something that had begun ten years earlier in the USA, where the whole concept of punk has its musical and stylistic origins. Even the very first followers of British punk, who were motivated by genuine ideals and for whom someone like Mick Jagger was as passé as a Windsor knot, would have had to concede that had it not been for the British beat invasion of America in the early sixties, spearheaded by bands like the Beatles, Stones and Kinks, there would never have been a grass-roots reaction from thousands of Americans who were raring to get stuck into what was virtually a British monopoly of the entire USA music scene.

The result was that around 1964, the aggression underlying rock & roll, re-awakened in high-school leavers and drop-outs from all over the USA by the British r&b boom, took on new and hybrid forms, reflecting, in some cases superbly, the angst of suburban living, the frustrations of repressive authority and of too much Bobby Vee on the radio. The fans were going to make their own music on their own terms, and although hundreds of amateur bands never even cut a record, the proliferation of small local labels multiplied to the extent that, by 1966, what had started as a rash had become an epidemic of 'garage bands', a loose but apt description of the self-taught outfits who were trying for a sound that would give new meaning to the word 'raw', but who didn't have the loot to buy studio time; after all, California surf bands like the Beach Boys had started up in similar fashion only three or four years previously.

Naturally the element of regionalism played an important part in the punk sound of the sixties: just as Liverpool, Manchester, London and Southend evolved their own discernible brands of r&b in Britain, so there were styles peculiar to cities and suburbs in the US, notably in Los Angeles, in San Jose and in Texas. Despite the stylistic divergences, however, what was it that characterized the punk sound of the middle sixties? The basic ingredients were a tinny Vox organ, guitars doctored, according to taste, from fuzz-tone to feedback, 4/4 drumming to keep everything moving forward at a steady pace, and an outrageously sneering vocal style delivered with a disaffected stance reminiscent of, say, Reg Presley of the Troggs, whose massive hit 'Wild Thing' was in most groups' repertoire, along with three other seminal influences, 'Gloria', 'Hey Joe' and 'Louie Louie', a riff so fundamental to rock that fifteen years later we find Eno feeding it through a computer in his spare time (all in the cause of art).

Those songs, of course, were hits, but groups that managed to reach the charts outside their own town were rarely able to repeat the success. It was only thanks to Dylan songs, a shrewd producer in Terry Melcher (who successfully americanized the English sound) and the positive backing of a giant company like Columbia, that the Byrds achieved what eluded hundreds of other groups – the ability to sell records. Garage-band activity was confined mainly to local Saturday-night dances and 'Battle of the Bands' competitions.

By the end of 1967, punk groups had either just disappeared or evolved into one of two very different directions – bubble-gum, like the Shadows of Knight, and psychedelia, like the Seeds. For a typical rise and fall saga of a main-stream punk band, Greg Shaw's appraisal of the Standells in *Who Put the Bomp!* magazine, summer 1974 (available from PO Box 7112, Burbank, California 91510), makes excellent reading. Their decline led them first to cabaret in Las Vegas, and thereafter, in a reformed version, to the small clubs in California – a full circle of sorts.

As Middle America absorbed the summer of love, the ever-increasing violence of cities such as New York was bound to spark off a rock sound that had more in common with personal rebellion than cosmic revolution. In Detroit the MC5 somehow managed to combine both qualities on a searing album of modern rock & roll called *Kick Out the Jams* – raw, electric music that was not to be forgotten by the British new wave of the mid seventies. 'If you take everything in the universe and break it down to a common denominator, all you've got is energy – it's the level we communicate from – that's the essence of the urban sound': this is how the MC5's Wayne Kramer saw the group's role in 1968. Iggy Pop of the Stooges, who, like MC5, came from Detroit, had a more 'heroic' influence on British punk due to his wild and distasteful sense of depravity, filtered onto record in three-chord fashion by the Velvet Underground's John Cale in 1969.

The Velvet Underground were a vital catalyst for all that was best in the British new wave. Their mechanically insistent rhythms, an extension of the organ-dominated sound of Sir Douglas Quintet and others, provided the raw material for groups like the Ramones, who needed only to speed it up to achieve a combination that was rarely missing from the speakers, if not the airwaves, of the UK in 1976–7.

In 1965, the Falling Spikes became the Velvet Underground, of which Lou Reed and John Cale were the hub. Their involvement with Andy Warhol has been grossly oversold; in effect, the band toured with a kind of 'total show', the Exploding Plastic Inevitable, which featured films, dancers and a light show – psychedelic self-expression NY-style. Over the next three years the Underground, in all its various forms (Doug Yule replaced Cale and Yule's brother Tommy later stood in for Mo Tucker), were to produce music that was very much of its time; the fact that on albums like *White Light, White Heat* they were also distinctly ahead of their time meant the inevitable lack of commercial success. Their influence was not to be felt at a popular level until Bowie emerged in 1971.

The early seventies saw bands playing in ever bigger venues, moving further away from their audiences in every sense and creating the astrodome mentality. James Taylor also appeared, the first of a series of singer/song-writers who churned out Hip Easy Listening, music marked by its bland sensitivity. Despite this trend, there were areas where groups kept alive and developed the garage-band approach. The New York Dolls strutted their trash aesthetic, sparking off en route a localized upsurge of new bands, the most commercially successful of which turned out to be Kiss, a gimmick-laden package at the fag-end of glam-rock. Interestingly, the Dolls' last manager was Malcolm McLaren, who tried to reactivate the band in early 1975 with an image of chic Marxism. It failed, but gave McLaren invaluable experience for his forthcoming Sex Pistols masterscheme.

Media coverage became increasingly important. It contributed hugely to another emergent scene that, during 1974, centred on two New York clubs, CBGB's and Max's Kansas City. Throughout the next two years, they played host to a vast influx of new outfits who frequently swapped personnel. Richard Hell, for instance, a pivotal figure whose approach (poetic neurosis) and dress style (spikey hair and ripped T-shirts) had a profound influence on British punks, moved from Television to the Heartbreakers and finally to his own band, the Voidoids.

This crop also included Blondie, the Ramones, Talking Heads and countless others, some of whom enjoyed brief fame on compilations like *Live at CBGB's* and *Live at Max's*, Volumes 1 and 2. The first act, however, to get hitherto unprecedented attention was Patti Smith, an occasional music critic who turned her rock-based poetry into electrifying songs.

In London, pub rock had begun as a reaction against heavy metal headbangers and the now moribund glitter-rock, whose originator, Marc Bolan, though very different in style, introduced the punk notion of a three-minute, arrogant flash. Pub rock was important because it brought music back into the small venues, at reasonable prices. It also provided an important breeding-ground for several figures who broke at the same time as British punk. Elvis Costello sharpened his teeth in Flip City, Nick Lowe had paid long dues in Brinsley Schwarz, while Ian Dury emerged from Kilburn and the High Roads.

Younger bands sprang up who would be even more closely allied to the '76 movement. The

101-ers yielded Clash member Joe Strummer, while Eddie and the Hot Rods, a more traditional r&b bluster band, gave some idea of the pure energy that was about to hit. Also, in France, the independent Skydog label kept alive the legacy left by the Stooges, the MC5 and the Velvet Underground. One French fanzine, *Rock News*, mirrored the nascent New York scene more comprehensively than any of its British counterparts (and there were precious few at that stage). Here the word 'punk', in fact, was being applied to artists like Nils Lofgren and Bruce Springsteen who, though they embodied a street toughness, had a sophistication that was in no way punk.

But then the Sex Pistols played their first gig at London's St Martin's College of Art and, almost immediately, gave the ensuing revolt its style, form, content and direction. Johnny Rotten became Public Enemy Number One, a rebel figure-head for the 'blank generation'. This was as much the result of Rotten's savage contempt for everyone and everything as of manager McLaren's Machiavellian expertise in playing the media and record business, who were desperate not to miss a good thing when they saw it. Throughout 1976 scores of bands started, with the Clash, the Damned, the Stranglers, the Jam and the Vibrators in the forefront. The coming-out party took place in September at a punk festival in London's 100 Club. The movement spread across the country and regional bands popped up everywhere: Manchester was especially productive (Buzzcocks, Magazine, John Cooper Clarke, Jilted John, the Fall). The punk umbrella embraced anything that convention considered amateurish, taboo, anti-social, antagonistic or downright subversive. By late 1977 the major record companies had signed up everything available, the scene had become swamped by blatant bandwaggoners, groups began to disown the 'punk' tag in favour of the less constricting 'new wave', the ideals had been quashed or forgotten and exploitation was widespread. Rotten's departure from the Pistols spelt the end.

And the future? Will Halifax (Yorkshire) or Halifax (Nova Scotia) become the new centre of punk? The current groups have either split up or moved in similar directions to their predecessors. Powerpop, an attempt to make punk into more mainstream pop, recalls such sixties bands as Paul Revere and the Raiders and Tommy James and the Shondells, while electronic outfits like Devo, who reflect the industrialization of modern society, have a cerebral quality reminiscent of psychedelia.

Stay tuned.

Punk : Albums

Various Artists

Nuggets – Original Artyfacts from the First Psychedelic Era 1966–1968

(ORIGINAL CATALOGUE NUMBER: ELEKTRA 7E–2006/
RE-ISSUE NUMBER: SIRE SASH 3716 – BOTH US IMPORTS)

I Had Too Much To Dream (Last Night) (The Electric Prunes)/Dirty Water (The Standells)/Night Time (The Strangeloves)/Lies (The Knickerbockers)/Respect (The Vagrants)/A Public Execution (Mouse)/ No Time Like The Right Time (The Blues Project)/Oh Yeah (The Shadows of Knight)/Pushin' Too Hard (The Seeds)/Moulty (The Barbarians)/Don't Look Back (The Remains)/Invitation To Cry (The Magicians)/Liar, Liar (The Castaways)/You're Gonna Miss Me (The 13th Floor Elevators)/Psychotic Reaction (Count Five)/Hey Joe (The Leaves)/Just Like Romeo And Juliet (Michael and the Messengers)/ Sugar And Spice (The Cryan Shames)/Baby Please Don't Go (The Amboy Jukes)/Tobacco Road (The Blues Magoos)/Let's Talk About Girls (Chocolate Watch Band)/Sit Down I Think I Love You (The Mojo Men)/Run Run Run (The Third Rail)/My World Fell Down (Sagittarius)/Open My Eyes (Nazz)/Farmer John (The Premiers)/It's-A-Happening (The Magic Mushrooms)

Released in 1972, *Nuggets* speaks loudly for itself as much through the twenty-seven artists that appear as through its compiler Lenny Kaye, who not only annotates each track but, in the main liner note, comes as close as anyone ever will to explaining what was happening to rock music at ground level in the States during the mid sixties.

He saw the influence that this transitional and, in the main, commercially ignored wave of music was to have in a few years' time. The diversity of songs on this album, in fact, proves beyond doubt that it was as much an era of experimentation (The Magic Mushrooms) as of emulation (The Beatles-drenched Knickerbockers) and everything in between.

Classic singles that don't appear in the index will be on this album, which even today is the only compilation that can honestly be called a musical primer. There is talk of a Volume 2 on the Sire label: let's hope it includes another track by the Blues Magoos (featured here with John D. Loudermilk's 'Tobacco Road'), a Bronx-bred outfit whose level of musicianship was generally considered to be sub-par even by garage-band standards ('basic', 'largely forgettable, rampant and discordant', etc, etc) but whose stage suits lit up with flashing lights and who dared to call their first album *Psychedelic Lollipop*!

Thus we encounter the truly classic refrain on one of their singles, 'We Ain't Got Nothin' Yet': 'Nothin' can hold us and nothin' can keep us down/some day our names will be spread all over town/we get in while the gettin' is good/so make it on your own and you know that's good.' You can't really sum up the street-corner punk ethos better than that. This was the world of *Nuggets*.

The Standells

Dirty Water (TOWER ST 5027: US IMPORT)

Medication/Little Sally Tease/There Is A Storm Comin'/19th Nervous Breakdown/Dirty Water/Pride And Devotion/Sometimes Good Guys Don't Wear White/Hey Joe/Why Did You Hurt Me?/Rari

Although there seem to be more copies of the album *Why Pick on Me?* circulating around Britain, the choice for the Standells has to be *Dirty Water*, a punk classic by a classic punk group.

They started in 1963 around Larry Tamblyn, and included Tony Valentino, Gary Lane and drummer Dickie Dodd, late of the Mouseketeers. They had it all down pat – long hair combed forward, riffs culled from English r&b bands, notably the Stones, an arrogant stance and nasty lyrics that reflected the frustrations of mundane authoritarianism.

It wasn't until Ed Cobb, who was producing the first wave of punk bands in San Jose, met them, both writing and producing *Dirty Water* (which also became a big hit single), that things gelled. On side one there are scorching versions of 'Hey Joe' and of the Stones' '19th Nervous Breakdown', plus a number of snarlingly delivered girl-jive songs including 'Little Sally Tease', also recorded by the Kingsmen.

Vying for honours with the title track as a sneering punk anthem, side two's masterpiece, which also appears on *Why Pick on Me*, is 'Sometimes Good Guys Don't Wear White'. Sample lyric: 'Some of my friends they've been in real trouble/and some say I'm no better than the rest/but tell your momma and your poppa/sometimes good guys don't wear white.'

The Standells appeared in the exploitation movie, *Riot on Sunset Strip*, but went the way of most punk bands, in this case drifting into cabaret and ultimate obscurity.

The Seeds

Legendary Master Recordings (SONET SNTF 746)

Can't Seem To Make You Mine/No Escape/Lose Your Mind/Evil Hoodoo/Girl I Want You/Pushin' Too Hard/Try To Understand/ Nobody Spoil My Fun/It's A Hard Life/You Can't Be Trusted/Excuse, Excuse/Fallin' In Love

There could have been no Seeds without their charismatic front-man Sky Saxon. Along with the Standells, the Seeds were at the core of LA's emerging underground rock scene of 1965 – aggressive on stage and no less so on this, a re-issue of their debut album, which was released in spring 1966 and which features the first two singles, 'Can't Seem To Make You Mine' and 'Pushin' Too Hard'. The latter was their most famous song, and others were based on it, almost to the point of being identical.

But then it *was* an archetypal punk sound – 'A relentless two-chord riff propelled by the distinctive electric piano and super-simplistic but entirely appropriate guitar break'. Re-released as a single and played incessantly on LA station KRKD (alongside 'Psychotic Reaction'),

'Pushin' Too Hard' eventually became a hit and the Seeds the rage of southern California.

Their second album, *Web of Sound*, included the pre-psychedelic 'Mister Farmer', and by their third album, *Future*, the Seeds had become the uncrowned kings of 'flower music'. Of course, from here it was a slow process of dissolution, due to lack of widespread commercialism.

In 1967 they inexplicably released a dreadful album called *A Spoonful of Seedy Blues*, an unwittingly apt title, but by now were playing smaller and fewer venues anyway. Sky Saxon shortly joined the legion of rock casualties who insisted that they had met God and could outsell the Beatles.

The 13th Floor Elevators

The Psychedelic Sounds of the 13th Floor Elevators (RADAR RAD 13)

You're Gonna Miss Me/Roller Coaster/Splash (Now I'm Home)/ Reverberation (Doubt)/Don't Fall Down/Fire Engine/Thru The Rhythm/ You Don't Know/Kingdom Of Heaven/Monkey Island/Tried To Hide

A force to be reckoned with in Texas during the middle sixties was undoubtedly International Artists, who released twelve albums, four of them by the Elevators, who are justly considered to be prime movers of the acid/psychedelic onslaught of that period.

Nevertheless, their first album is appropriate to this survey since it illustrates both the wide range of musical ideas that were current in 1966 and the way in which those ideas could be brought together. This album (produced by Kenny Rogers' brother, Lelan, and with a psychedelic poster cover by John Cleveland) centres on the guitars of manic Roky Erikson and Stacy Sutherland, and the 'quest'-filled lyrics of Tommy Hall.

In rock terms, the most 'conventional' tracks are a version of the single 'You're Gonna Miss Me', which also appears on *Nuggets*, and 'Tried To Hide', plus the hallucinatory 'Fire Engine', which Tom Verlaine used to feature when Television were first starting to play the clubs in New York.

Although the Elevators were a band essentially (and ever more obviously) concerned with 'consciousness expansion', what do we find on their third album, *13th Floor Elevators Live*, but Bo Diddley's 'Before You Accuse Me', Buddy Holly's 'I'm Gonna Love You Too' and a version of 'Everybody Needs Somebody To Love', a favourite from the Stones' repertoire.

There also exists a tape of the band playing the Avalon ballroom in 1966, where they perform a Beatles' song and the Kinks' 'You Really Got Me': all in all, a revealing choice of influences and proof that they were ready to rock.

Sir Douglas Quintet

The Best of Sir Douglas Quintet

(CRAZY CAJUN CC–LP 1003: US IMPORT)

She's About A Mover/Beginning Of The End/The Tracker/You're Out Walking The Streets Tonight/It Was In The Pines/In The Jailhouse Now/Quarter To Three/It's A Man Down There/The Rains Came/Please Just Say So/We'll Take Our Last Walk Tonight/Walking The Streets

Sir Douglas was the band of Doug Sahm, a Texan from San Antone who had been playing country music since the age of ten, and who veered towards rock & roll in the late fifties. The Quintet were formed in 1964 and the combination of Sahm's writing style, the inimitable organ sound of Augie Meyer and a restrained production by r&b veteran Huey Meaux gave the band a nation-wide hit the following year with 'She's About A Mover'.

Meaux claims they were the first American group to have a hit 'with the very famous English sound', but this record went way beyond mimicry: it was that part of the American mid-sixties punk sound which later survived as bubble-gum, and it inspired many other bands of lesser talent to adopt an organ-dominated rhythm base (for example Sam the Sham and ? and the Mysterians), giving rise to a local teen-scene in Texas which could truly claim a sound of its own.

Apart from 'The Tracker', which is virtually a re-working of 'She's About A Mover', 'In The Jailhouse Now', a kind of 'punk-blues' rendering of the Jimmie Rodgers song, and the band's other big single 'The Rains Came', the country influence tends to win through.

Sahm later moved to San Francisco, recording his best-selling album *Mendocino* in 1969 and (with Meyer) three others, all commercial disasters, before going solo.

MC5

Kick Out the Jams (ELEKTRA K42027)

Ramblin' Rose/Kick Out The Jams/Come Together/Rocket Reducer No. 64 (Rama Lama Fa Fa Fa)/Borderline/Motor City Is Burning/I Want You Right Now/Starship

Recorded in Detroit's Grande Ballroom in October 1968, there has rarely been such a show of high energy on vinyl since its release. The sheer force of the rhythm section, with Dennis Thompson on drums and Mike Davis on bass, allied to the dual attack of Wayne Kramer's and Fred 'Sonic' Smith's guitars, and the rabble-rousing vocals of Rob Tyner, is one reason why this band are often thought of as pioneers of the British punk explosion.

But the MC5 were hardly a 'punk' band: they formed a partnership with Trans-Love Energies, John Sinclair's militant White Panther organization, smoked plenty of dope, used an energy chant on stage and from 1967 to 1969 generally led rock & roll audience communication through changes that put Jefferson Airplane to shame.

Soon the band would be ceremoniously ripping up the American flag as part of their act: anarchy was just a shot away and when Tyner sang 'Motor City Is Burning' in 1968, the urban nightmare that had been Detroit a year before would still have been fresh in the mind.

Although their second (studio) release *Back in the USA* is also a great rock album, it is the total energy of *Kick Out the Jams* which boots it into the hall of fame.

Academic postscript: this re-issue has the refurbished 'Kick-out-the-jams' chant (no 'motherfuckers') and lacks the original liner notes by John Sinclair.

The Velvet Underground

The Velvet Underground and Nico Produced by Andy Warhol (POLYDOR 2315 056)

Sunday Morning/I'm Waiting For The Man/Femme Fatale/Venus In Furs/Run Run Run/All Tomorrow's Parties/Heroin/There She Goes Again/I'll Be Your Mirror/The Black Angel's Death Song/European Son

Recorded in 1967, 'in an hour, an hour and a half' if we are to believe Lou Reed, this album became a model for the decadence-obsessed rock fans of the early seventies, soon to become weekend-Berliners and finally glitter-merchants. There is even a sleeve note quoting a review by *LA* magazine, which describes the record as reminiscent of 'Berlin in the decadent '30s' and in the same breath tells us that it is 'screeching rock & roll' – a laughable anomaly.

Dark themes there certainly are: sex, sado-masochism and heroin are not subjects that translate into rock in any but the most direct fashion, and the Velvets were a rock & roll band, not a cabaret, a point that was obviously lost on some critics of the period.

'Heroin', along with 'Run Run Run' and the absolute quintessence of the Velvet Underground sound, 'I'm Waiting For The Man', form a triumvirate of songs which, taken a stage further in 'Sister Ray' from the next album (where the central riff has become so monotonous as to be almost free-form), brought rock to a limit beyond which, in some ways, it was impossible to go. As a sound it was heavy, metallic, industrial, mechanical – and you could dance to it. Lou Reed's brilliant lyrics merely make the whole achievement more formidable.

The Velvet Underground

1969 Velvet Underground Live

(MERCURY SRM–2–7504: US IMPORT)

Waiting For My Man/Lisa Says/What Goes On/Sweet Jane/We're Gonna Have A Real Good Time Together/Femme Fatale/New Age/Rock

And Roll/Beginning To See The Light/Ocean/Pale Blue Eyes/Heroin/ Some Kinda Love/Over You/Sweet Bonnie Brown – It's Just Too Much/ White Light, White Heat/I'll Be Your Mirror

No apologies for including this double album: it contains invariably the best versions of any songs that appeared on the studio albums, although 'Sweet Jane' is so different from the one on *Loaded*, their 1970 swan-song release which was ironically their most commercially successful, that comparison is unfair.

Some songs clock in at over seven minutes and show how the band were able to build slowly on the originals, in some cases (on 'Rock And Roll' and especially 'What Goes On') reaching a frenzied peak that was sustained to the point of hypnotism.

At 7, 9.42 and 8.32 minutes respectively, 'I'm Waiting For The Man', 'Heroin' and 'White Light, White Heat' are allowed to expand to an extent where the threatening nature of those songs hits you with an even greater force. There are also three tracks unavailable on any other Velvet Underground album, including 'We're Gonna Have a Real Good Time Together', a great rocker which Patti Smith has consistently featured in her gigs right from the start. Taped in Texas and San Francisco, this is live rock & roll at its very best.

As far as British rock was concerned, the Velvet Underground's influence was enormous, starting with David Bowie's 'Queen Bitch', through Roxy Music's 'Virginia Plain', right up to such new wave acts as Siouxsie and the Banshees.

The Stooges

Fun House (ELEKTRA 42 055)

Down On The Street/Loose/T V Eye/Dirt/1970/Fun House/L A Blues

Iggy Pop was an original: the genuine article. Long before the term 'heavy metal' was coined, the Stooges picked up on that 'real life as nightmare' feeling with which the Doors' death-obsessed Jim Morrison had recently unsettled us, and matched it with music to assault the senses and go truly insane by.

The relentless, power-drill sound of guitarist Ron Asheton and bassist

Dave Alexander matched the uniquely demented vision of their first album, *The Stooges* (1969) (witness 'No Fun' and 'Real Cool Time'). *Fun House* (1970), their second album with added sax, is the Stooges' finest hour. 'Down On The Street' and 'TV Eye' scream out the stuff of paranoia. Producer Don Gallucci roughed up the edges and, on tracks like 'Fun House' itself, every guitar note is precision-wrenched from the fret.

After two years of inactivity, Iggy Pop was produced by David Bowie for the fine *Raw Power* album (1973), with James Williamson now in the guitar seat, and the mentor's style in evidence. With the arrival of the British punk scene, Iggy continued to surprise those who expected more of the same. *The Idiot* (1977), with its very Morrisonesque 'Baby' and the underrated 'Kill City' (tracks from '75 released in '78), is recommended.

Third World War

Third World War (FLY RECORDS HI FLY 4)

Ascension Day/MI5's Alive/Teddy Teeth Goes Sailing/Working Class Man/Shepherds Bush Cowboy/Stardom Road, Part 1/Stardom Road, Part 2/Get Out Of Bed You Dirty Red/Preaching Violence

A genuine oddity, but interesting for its tough preoccupation with British street violence and system-smashing, years before it became even a fringe of the rock scene. 'Let's free the working class/we're tired of kissing the monarchy's arse' is not a million miles away from the Pistols' 'God Save The Queen', and the overall 'sten-guns-in-Belgravia' outlook is treated far more viciously than on anything the Clash ever did.

Third World War were Terry Stamp (vocals) and Jim Avery (bass), who gigged in and around London and recorded two albums, the first in late 1970, which contained stark and unsubtle urban themes with titles like 'Preaching Violence', 'Get Out Of Bed You Dirty Red' and 'Shepherds Bush Cowboy' with its boozers, queer-bashing, skinheads and football fans.

The sound was harsh, to say the least, and although backed up by 'name' session-men like Jim Price, Bobby Keyes and Tony Ashton there are some tracks (like 'Ascension Day') which are so unmusical that they make for painful listening.

Third World War's second album was recorded just over a year later but not released by Track until 1973. The ingredients were similar, with its West London references ('Hammersmith Guerilla') and 'commie' taunts ('I'd Rather Cut Cane For Castro'), but lyrically it was even more extreme ('So I grabbed myself a bottle/smashed it on the table/and screwed it straight in his face'); musically it was a marked improvement.

The Modern Lovers

The Modern Lovers (BESERKLEY BSERK I)

Roadrunner/Astral Plane/Old World/Pablo Picasso/She Cracked/Hospital/Someone I Care About/Girl Friend/Modern World.

Released in 1976, five years after it was recorded and just prior to the punk revolution, this was the band's first and finest album.

The 'suburban misfit', Jonathan Richman, formed the group in 1970 with Ernie Brooks, Jerry Harrison (now in Talking Heads), and David Robinson (now in Cars) because he was lonely – honestly!

They cut half-a-dozen demo tapes with John Cale but the project nose-dived. Kim Fowley replaced Cale but he also proved unsatisfactory. Things only started to pick up when Matthew Kaufman, Beserkley's headman, got hold of the tapes, added three more from the same era and put them out.

Not only did Richman contravene every psychedelic dictate of the time (for example, he rejected all drugs) but he also anticipated many new wave attitudes. He turned a fanatical devotion to the Velvet Underground into a music that distilled US teen-dream imagery for the seventies. Through a perpetual sense of wonder and fractured innocence, he translated everyday realities into screwball or chilling surrealism. He created the now clichéd distinction between the old and modern world, singing in an unconventional blur and keeping the sound tough, tight and sizzling with poker-faced fun. He has since espoused acoustic-based, kindergarten escapism.

New York Dolls

New York Dolls, Volumes 1 and 2

(MERCURY 6641 631)

Personality Crisis/Looking For A Kiss/Vietnamese Baby/Lonely Planet Boy/Frankenstein (Orig.)/Trash/Bad Girl/Subway Train/Pills/Private World/Jet Boy/Babylon/Stranded In The Jungle/Who Are The Mystery Girls?/(There's Gonna Be A) Showdown/It's Too Late/Puss 'N' Boots/Chatterbox/Bad Detective/Don't Start Me Talkin'/Human Being

Surfacing in the early seventies, the Dolls didn't so much play classic punk as epitomize an attitude that became crucial to the post-1976 bands.

The Sex Pistols' song, 'New York', for example, was a vicious attack on the more recent antics of Doll vocalist David JoHansen – you only show that much passion if you really care.

Johnny Thunders (guitar), Arthur Kane (bass), Sylvain Sylvain (guitar, piano), Jerry Nolan (drums) and JoHansen – the line-up during their heyday of 1972 to 1974 – championed a heady mixture of advanced narcissism, tenement toughness, sparse musical know-how, shambolic firepower and enormous visual flair, which was glitter-rock at its tackiest. In direct descent from Eddie Cochran and the Stones, they played raw rock & roll which dealt with hard-core teenage obsessions like 'luv', girls, drugs, neurosis and round-the-clock kicks.

Through a combination of record company reluctance, massive ego problems, their excessive life-style (original drummer Billy Murcia overdosed at seventeen while Thunders was treated for heroin addiction) plus two ill-fitting producers (Todd Rundgren and Shadow Morton), the band effectively collapsed when Nolan and Thunders left in Florida during a club tour.

Ramones

Ramones

(SIRE SR 6020)

Blitzkrieg Bop/Beat On The Brat/Judy Is A Punk/I Wanna Be Your Boyfriend/Chain Saw/Now I Wanna Sniff Some Glue/I Don't Wanna Go Down To The Basement/Loudmouth/Havana Affair/Listen To My Heart/53rd and 3rd/I Don't Wanna Walk Around With You/Today Your Love, Tomorrow The World

The Pistols opened the floodgates, the Clash perfected the stance, but the Ramones determined the sound of new wave with this, their debut album, released in May 1976. It sparked off endless imitators, who ranged from photostats like the Lurkers to intelligent interpreters like Buzzcocks.

Stripping away all unnecessary intricacy, they bolted pure pop onto power-chord hard rock, keeping everything short, sharp and breathlessly fast. There were no guitar solos and each track rarely exceeded three chords in structure or two-and-a-half minutes in length. The result was an irresistible melodic drone overlaid by Joey Ramone's deadpan vocals.

Pretending to be brothers, Joey, Dee Dee, Johnny and Tommy (now replaced by Marky) presented a near-faultless image of street-corner dumbness (lank moptops, leather bomber-jackets, shredded jeans, rancid sneakers and a pinhead mentality), which in fact belied their acute understanding of the medium.

The lyrics painted ludicrously black cartoon pictures of New York's gutter life, setting ritualized violence and depersonalized brutality alongside teen affection. Their sardonic humour staves off the charge of wilful irresponsibility.

Patti Smith

Horses

(ARISTA ARTY 122)

Gloria/Redondo Beach/Birdland/Free Money/Kimberly/Break It Up/Land/Elegie

Hitting New York in 1967, Patti Smith began performing her compulsively frenetic poetry during the early seventies, frequently accompanied by rock critic and *Nuggets* compiler Lenny Kaye on guitar.

Both shared a ferocious allegiance to rock and, gradually, Smith stopped reciting and started singing. In late 1974 they cut, together with pianist Richard D. N. V. Sohl, their first single, an idiosyncratic version of 'Hey Joe' that updated the garage-band staple through a sustained reference to urban terrorist Patty Hearst.

After guitarist Ivan Kral and drummer Jay Dee Daugherty had joined the band, they signed to Arista and released *Horses* in November 1975. An awesome debut expertly produced by John Cale, it broke ground in many ways.

Smith experimented with the traditional forms, combining poetry and rock with the kind of intuitive brilliance that can only grow out of limited technique and intense feeling. The result was like the Velvet Underground meeting the Stones, Rimbaud and sixties black vocal groups.

She showed women could rock, not by apeing male archetypes but by creating their own approach – here at last was a fiercely active rather than a passive female performance. The new wave brought more women than ever before into rock, and Smith must take much of the credit for that.

The Damned

Damned Damned Damned

(STIFF RECORDS SEEZ 1)

Neat Neat Neat/Fan Club/I Fall/Born To Kill/Stab Your Back/Feel The Pain/New Rose/Fish/See Her Tonite/I Of The 2/So Messed Up/I Feel Alright

They may have formed nine months after the Pistols, but the Damned turned out to be the new wave band that did most things first – though by no means best. They were the first to sign a contract (with Stiff); first to release a single ('New Rose'/'Help!' in October 1976) and an album (the above, in February 1977); first to play the States; first to be sacked from a label; and first to break up (though three quarters of them later revived the group).

Pretty incompetent musically, even at the end of their first lifespan, they compensated with a hyper-energetic stage show and an image of rowdy, slapstick burlesque. Vocalist Dave Vanian wore B-feature, Count Dracula togs and had gestures to match. Bassist Captain Sensible would wear anything, from a nurse's uniform to a ballerina's outfit. Drummer Rat Scabies played the beefy and obnoxious bully-boy to perfection while guitarist Brian James was more studiously introverted. He wrote their material, managing three great songs, 'Neat Neat Neat', 'Fan Club' and 'New Rose', all included here. Nick Lowe produced the debut in his characteristic 'bash-it-down-and-then-tart-it-up' manner.

The Damned were a classic example of a fun band with few pretensions, limited imagination, flamboyant style and huge popular appeal.

The Clash

The Clash (CBS 82000)

Janie Jones/Remote Control/I'm So Bored With The USA/White Riot/Hate And War/What's My Name/Deny/London's Burning/Career Opportunities/Cheat/Protex Blue/Police And Thieves/48 Hours/Garageland

Inspired by but always second to the Pistols in the early punk hierarchy, the Clash released this debut at a time (April 1977) when they had not yet stabilized their line-up.

Drummer Terry Chimes, considered politically 'unsuitable', was to be replaced by Nicky 'Topper' Headon, joining the hard core of Joe Strummer (lead vocals/guitar), Mick Jones (lead guitar/vocals) and Paul Simonon (bass).

The album epitomized punk in the late seventies. Matched by a suitably scrambled production by Clash sound-man Micky Foote, Jones and Strummer wrote songs that mirrored reality, for many white working-class teenagers; high-rise living, the lack of career opportunities, angry confusion, football-terrace aggression (one track, 'Hate And War', reversed the sixties peace and love mantra), police harrassment after closing time, a growing kinship with West Indian culture (they did a version of the reggae standard 'Police And Thieves') and boredom.

Their politics, although intensely felt, were naïvely expressed, creating an image of urban commando chic that was – thankfully – offset by a strong sense of humour and a genuine humanity.

When the Pistols disintegrated, the Clash assumed the number one position.

The Sex Pistols

Never Mind the Bollocks Here's the Sex Pistols (VIRGIN V2086)

Holidays In The Sun/Bodies/No Feelings/Liar/God Save The Queen/ Problems/Seventeen/Anarchy In The UK/Submission/Pretty Vacant/ New York/EMI

When a band becomes an enormous media symbol – as befell the Pistols – the actual music is often pushed to one side.

A frequent criticism was that they couldn't play, but *Bollocks*, the only official album they made while Johnny Rotten was still in the group, showed how their technical expertise easily met their requirements.

Steve Jones played with simple but effective density, creating a stinging, siren guitar sound that was as integral to the band as Rotten's vocals. Paul Cook's drumming was clean, tough and propulsive while even Sid Vicious, who replaced Glen Matlock, managed a basic bass throb.

Rotten's delivery, a uniquely British blend of amphetamine sneer and bored nonchalance, was ideally suited to his relentlessly acidic attacks on all forms of hypocrisy, complacency, intolerance and unthinking acceptance.

Good though the album is (it contains all four of their chart-busting singles), they excelled in live performances, which were not only sparse because of internal bickerings and local council vetoes but also wildly erratic.

Their music bristled with pioneering energy, black humour, emetic disgust, aggressive confusion, a desperate yearning to understand these contradictions, and pure power – elements central to the punk mentality.

Various Artists

The Roxy London WC2 (January–April 1977)

(HARVEST SHSP 4069)

Runaway (Slaughter and the Dogs)/Boston Babies (Slaughter and the Dogs)/Freedom (The Unwanted)/Lowdown (Wire)/12XU (Wire)/ Bored Teenagers (The Adverts)/Hard Loving Man (Johnny Moped)/ Don't Need It (Eater)/15 (Eater)/Oh Bondage! Up Yours! (X Ray Spex)/Breakdown (Buzzcocks)/Love Battery (Buzzcocks)

Musical explosions often start from a specific club which has the courage to showcase new bands. The Roxy in London's Covent Garden provided a short-lived but vital home for punk when venues generally barred their doors. Masterminded by Andrew Czezowski, who had briefly managed the Damned and Generation X, it opened on 1 January 1977, with the Clash as the first act.

The club rapidly became a breeding-ground for a second wave of punk bands, many of whom are featured here. Released in July 1977, the lion's share of the acts (like X Ray Spex, Buzzcocks and the Adverts) have since gone on to make lucrative record deals with varying degrees of success.

The others have either disintegrated or are treading water on the sidelines. As an enjoyable experience the album ranks low, but as a chronicle of that squalid basement's 100-day run it's fascinating.

Inevitably, the club fell victim to malicious back-biting, self-conscious posing and record company enticements. An interesting spin-off came in *The Original Punk Rock Movie*, assembled by resident Roxy DJ Don Letts. Much of the footage was filmed at the Roxy, and its 'do-it-yourself' quality succeeds in capturing the atmosphere of the place.

The Afrika Korps

Music to Kill By

(IRON CROSS RECORDS 4001: US IMPORT AVAILABLE FROM IRON CROSS RECORDS, BOX 253, TEANECK, NEW JERSEY 07666, USA)

Jailbait Janet/Fox Lane/Too Cool To Fool/Everyday/Buzz Stomp/Make Her Know/Juvenile Delinquent/Wild Mouse/Refrigerator Rappin'/Till The End Of The Day/Breaking Out/NY Punk/You're A Tease Baby/ Creep Skin/Happy Person/Heartful Of Soul/Iggy/Ellen No/I Laffed Out Loud/Crazy Jill/Lorraine/Death To Disko!

Garage band-classics should always come out of the blue, and *Music to Kill By* did exactly that in the middle of 1977.

For a one-off experiment, the Afrika Korps (Kenny Kaiser, Ken Gizmo Highland, plus brothers Jay and Solomon Gruberger) swelled their ranks to include like-minded neighbours from New Jersey/ Washington DC bands like the Slickee Boys, the Gizmos, the Look, the Teenage Boys, O Rex and the Kaiser's Kittens.

The result is like a cross between the Ramones and primitive Velvet Underground: a mammoth twenty-two songs written mostly by the Korps, and about the kind of things that dominate suburban teenage life – for example, acne ('Creep Skin'), anti-social dumbness ('Happy Person'), high school rebellion ('Juvenile Delinquent'), growing up and getting dangerous ('Breaking Out') and first sex ('Make Her Know' and 'Jailbait Janet').

They also pay tribute to the Kinks (in 'Till The End Of The Day'), the Yardbirds (in their version of 'Heartful Of Soul') and Iggy Pop in a specially written paean. Each track is a ramshackle snippet, a first-take chorus that reveals, beneath the snarling veneer, an authentic innocence.

Siouxsie and the Banshees

The Scream (POLYDOR DELUXE POLD 5009)

Pure/Jigsaw Feeling/Overground/Carcass/Helter Skelter/Mirage/Metal Postcard (Mittageisen)/Nicotine Stain/Suburban Relapse/Switch

Formed from the Bromley contingent, an outrageous coven of early Pistols' fans, Siouxsie and the Banshees played their first-ever gig at the 100 Club Punk Festival, disembowelling the Lord's Prayer for twenty minutes of excruciating ineptitude. The band included for that one performance Siouxsie, Steve Havoc (now Steven Severin), Sid Vicious and Marco, who acted out the musical anarchy that many new groups preached but rarely practised.

Siouxsie and Steven were joined by Kenny Morris and P. T. Fenton (whom John McKay replaced) and though they improved by leaps and bounds, an unwavering commitment to ideals together with some appalling shock-horror tactics during their early stages (lines like 'too many Jews for my liking') scared many record companies away until Polydor signed them in mid 1978. Almost immediately afterwards they scored a Top Ten hit with their first single, 'Hong Kong Garden'.

The Scream, released a couple of months later, lived up to its title – intelligent, abrasive rock that developed the rhythmic textures of the Velvet Underground as well as drawing from experimental German bands like Can. This is where punk meets the avant-garde.

Punk : Singles

The Kinks: *You Really Got Me* (1964)

Their third single and first hit, this Ray Davies song had the kind of howling primitivism tailor-made for garage bands.

The Kingsmen: *Louie Louie* (1964)

A revival of Richard Berry's original, this became another standard which can still score today (viz Motorhead's 1978 chart version).

The Beau Brummells: *Laugh Laugh* (1964)

The San Francisco-based Brummells featured twelve-string guitars (before the Byrds) and this half-million seller stood out in a year dominated by the British sound.

Them: *Gloria* (1965)

Van Morrison's r&b classic with its virtual one-chord riff was bread and butter to the sixties garage-band repertoire (viz the Shadows of Knight).

Sam the Sham and the Pharaohs: *Wooly Bully* (1965)

A 'Tex-Mex' quintet – this piece of glorious nonsense became another favourite, revived by Eddie and the Hot Rods in 1976.

The Strangeloves: *I Want Candy* (1965)

Revived by the Bishops in 1978, this was a hit for a trio of producers which included Richard Gottehrer, who was behind Blondie's first album.

The McCoys: *Hang On Sloopy* (1965)

Rick Derringer's first band, the McCoys, achieved a US and British monster with this hand-clapper by Bert Berns, producer of Them's 'Gloria'.

Paul Revere And The Raiders: *Good Thing* (1965)

With four-part harmonies and a powerful sound produced by Terry Melcher or Bruce Johnston, Top Ten hits kept on coming ('Kicks', 'Just Like Me', etc).

The Troggs: *Wild Thing* (1966)

With this Chip Taylor-penned smash and subsequent singles, the Troggs were the closest a *British* band came to the sixties idea of punk.

Syndicate of Sound: *Little Girl* (1966)

Like the Count Five and Chocolate Watch Band, they put San Jose on the punk map with this misogynistic ditty, faithfully revived in 1978 by the Banned.

? and the Mysterians: *96 Tears* (1966)

Along with 'I Need Somebody', this Cameo release epitomized the 'Tex-Mex' sound of punk – adenoidal vocals and treble-increased organ.

John's Children: *Desdemona* (1967)

A quasi-psychedelic punk single from the short-lived British underground group, which included Marc Bolan and anticipated that man's reign as glam-rock king.

Electric Prunes: *Get Me To The World On Time* (1967)

Superficial drug references, echo chambers and reverb – all geared to the A M singles' market of the day. Cheap, exploitative and fun.

Richard Hell: *Blank Generation EP* (1976)

Performed originally in Television, the title track helped christen and define new wave on both sides of the Atlantic.

The Saints: *(I'm) Stranded* (1976)

From Australia's ambassadeurs-de-punk, 'Stranded' contains all the essential ingredients of post-Ramones rock with its whirlwind guitars and headbanging rhythm.

Buzzcocks: *Spiral Scratch* (1977)

An inspirational, four-track EP from the Manchester new wave band that Howard Devoto subsequently left to form Magazine.

The Heartbreakers: *Chinese Rocks/Born To Lose* (1977)

Formed from the ashes of the New York Dolls, the Heartbreakers had strong material which was ill-treated by diabolical production.

Public Image: *Public Image* (1978)

The band Johnny Rotten formed after quitting the Sex Pistols, they made their debut with an ingenious song built around a ringing guitar sound.

STEVE TAYLOR

The Seventies

Taking another look at the music press in Britain from the turn of the last decade wouldn't reveal any great surprises; quite the opposite. The 'New Year Pop Shocks' were the fact that the Bonzo Dog Band had split after four years together, that singer Steve Ellis had left Love Affair and that King Crimson had lost two members, just a year after the band's inception.

Hardly the names that fill today's news, musical or otherwise. The charts showed a similar pop innocuousness: Rolf Harris's 'Two Little Boys' was the Number 1 single; less depressingly, the Beatles' *Abbey Road* was the best-selling album. The papers for the following months were filled with several recurring obsessions: which major American bands and singers were to be visiting Britain in the coming year, which festivals were going to brighten the summer, which defunct groups – Traffic and Cream, for example – were rumoured to be reforming. And the other big space-taker was a sociological concern with the practices and ideals of the late-sixties youth culture; drugs, festivals, political change.

Taken as a whole the mood is one of uncertainty, of both looking back to the heroes of the sixties to get it (and themselves) together once more, and cautiously casting a sideways glance at the newer developments in rock. While articles appeared bemoaning the destruction of the creative urge with drugs, and questioning the motives behind the Woodstock gathering, the *Melody Maker* of 6 June 1970 devoted a two-page spread to the opinions of rock musicians over the forthcoming British Heath *v.* Wilson election. What it revealed was a mixture of cynical support for Labour and a not too enlightened self-interest. Eric Clapton wryly suggested that he'd vote for any government who'd be prepared to develop a self-tuning guitar. What was most clear was a complete lack of the slightest hint of a connection between rock and politics.

Still, that is probably an accurate reflection. How any genuine revolutionary change could have come out of such a self-regarding drug as LSD or from such self-congratulatory events as Woodstock is now very hard to see. There is little doubt that the sense of communication and togetherness between the members of one generation was powerful. But isolation, even geographical – Haight-Ashbury, Ladbroke Grove – was common and the connections outwards into a wider society were few.

Events in Europe in 1968 cast things in a different light; street-fighting man rather than Woodstock man. The two camps came to a muted confrontation in the summer of that year at the Third Isle of Wight Festival. Joni Mitchell hadn't performed at Woodstock, but she had written a song about it, which she interrupted her IOW opening number to sing, presumably moved by the event. However, the song was disrupted twice, first by appeals for help from the VIP enclosure, where a figure in the throes of a bad trip drew everyone's attention, and then by a man who leapt on stage, took over the microphone and delivered a message to the 10,000 listening for free on Desolation Hill.

Worse was yet to come. In September 1970 Jimi Hendrix was found dead in a London flat from inhalation of vomit following barbiturate intoxication. On 4 October Janis Joplin died of a heroin overdose in a Hollywood hotel room. Hendrix's death posed fundamental musical questions: rock had lost one of its most singular and charismatic innovators, for, apart from the image and the sexuality, Hendrix's electrification of the blues guitar was central to an understanding of how, in the right hands, electricity could transform music.

Hendrix himself had played at the Isle of Wight festival and, portentously, hadn't come over very well. Personal survival began to seem as much at stake as a youthful generation's naïve ideals, and the deaths of idols corresponded with broader changes: the telling disruption of the IOW festival by French, Algerian and American revolutionaries, the killing of four students at Kent State University, Ohio, by national guardsmen earlier in the year.

The following year Jim Morrison, lead singer and embracer of excess with the Doors, was found dead of a heart attack in a bath in Paris. 1971 was the year of the Manson killings and the year the US broadcast licensing authorities warned radio stations that they would be subverting the government's campaign against drug abuse if they played lyrics which mentioned dope.

The overall meaning was clear; the more grotesque consequences of the indulgences of the late sixties were becoming clear, and in response the 'liberal' establishment was closing ranks. But did the freeing of rock from its somewhat spurious social associations leave the music more space in which to develop – as music?

Sadly, the answer must be – No. What it did ensure was that rock became even more a prey to the machinations of the corporate rock business. For a long time the music suffered accordingly.

Musically, the problem facing rock at the end of the sixties can be stated fairly plainly; rock was a reduction and a debasement of the traditional forms which had originally combined in its gestation. By the end of the decade the dominance of 'progressive' rock meant the dominance of a 4/4 rhythmic stranglehold, of endless riffing and of the repetitious production of 'solos' or 'improvization' over the beat. The band often hailed as the 'best' band of the era exemplified the approach: Cream, whose music began, according to their guitarist Eric Clapton, as that of a blues trio – 'like Buddy Guy with a rhythm section'.

Early numbers like 'Sunshine Of Your Love' and 'Strange Brew', with their strong, vaguely disturbing melody lines and controlled admixture of wailing guitar (that vocal-simulating tone taken directly from black electric blues players) soon gave way to the lengthy group 'improvizations' of their live sets, recorded on the 1968 double album *Wheels of Fire*. In reality the music was more like the extended patterning of Indian ragas than the genuine improvization of American post-war jazz. Only bassist Jack Bruce was a musician of sufficient imagination and intelligence to sustain the interest of the pieces for long enough. As his later recordings such as the hit single 'Layla' have shown, Clapton is much more at home within the confines of a tightly structured song.

In taking rock's severely limited rhythms to such indulgent extremes, bands like Cream merely highlighted in the end the need for revitalization from other sources. At the beginning of the seventies the area of music most frequently looked to was jazz, and the most hopeful-looking figure was that of black trumpeter Miles Davis.

Davis had been the perpetrator of a string of

musical innovations, as a junior member of Charlie Parker's band in the late forties, as an apostle of the orchestrations of Gil Evans, as a member of John Coltrane's quintet and – on a trio of albums, *Miles in the Sky*, *Filles de Kilamajaro* and especially *In a Silent Way* – as the originator of a jazz/rock synthesis. It was Davis's 1971 album *Bitches Brew*, with its long improvizations, which attracted rock audiences. Although they had the apparent harmonic single-mindedness of a Cream workout, Davis's numbers utilized fragmented rhythms and a searing range of tones – bass clarinet, electric keyboards, Miles's own distorted trumpet – to continually hit the listener anew.

But the school of disciples raised in Davis's 1968–72 bands failed to build on those initial achievements and, perhaps succumbing to the temptations of radio plays and album sales, figures like Herbie Hancock, Billy Cobham and John McLaughlin have regressed into super-clever jazz/rock excess or – worse still – Top Forty disco/funk (Hancock). Only Zawinul and Shorter's Weather Report still offers rock any hope in that particular direction.

It's apparent from the music press at the time that the loss of faith in jazz hit pretty soon, and by 1971 attention was already being turned to European sources for aid. There was then no market for dance music, and the quality of European pop was persistently mundane. Such bands as Burning Red Ivanhoe, Magma and Amon Duul II therefore concentrated instead on composition, technically complex playing, electronics and studio techniques.

The continental musicians' affiliations with late sixties rock were predictably with those bands who had espoused 'improvization' and electronics; Grateful Dead, Jefferson Airplane, Cream, Pink Floyd and Soft Machine. There were acknowledged debts to twentieth-century classical composers, too: to Satie, Messiaen, Varese, Stravinsky, Stockhausen. Although many of the individual bands have disappeared, the innovatory forces of 'Eurorock' have still to be really felt and are likely to figure strongly in the grass-roots rock activity of the eighties.

Meanwhile, mainstream rock in the seventies looked not outwards towards other cultures for its badly needed remedy, but backwards towards its Anglo-American roots in country, blues, rock & roll and the broader sweeps of popular music. Van Morrison's *Astral Weeks* and the Band's *The Band* – both 1969 – are remarkable records in that they appeared right at the nadir of sixties 'progressive' ramblings, and presented, in an integrated and understated way, a synthesis of the multifarious musical movements they had absorbed. Ry Cooder did much the same thing, in a more documentary form, on his 1971 *Into the Purple Valley*.

In that same year the Stones produced their own manifesto of refined seventies eclecticism on *Sticky Fingers*. And so it goes on. The upshot for historical criticism is that the musicological approach becomes not only circular, tautological and downright tedious but a major red herring. As in any other history of a cultural form, tradition is in the mind of the beholder, and to trace the lines which connect Ry Cooder's work backwards through fifty years of American popular music, and thence forwards through bands as diverse as Little Feat, Dan Hicks and His Hot Licks, Commander Cody and his Lost Planet Airmen or the Rolling Stones seems as ultimately unhelpful as starting with modern 'experimental' composers, going through the music of Brian Eno, Can, Robert Fripp, and Kraftwerke and ending up with the 'electronic garage bands' of the early eighties.

The rampant eclecticism of the decade has only confirmed the gradual tendency towards 'sophistication' in the tastes of the record-buying public and mass concert-goers, leaving the ground-floor innovators as always largely unknown. David Bowie stands out as a singular figure in this respect; he is one of the few artists who has managed to combine popularity and record sales, including singles, with genuine musical experimentation and progress.

While unknown musicians with the necessary energy and lack of commitments work away, the broad view of seventies rock still shows a panorama of business values and business problems, debts and profits, contracts made and broken. If that offends the sensibility of anyone with a personal affection for particular records (think of the hundreds of thousands of individual associations with Elton John's 'Your Song', for example) it's not meant to; it is intended rather to draw attention to the overwhelming dominance of business factors in establishing 'important' records.

By the seventies, rock appeared to be organized into a large number of small business concerns; take the example of the British 'independent' record companies: Island, Charisma, Chrysalis. Yet what was going on in fact was much more disturbing; record companies were buying up not only smaller record companies but the many other subsidiary firms who held the capital-intensive resources of all the concerns involved in getting rock to the public: instrument sales, studios, distribution, record shops, publishing, concert halls, even, in the case of EMI, film and TV companies.

The recent activities of Virgin Records (a supposedly 'independent' new company) illustrate this perfectly: they began as a mail-order record sales firm, moving into retail outlets in major towns and establishing their own studios (the Manor and Town House), record labels, publishing company and a London concert theatre, the Venue. These inter-relationships guarantee success; Virgin can push an artist's records in their shops, give them studio time as Virgin boss Richard Branson did indefinitely for Mike Oldfield, later putting out the multi-million-selling *Tubular Bells* on the fledgling Virgin label.

As the generation of album buyers who attended Woodstock or who identified with its ethos got older and more affluent in the seventies, home stereo equipment became more sophisticated, soaring studio costs became the main inflationary figure in the production costs of a rock LP, and the sales break-even point rose from around 20,000 copies to nearer 100,000. What the vertical integration of subsidiary concerns into major companies meant was that many of the costs returned as profit. This has been incorporated into rock contracts, so that the band has to pay back many of the fixed costs – particularly studio time – before the royalty rate brings it direct financial benefit.

The rising costs, too, of getting a band on the road mean that most lose money when they play in public, much of the fee being immediately paid out to promoters, staff, publicity, and particularly to PA and lighting hire companies. There has again been a decrease in self-ownership of PA, lights etc – once the norm for bands like Pink Floyd – towards small companies who are actually corporately owned.

What all this adds up to is that only the giant corporations have the necessary capital to 'float' new artists; it is now estimated that in the US the pattern is for companies to lose on tours and albums for up to three years before returns start to come in. The early records of the Band, Joni Mitchell, Van Morrison and Little Feat have followed this pattern of relatively low initial sales followed by good long-term ones. (And, incidentally, they are all now sold by the multi-media Warner Brothers.)

Increasing costs have also led to the need for vast promotional campaigns, like the overblown hype which surrounded Bruce Springsteen at the time of *Born to Run*, or the £145-a-week services of independent publicist Tony Brainsby employed to maintain the Clash's punk credentials after their £100,000-plus signing to CBS.

Because of the vast scale of rock's economics, the British market now occupies an increasingly insignificant part, the main areas being the US and Japan. In the States radio promotion plays a crucial role, particularly the FM bands with their high sound quality. After their initial 'underground' phase the FM stations soon became the show-case merely for a different slice of the market: the rock tastes of 18–30 year olds. The tendency of American stations to specialize, made possible by their large numbers, has led to the domination of FM by a particular genre of easy-listening music, which is the result partly of conservatism of taste and partly of a change in function – rock ceasing to be a physically moving force and becoming yet another purchase in a life-style of hip consumerism. In practice it consists of various watered-down rock styles: the country rock of the Eagles, Linda Ronstadt or Fleetwood Mac (which is what *Rumours* boils down to) or the 'funked-up muzak' to which Steely Dan referred in their 'FM' single.

To sum up, rock in the seventies has freed itself from the dubious 'social' associations that it acquired in the late sixties – not because these things are inherently and necessarily separate, but because the links were superficial and the social philosophies deeply flawed. That has left the musical reality a little thin and nowhere near as 'progressive' as it was once blown up to be. Rock's social dimension has been reduced to grotesques and parodies: the Stones' chic satanism and the Altamont killing, the same band's exile to the south of France and 'society', the flirting with sexual doubts which 'glitter-rock' exploited. Bowie had it taped on *Ziggy Stardust*; taking on the persona of a member of his imaginary backing band, he foresees the time when the rock star, living 'on the edge' on behalf of a generation with few economic or political pressures to focus its psychic energies, acts by proxy to the point of self-destruction. 'When the kids had killed the man I had to break up the band,' he states baldly.

All is not lost, however. Punk put iconoclastic social forces once more in context – a context of economic depression, mongrel style, conglomerate-dominated industry and the embittered failure of youth rebellion – paving the way for more genuine innovation and mutual respect between styles. In the eighties, rock may once more be a real contender.

The Seventies : Albums

The Band

The Last Waltz (WARNER BROS. K66076)

Theme From The Last Waltz/Up On Cripple Creek/Who Do You Love/Helpless/Stagefright/Coyote/Dry Your Eyes/It Makes No Difference/Such A Night/The Night They Drove Old Dixie Down/Mystery Train/Mannish Boy/Further Up The Road/Shape I'm In/Down South In New Orleans/Ophelia/Tura Lura Lural (That's An Irish Lullaby)/Caravan/Life Is A Carnival/Baby Let Me Follow You Down/I Don't Believe You (She Acts Like We Never Have Met)/Forever Young/Baby Let Me Follow You Down (Reprise)/I Shall Be Released/The Well/Evangeline/Out Of The Blue/The Weight/The Last Waltz Refrain/Theme From The Last Waltz

The Band came together in the late fifties to back Toronto-based rockabilly singer Ronnie Hawkins, later re-christening themselves with self-confident aplomb. Guitarist Robbie Robertson's song-writing drew from broad areas of American history and culture, and was heavily influenced by the breadth of imagery and reference in the lyrics of Bob Dylan, who they began backing in 1966 after contributing to parts of *Blonde on Blonde*. The crucial difference with them was that Robertson, like four more of the Band, was Canadian, seeing America through the eyes of an outsider.

The stylistic mélange of their first two albums, *Music from Big Pink* and *The Band*, was directly at odds with the excess and self-indulgence into which 'progressive' rock had nose-dived in the late sixties, and owed much to their long communal retreat in Bearsville/Woodstock. When they took to touring extensively, the disillusionment of the immediate American present diluted their songs' mythical sweep, resulting in 'Stagefright'.

They never recovered that initial synthesis, and in the autumn of 1976 announced their decision to cease playing live; they fixed a farewell concert for Thanksgiving Day (6 December) at the San Francisco Winterland, the venue where they had made their live debut sixteen years previously.

Although *The Last Waltz* has the air of a swan-song for a whole generation of ageing rock performers, the celebratory ambience and the seemingly limitless flexibility of the Band's playing brought renewed fire to the music of many 'guest' artists, most notably Joni Mitchell, Neil Young, Van Morrison and Dylan himself.

Van Morrison

Moondance (WARNER BROS. K46040)

Stoned Me/Moondance/Crazy Love/Caravan/Into The Mystic/Come Running/These Dreams Of You/Brand New Days/Everyone/Glad Tidings

In a way that was very similar to the Band's, Van Morrison suddenly shifted the foundations of rock as the decade turned, moving them away from r&b and r&r. His 1969 album *Astral Weeks* is often regarded as *the* essential rock album, a true classic, although on first listening it's such an unassuming and gentle record you'd hardly think so.

What made *Astral Weeks* even more of a surprise was that Morrison, born in Belfast, served his apprenticeship with a 'punk' r&b outfit, Them, who were responsible for one of rock's all-time great singles, 'Gloria'. *Astral Weeks* was utterly different: the music was jazz-based, romantic and impressionistic, and the lyrics conveyed a stream of images caught as if in the window reflections of a passing car; back streets, railroads, women caught in doorways, children bending to pick bottle-tops from the gutter.

The soft instrumentation of *Astral Weeks* gave way on *Moondance* to more brass and shorter, tighter song-structuring, which allowed Morrison's voice a freer rein. Morrison's soulful tone – unique in a white singer – made his singing an irresistible mix of the intensity of the blues (his father had been an avid collector of records by blues singers like Leadbelly) and the inventiveness of jazz. Although the songs on *Moondance* are superb, particularly 'Into The Mystic', the quality of Van's writing has slowly declined over the span of a decade; his influence nowadays is on a new generation of white soul/r&b singers like Graham Parker, who are impressed by the controlled emotional power of his sensitive rock singing.

The Who

Who's Next (TRACK 2408 102)

Baba O'Riley/Bargain/Love Ain't For Keeping/My Wife/Song Is Over/Getting In Tune/Going Mobile/Behind Blue Eyes/Won't Get Fooled Again

By the turn of the decade Pete Townshend had long ago written the definitive expression of a restless generation's angst in 'My Generation'. In many ways his ideas have remained suspended between those datum points – of stammering teen rebellion and the insidious encroachment of one's twenties (thirties, these days). *Tommy* (1968) reflects the logical development of a song-writing talent with a penchant for suggestively eccentric characterization and spiritual preoccupations.

Wholly out of proportion to the importance of its actual content, *Tommy* dominated the Who's working life in the seventies, forming the core of their live performances and, despite Ken Russell's 1975 movie, making the West End stage in early 1979. Nevertheless they entered the seventies with a reputation as rock's greatest on-stage phenomenon, a status confirmed by their appearance at Woodstock in 1969, and captured on the 1970 *Live at Leeds*.

Who's Next followed, including material from Townshend's abandoned solo album *Lifehouse*, which was to have been based on the writings of his guru Meher Baba. The opener, 'Baba O'Riley', showed the significant advance Townshend's compositions had made; the basis was still a simple power-chord sequence, but this was underpinned by a mesmerizing dance of synthesizers and crashing piano. The subject-matter was a mixture of love songs and a powerful melancholy, brilliantly articulated by Roger Daltrey's stratospheric vocals.

Rolling Stones

Exile on Main Street

(ROLLING STONES RECORDS COC 69100)

Rocks Off/Rip This Joint/Hip Shake/Casino Boogie/Tumbling Dice/Sweet Virginia/Torn And Frayed/Black Angel/Happy/Turd On The Run/Ventilator Blues/Just Wanna See His Face/Let It Loose/All Down The Line/Stop Breaking Down/Shine A Light/Soul Survivor

On the cover of *Exile* Mick Jagger poses self-depreciatingly in front of a barely readable porn-palace poster which promises 'Hedonistic Pleasures'. Don't you believe it. After their overblown skirmish with psychedelia, the Stones entered the decade without Brian Jones, who had been found dead in his swimming pool on 3 July 1969. Ex-John Mayall guitarist Mick Taylor joined, and the day after Jones was buried they released 'Honky Tonk Women', which sold as much on the celebratory decadence of its lyric as on its cracking dance beat.

After the eclectic pleasures of their excellent 1971 *Sticky Fingers*, the first on their own label, *Exile on Main Street* appeared to a critical thumbs-down, although it's now usually reassessed as their best; frankly I'm undecided. It's a muddy album, an ill-defined mix of sliding guitars, thudding bass and cash-register piano jangles which seems suffused with contempt for the listener – an impression strengthened by the cover, with its gloomy collage of American freak-show and low-life shots, its cellotaped freehand annotations and its contemptuously vulgar catalogue number.

In some ways the generation of rock commentators who grew up with the Stones desperately want to believe in them. The band – Jagger in particular – stands as a symbol of the rock life-style's resilience to growing old. Also, Jagger and Richards' example as purveyors of white r&b remains central and influential, especially to the many r&b pub-rock bands of Britain's late seventies. However, their burgeoning eclecticism, taking in country, reggae (*Black and Blue*) and disco (*Some Girls*) may get to them before middle age does.

Elton John

Elton John

(DJM DJF 20406)

Your Song/I Need You To Turn To/Take Me To The Pilot/No Shoe-strings On Louise/First Episode At Hienton/Sixty Years On/Border Song/The Greatest Discovery/The Cage/The King Must Die

It would be inapposite to talk about Elton John influencing seventies rock, unless it be in setting an example by resurrecting a wide range of styles: his music has always been restlessly eclectic and looked longingly across the Atlantic in its instrumental styles (the post-Band *'Tumbleweed Connection'*, for example) or in its vocal inflection (the Jagger country drawl in 'No Shoestrings On Louise').

Elton John's career reads like that of a Bowie without the irony; the bespectacled, overweight r&b pianist with the doom-laden name Reginald Dwight fails an audition for Liberty Records, singing amongst other material Jim Reeves' 'I Love You Because'. But he is given a sheaf of lyrics by an equally unknown lyricist from Lincolnshire, Bernie Taupin. Publisher Dick James offers them each £10 a week to knock out Top Forty songs, but one of James's song pluggers, Steve Brown, encourages them to pursue their own muse, resulting in the 1969 *Empty Sky* followed in 1970 by *Elton John* in April and *Tumbleweed Connection* in October. Both albums' material came from the same recording sessions.

Then came a string of outrageously successful albums and singles, arduous and phenomenally well received international tours, repeated bouts of nervous exhaustion and, from MCA Records in the States, one of the most expensive recording deals ever. *Elton John* displays the styles in which John's workmanlike talents produce their finest results; soulful balladry ('Border Song'), delicate love songs ('Your Song') or medium-power raunch ('Take Me To The Pilot'). His later work succeeds when he sticks to what he does well, and falls down if he's too clever or tries to rock too hard.

Rod Stewart

Every Picture Tells a Story (MERCURY 6338 063)

Every Picture Tells A Story/I'm Losing You/Maggie May/Mandolin Wind/Reason To Believe/Seems Like A Long Time/That's All Right/Tomorrow Is A Long Time

It is sometimes hard now to connect the rampaging satin posturing and merciless plundering of popular song idioms, which characterized the late-seventies Rod Stewart, with the fine interpreter and sensitive song-writer of earlier years. *Every Picture*, his third solo album, seems a long way off, with its superb renderings of David Ruffin, Tim Hardin and Dylan songs, and the classic Stewart original, 'Maggie May'.

At the time, Stewart was pursuing two parallel careers; as a solo artist and as the lead singer with the Faces, whom he'd joined in 1969 after he and Ron Wood parted company with Jeff Beck. The Faces had a reputation as one of the best world-class live draws, a status they had never been able to match on record. Stewart's solo projects, in contrast, were models of sympathetic studio collaboration, using a sensitive variety of instruments, including mandolin and fiddle, and a tasteful selection of material.

Every Picture is the culmination of a progression from *An Old Raincoat Will Never Let You Down* and *Gasoline Alley*, and as an indication of the commercial success of Stewart's method it occupied the Number 1 album slots in both Britain and the US in September 1971; at the same time 'Maggie May' was the top single both sides of the water, too.

It proved to be a high point; the inevitable break-up of the Faces and Rod's increasingly money/Hollywood/society life-style seemed to undermine his taste and inspiration, and the poor sales and response generated by *Smiler* led to a change of label – to Warner Brothers – and a change of style, to the session-men-dominated *Atlantic Crossing* in 1975. Since then his output has been increasingly commercial and – to these ears – increasingly disappointing.

Led Zeppelin

Fourth (Untitled)

(ATLANTIC K50008)

Black Dog/Rock And Roll/The Battle Of Evermore/Stairway To Heaven/ Misty Mountain Hop/Four Sticks/Going To California/When The Levee Breaks

Zeppelin's achievement was to distil a wide selection of sixties borrowings into a new and virtually self-defined genre – heavy metal – which they have continued to set absolute standards for. Signed to Atlantic on the strength of their reputations as musicians, Zeppelin released their first LP in late 1968: it was a stunning all-out assault which utilized the whole armoury of white blues and r&b, laying down the sounds in an exaggeratedly raw state.

Right from the start, under the uncompromising and astute management of Peter Grant, the band concentrated on the huge American market, and by early 1970 their anthem 'Whole Lotta Love' was a US smash. It ended up as the most requested track on American radio that year. By the end of January they had a top US album – *Led Zeppelin II* – and toured the States breaking many of the concert attendance records previously held by the Beatles. On a par with the Who as supreme exponents of essential live rock, Zeppelin created such a powerful demand for ultra-heavy arena-scale rock in the US that when they stopped touring for any time a host of imitators or hard-rock substitutes stepped into the breach.

By their fourth, *The Runes Album*, the band were stretching their musical abilities, mixing heavy metal with semi-acoustic material, adding a deep drug/hippie mysticism to the blatant eroticism they had plagiarized from their blues antecedents. Guitarist Jimmy Page's private passion for the occult became as much a focus for imitators as the wall-of-sound musical approach, and a line of bands that includes Black Sabbath, Uriah Heep and Deep Purple were spawned. Stateside, the gap left when Zeppelin were not performing has been filled by second-league heavies like Ted Nugent, Styx or Kansas, although the addition of more melodic bands like Boston has made the genre a little less lumpen.

Pink Floyd

The Dark Side of the Moon (HARVEST SHLV 804)

Speak To Me/Breathe/On The Run/Time/The Great Gig In The Sky/ Money/Us And Them/Any Colour You Like/Brain Damage/Eclipse

The Floyd were London's foremost psychedelic band in the late sixties, managing, with one exception, to keep themselves and the band together into the next decade. The exception was Syd Barrett, whose whimsical song-writing talents illuminated the band's debut album *The Piper at the Gates of Dawn* (1967). After he had left, evidently an acid casualty, and had been replaced by guitarist Dave Gilmour, the band moved into 'spacey' instrumental pieces which stretched lengthily in performance but still worked well compressed onto their second album, *A Saucerful of Secrets*.

Live, their shows became more theatrical and elaborate, but as regards composition they had an arid few years until their 1973 *Dark Side of the Moon*. With a studio production which set new standards, they put together instrumental passages which extended their previous style, with much cyclical use of synthesizers in the manner of composer Terry Riley – his ideas crop up on Soft Machine's *Third* and much of Eno's work, too.

These sections were interspersed with songs that wedded the soulful, funky elements that had surprised many listeners in *Atom Heart Mother* to their usual plodding intensity. Colouring by saxophone and girl singers provided the necessary human sound, poignantly contrasting with Roger Waters's lyrics. These had moved from the heady optimism of the late sixties to face resignedly the realities of work, money, growing old, going mad; the depressing repetition and circularity of it all is expressed in a song- or life-cycle which begins with the words 'Breathe, breathe in the air' and ends with a fading heartbeat. An almost unsurpassable achievement, *Dark Side* remains a pinnacle of studio perfection, and the Floyd may yet influence a new generation of neo-psychedelic bands, or perhaps the impecunious 'electronic garage bands' of the early eighties.

Weather Report

Mysterious Traveller (CBS 80 027)

Nubian Sundance/American Tango/Cucumber Slumber/Mysterious Traveller/Blackthorne Rose/Scarlet Woman/Jungle Book

Miles Davis's 1969 album *In a Silent Way* set a precedent for one of the dominant tendencies of seventies rock, the 'fusion' of elements from jazz and rock into an often tiresome, often profitable and occasionally creative compromise. Two of the musicians from those *Silent Way* sessions, Vienna-born pianist Josef Zawinul and black American saxophonist Wayne Shorter, decided to explore the possibilities of electronic instrumentation and rock rhythms in a band whose trademark would be constant change and evolution, issuing its own periodic Weather Report.

Jazz, in terms of album sales, had been regarded as commercially dead in the sixties but Miles Davis's *Bitches Brew* changed all that, selling more than a million copies in 1970 and grabbing its share of rock radio plays. There was money in jazz rock and Clive Davis, then head of CBS Records, signed Weather Report to cash in on the increasing 'sophistication' of the album-buying population.

The group's commercial potential, however, has only lately become evident, with their 1977 album *Heavy Weather* and the instrumental hit it contained, 'Birdland'. Stylistically they have never repeated the subtle successes of *Mysterious Traveller*, which combines driving rhythm and percussion with atmospheric 'natural' timbres that leave a nagging emotional and tonal resonance in the mind. The strongest ingredient in their mix is the exemplary use to which Zawinul has put the synthesizer, abandoning orthodox keyboard technique for a quasi-orchestral layering of sounds.

Little Feat

Sailin' Shoes (WARNER BROS. K 46156)

Easy To Slip/Cold, Cold, Cold/Trouble/Tripe Face Boogie/Willin'/Apolitical Blues/Sailin' Shoes/Teenage Nervous Breakdown/Got No Shadow/Cat Fever/Texas Rose Café

This, Little Feat's second album, contains eight peerless songs by Lowell George, who founded the band in 1970 along with fellow ex-Mother of Invention Roy Estrada. George's songs are characterized by his superb slide guitar playing, unique sense of musical time and some of the best rock lyrics around: perfect stoned blues, crazy and eloquent as on 'Teenage Nervous Breakdown' or warmly empathetic in 'Willin'', one of *the* all-time classic rock songs.

If their early albums crafted blues, country and rock & roll in a way that has led to Little Feat being called 'the Californian equivalent of the Band', the later *Feats Don't Fail Me Now* and *The Last Record Show* showed a growing interest in black rhythms, strengthened by the addition of three new musicians after Estrada's departure. This – together with the band's ever-growing instrumental skill and interplay, qualities which have made them highly regarded by musicians and critics – contributed to the relative commercial success of *Feats.*

However, the diminishing role of George within the band led to the jazz-rock indulgences of *Time Loves a Hero*, and fewer new compositions by him. Live, he began to leave the stage for some of the more indulgent instrumental passages; splits were rumoured. George died in 1979 leaving behind a solo album, *Thanks, I'll Eat It Here*, but the band's best work is still on their earlier albums. Just listen to the sparing instrumentation on George's poignant 'Long Distance Love' from *The Last Record Album*, and you'll know exactly what I mean.

Ry Cooder

Into the Purple Valley (REPRISE K44142)

How Can You Keep On Moving/Billy The Kid/Money Honey/FDR In Trinidad/Teardrops Will Fall/Denomination Blues/On A Monday/Hey Porter/Great Dreams From Heaven/Taxes On The Farmer Feeds Us All/Vigilante Man

Through an early, and in part first-hand, knowledge of blues guitar styles, Ry Cooder became one of the top Los Angeles session players by the end of the sixties, after spells with Taj Mahal and Captain Beefheart. Cooder's slide guitar playing is a major element on the Captain's first album with his Magic Band, *Safe as Milk*.

Although he grew up on the West Coast, Cooder became steeped in the American folk heritage; he was interested not merely in its song content, but (as with Taj Mahal) in the resurrection of specific instrumental techniques. Cooder became an expert bottleneck guitar player, contributing to the scores of *Candy* and *Performance*, and to albums by the Rolling Stones (*Let It Bleed*), Randy Newman and Maria Muldaur, among many others.

His own albums see him sifting back through several decades of American popular music; *Into the Purple Valley* concentrates on songs from the Depression of the thirties, whereas *Jazz* delves even further back into forgotten aspects of *that* genre. Although Cooder has been reluctant to perform live, he did bring to Europe the band of Texan/Mexican musicians who played with him on the excellent *Chicken Skin Music*.

In acting as an archivist for the American folk tradition, and at the same time remaining a player of great understatement and tightly coiled toughness, Cooder has helped to put the retrospective movement of seventies rock in its proper historical context.

Roxy Music

For Your Pleasure (POLYDOR 2302 049)

Do The Strand/Beauty Queen/Strictly Confidential/Editions Of You/In Every Dream Home A Heartache/The Bogus Man/Grey Lagoons/For Your Pleasure

If the profitable entente between jazz and rock in the seventies was to produce little beyond endless super-slick million-sellers, perhaps the input of ideas and approaches from modern classical music could be the answer to the stranglehold of banal, repetitive rhythms. In London during the early months of 1972 an answer was being formulated by the embryonic Roxy Music, who boasted two ex-teachers, a superbly muscular rock drummer, an informed interest in avant-garde composition and lots of ideas.

Dangerously, Roxy had two focal points – the enigmatic and androgynous Brian Eno, who distorted sounds, played with tapes and worked the synthesizer, and singer Bryan Ferry, whose concern with appearances and high art-school camp have led to his being labelled the originator of glam-rock.

For Your Pleasure, the band's second, refined the pastiche and experimentation of *Roxy Music* into a stylish mélange of electronics and rock & roll, with Ferry's affected vocal, penetrating lyrics and sense of occasion very much to the fore. Ego-tussles between him and Eno forced the latter to leave, and although *Stranded* and *Country Life* remained excellent, the innovations faded and Ferry's song-writing weakened.

In the face of declining commercial response to their solo efforts, the band – minus Eno – got together again in early 1979 to record *Manifesto*. A nigh-perfect example of late-seventies rock, *Manifesto* was a reminder more of their former expertise and sophistication than of their role as innovators: but Roxy Music changed the face of rock once – nobody really expected them to pull it off twice, did they?

David Bowie

Station to Station (RCA APLI 1327)

Station To Station/Golden Years/Word On A Wing/TVC15/Stay/ Wild Is The Wind

Like Roxy Music, David Bowie's substantial musical achievements are often obscured, in his case by the clouds of superficial adulation created by his self-advertised bisexuality, transvestitism, sexual omnivorousness, etc. An admirer of such wayward talents as Syd Barrett, Lou Reed and Iggy Pop, Bowie first came into the public eye and ear with his 1969 single, 'Space Oddity', afterwards 'retiring' to found and run the Beckenham Arts Lab.

His 1972 album *Hunky Dory* highlighted his excellent song-writing; a unique combination of attractive 'poppy' music and intense lyrics, it was capped by the 1972 *Ziggy Stardust and the Spiders from Mars*, a record that showed him to be deeply involved in the self-destructive rock star myth. After Bowie's 1974 American tour to promote his *Diamond Dogs* release, he began to move away from rock towards r&b and soul-influenced compositions, recording *Young Americans* in Philadelphia's Sigma Studios with local musicians.

Bowie referred to *Young Americans* as 'unrelenting plastic soul' but the directly imitative approach gave way on *Station to Station* to disintegrated and fragmented funk rhythms, which aptly reflected the desperation and depression of Bowie's words. It was as if the destruction that Bowie had foreseen for himself had caught up with him, the 'stations' becoming refuges of emotional security in a fundamentally devalued existence.

The depression deepened on *Low* (1977) but for the second time in his career Bowie changed direction, getting into cut-up lyrics à la William Burroughs and experimental systems of composition with his collaborator, Brian Eno, late of Roxy Music. That approach was again turned from an experiment into a powerful musical dimension on *Heroes*.

Joni Mitchell

The Hissing of Summer Lawns (ASYLUM K 53018)

In France They Kiss On Mainstreet/The Jungle Line/Edith And The Kingpin/Don't Interrupt The Sorrow/Shades Of Scarlet Conquering/The Hissing Of Summer Lawns/The Boho Dance/Harry's House-Centerpiece/Sweet Bird/Shadows And Light

As Joni Mitchell's lyrical technique became more oblique, suggestive and imagistic, her musicianship revealed a flair for imaginative arrangements that used the wider possibilities of jazz-based musicians and instrumentation. *Court and Spark* (1974) used Tom Scott's LA Express to help chart a mood of personal disillusionment and inertia through barely disguised identifications with various compromised and weakened characters; the mood is only relieved in the end by the wry comment on insanity made by Annie Ross's song 'Twisted' – the first non-original Joni had recorded.

The 1975 *The Hissing of Summer Lawns* represents the pinnacle of her work as an arranger; contributions from individual players coalesce into a uniquely musicianlike and mutually responsive final sound, but one that still retains her characteristic melancholy. Lyrically, it's her most dense and externalized work, focusing on the fate of women in contemporary American life, and on her own duality and rootlessness; each song is located in a sharply drawn setting.

In a field of music characterized by facile and inept lyric writing, Joni Mitchell distinguishes herself along with Dylan as a wordsmith supreme, and like him was not content to remain an acoustic guitar-toting singer/song-writer. Recently her musical contemporaneity may have overtaken her lyrical growth; on *Hejira* (1976) she found a new setting for her earlier stark instrumental colourings, playing with Weather Report bassist Jaco Pastorious in evident empathy, but mostly retracing old preoccupations in her lyrics. Another project to write lyrics to a set of melodies furnished by the late Charlie Mingus pointed towards even more important developments.

Genesis

Seconds Out

(CHARISMA GE 2001)

Squonk/The Carpet Crawl/Robbery, Assault And Battery/Afterglow/ Firth Of Fifth/I Know What I Like/The Lamb Lies Down On Broadway/ The Musical Box/Supper's Ready/Cinema Show/Dance On A Volcano/ Los Endos

'Symphonic rock', with its Mellotron-dominated backdrop of classically influenced chording, was the style that put the Moody Blues in the Number 2 position in the American charts in 1972 with their re-released single 'Nights In White Satin'. Trading on a spurious identification with orchestral music and 'meaningful' poetic imagery, the genre has produced many varieties of bombast: the flashy 'techno-rock' of bands like ELP and Yes (who rapidly ditched early melodicism and economy), the folksy strains of Barclay James Harvest or the 'electric Edwardian' of current practitioners the Enid.

Genesis' idiosyncratically English version made a first impact on their 1971 *Nursery Cryme*, and their live performances began to feature increasingly elaborate visual and theatrical effects, attention being centred on their lead singer, Peter Gabriel. He wrote their eccentric lyrics and developed an increasingly bizarre parade of costumes and stage personae, culminating in the 1974 tour on which Gabriel acted out the narrative of their ambitious double story-album *The Lamb Lies Down on Broadway*.

Although *Seconds Out*, four sides recorded in Paris in 1977, followed Gabriel's shock split with Genesis, it is a fitting record of the uninterrupted washes of sound that they were providing at the peak of their success. Genesis continued as a three-piece and Gabriel joined rock's experimenters, while still remaining an astute and magnetic live performer.

Fleetwood Mac

Rumours (WARNER BROS. K56344)

Second Hand News/Dreams/Never Going Back/Don't Stop/Go Your Own Way/Songbird/The Chain/You Make Loving Fun/I Don't Want To Know/Oh Daddy/Gold Dust Woman

Despite the numerous personnel changes, shifts of musical direction, legal hassles and periodic retirements, Fleetwood Mac have never been long without chart success right from the time of their 1968 album *Fleetwood Mac*, which stayed a best-seller for thirteen months even though it was composed of blues material.

After losing founder Peter Green in May 1970 and Jeremy Spencer in February 1971, both to private religious convictions, the Mac were joined by Californian writer/guitarist Bob Welch, and released the West-Coast-sounding *Future Games*, with which they made inroads into the American charts for the first time. But they almost split in 1973 after more leavings and joinings, and their career was further damaged by attempts to launch another band to capitalize on their name in the US.

When the lawyers left the scene, they set up base in LA with American husband and wife team Lindsey Buckingham and Stevie Nicks, who wrote commercial country-tinged rock with just the combination of melody and punch demanded by the American AOR (Album Oriented Rock or Adult Oriented Rock). *Fleetwood Mac* (1975) sold enormously, and *Rumours* (1976) has done even better. It is included here not just because of its almost unparalleled commercial success, but because it typifies the highly competent, easy-listening, 'laid-back' style which currently dominates the West Coast.

Bruce Springsteen

Born to Run (CBS 69170)

Thunder Road/Tenth Avenue Freeze Out/Night/Backstreets/Born To Run/She's The One/Meeting Across The River/Jungleland

Bruce Springsteen did the impossible; in what Bowie called 'this age of grand illusion', the American singer stood for all the old street-credibility values of the traditional rock hero, was sold to the world in a flurry of unprecedented hype and, miraculously, survived as one of rock's great individual talents. That he stood out from the tanned and tinselled seventies prima donnas is unquestioned: when, in October 1975, he appeared on the front cover of *Time* magazine under the banner 'Rock's New Sensation', they said that the 'glorified gutter rat from a dying New Jersey resort town' was 'not a golden California boy or a glitter queen from Britain,' and were relieved.

Springsteen's achievement has been to stalk the rock stage with an authority and presence given to only a handful of seventies rock luminaries: Bowie, Patti Smith, the Who, Dylan and so forth. Musically he grew up through bands and hassles, keeping a firm – and often impressively poetic – grasp on the preoccupations of an East Coast small-town teenager: oppressive work by day, hard-to-find good times by night, the emptiness of the movie-engendered myths the kids tried to live up to, the rackets, the gangs, and the half-grasped, half-doubted possibility of escape with your best girl in the passenger seat – if she's still yours.

The third album, *Born to Run*, was dramatically produced in a style which suggested Phil Spector on speed, and demonstrated Springsteen's fine understanding of the ethos of black r&b; the arrangements, which were driven by Springsteen's exemplary backing group, the E-Street Band, also showed a strong affinity with *Blonde on Blonde* – period Dylan. *Darkness on the Edge of Town*, delayed until 1978 by legal and business hassles, showed no evidence at all that his singular talent was on the wane.

Steely Dan

Greatest Hits (ABC ABCD 616)

Do It Again/Reeling In The Years/My Old School/Bodhisattva/Show Biz Kids/East St Louis Toodle-Oo/Rikki Don't Lose That Number/Pretzel Logic/Any Major Dude/Here At The Western World/Black Friday/Bad Sneakers/Doctor Wu/Haitian Divorce/Kid Charlemagne/The Fez/Peg/Josie

Bass player/guitarist Walter Becker and keyboard player/singer Donald Fagen met at a New York liberal arts college and decided to sell the songs they wrote together; in their words, 'Peddle them in the New York sleazo music business.' They wrote as staff songsmiths for ABC, before forming Steely Dan as a vehicle for their eclectic jazz-influenced tunes and intriguing, often bizarre lyrics. As jazz models for their work, they listened to band music heavy on complex structure; even in jazz, Fagen arrogantly says, 'I've heard nothing new since 1965.'

Working with a traditional, composition-based approach, which included written solos (e.g. Dean Park's guitar solo on 'Rose Darling' from *Katie Lied*), they were aided by producer Gary Katz in recording a stunning debut with their 1972 *Can't Buy a Thrill*, which gave them two US hit singles in 'Do It Again' and 'Reeling In The Years'. *Countdown to Ecstasy* was more musicianly and solo-oriented, but *Pretzel Logic* repeated their debut success with a gamut of impeccably rendered styles.

By 1974, the duo's unwillingness to tour led to a split, Fagen and Becker insisting that the Dan would continue, 'more a concept than a rock band'. They stepped back to direct an array of session players on the patchy *Katie Lied* and on *The Royal Scam*, which saw a further refinement and strengthening of their eccentricity. That was followed by the blander, more AOR, *Aja*. As a model of complex intelligent writing and clear-headed execution, Steely Dan are sure of a high position in any rock retrospective; only their absence from the concert-halls of the late seventies is a cause for regret.

Elvis Costello

My Aim Is True (STIFF SEEZ 3)

Welcome To The Working Week/Miracle Man/No Dancing/Blame It On Cain/Alison/Sneaky Feelings/(The Angels Wanna Wear My) Red Shoes/Less Than Zero/Mystery Dance/Pay It Back /I'm Not Angry/ Waiting For The End Of The World

Rock has been just as susceptible to the creation of anti-heroes as any other mass cultural form, and the rapid rise of Elvis Costello, from a computer operative and part-time country singer to the first new wave artist to break big commercially, is a classic example, the death of his namesake notwithstanding. Costello's first album, with its down-market packaging, and the image of the overgrown class weed complete with Woolies jeans and Buddy Holly specs, were the creation of the wacky entrepreneurial skills of Stiff, a fledgling shoestring independent record company who later lost the singer to Radar.

Radar, a 'creative unit' attached to the massive Warner Communications empire, produced the following albums, *This Year's Model* and *Armed Forces*, breaking Costello in an American market that had remained resolutely indifferent to punk and new wave acts. Although *This Year's Model* is often cited as his better work, *My Aim Is True*, tagged by one critic as a 'song-writer's demo album', is classic late-seventies beat music, furnished with a set of lyrics which attack the sexual mores of the last two decades from the embittered viewpoint of a jilted, nerve-jangled victim; anger burns and long-overdue tears are contained.

By *Armed Forces* the dream was starting to fade. Filing a suit for divorce, reputedly living with a model, and with his manager now ensconced in a new Chelsea office, Costello – admittedly in part through the sheer exhaustion of constant touring – seemed to be running himself beyond the reach of the ironies which inhabit the gap between the songs and the man. Such, one is tempted to conclude, is the voracious efficiency of rock's corporate machine. It's a little depressing.

Various Artists

Saturday Night Fever (RSO SUPER DOUBLE 2658 123)

Staying Alive/How Deep Is Your Love/Night Fever/More Than A Woman (The Bee Gees)/If I Can't Have You (Yvonne Elliman)/A Fifth of Beethoven (Walter Murphy)/More Than A Woman (Tavares)/Manhattan Skyline (David Shire)/Calypso Breakdown (Ralph McDonald)/Night On Disco Mountain (David Shire)/Open Sesame (Kool and the Gang)/Jive Talkin'/You Should Be Dancing (The Bee Gees)/Boogie Shoes (K. C. and the Sunshine Band)/Salsation (David Shire)/K-Jee (MFSB)/Disco Inferno (Tramps)

Saturday Night Fever bears witness to several phenomena in rock: the rise of disco, the late-seventies rash of rock movies and accompanying sound-track albums, and the resurgence of the Bee Gees. As a film about disco, *Fever* didn't really cut it; it was more a film *set* in a disco, and a spacious, not very noisy one at that. Similarly, in musical terms it is the result of slick, clean, white repackaging of black music, something the Bee Gees have had plenty of previous experience in.

Disco has been the subject of a welter of 'serious' commentary, but it is primarily functional dance music, hence its emphasis on mechanized beat. As clubs in which to dance and meet, discos grew up in America in the seventies to serve high society, blacks and homosexuals. They rapidly spawned an industry of specially made records, inevitably singles, like George McCrae's 'Rock Your Baby' or K. C. and the Sunshine Band's 'That's The Way I Like It'.

But it was an Englishman, David Bowie, who made disco such a big seller in America, by building on the massive audience attracted to his live shows and zapping them with the sudden change of direction of *Young Americans*. The result has been disco outings by many top white rock acts, for example the Stones' 'Hot Stuff' and 'Miss You' and Rod Stewart's 'Do Ya Think I'm Sexy'.

Commercially this has proved very effective; witness the phenomenal sales of Blondie's 'Heart Of Glass' in early 1979. In a broad context it has paved the way for the introduction of even more primordial Afro-American rhythms into rock in the music of Kraftwerke (who had a massive US disco hit with 'Trans-Europe Express'), the later Bowie, Talking Heads, and on Devo's revival of 'Satisfaction'. It may well prove to be one of rock's saving inputs in the eighties.

The Seventies : Singles

Jimi Hendrix: *Voodoo Chile* (1970)

As the posthumous exploitation of Hendrix began with a Number 1 single, rock mourned the seventies' prospective loss.

T. Rex: *Ride A White Swan* (1970)

Seduced by an electric guitar, the stoned elf left the garden and became a glitter king.

The Beatles: *Let It Be* (1970)

Phil Spector notwithstanding, McCartney acquits himself with grace – probably for the last time.

Rod Stewart: *Maggie May* (1971)

Cross-Atlantic hit story of schoolboy and happy hooker.

The Rolling Stones: *Brown Sugar* (1971)

Spot-on riff, sassy sax break and a perfect early-seventies rock dance beat.

Roxy Music: *Virginia Plain* (1972)

Another claimant in the glitter stakes, Bryan Ferry, found in an unusually happy rapport with Eno; very danceable results.

Mott the Hoople: *All The Young Dudes* (1972)

With Bowie's help an archetypal youth anthem, prefiguring the concerns of punk.

Alice Cooper: *School's Out* (1972)

Son of a preacher-man, sometime amateur snake-handler with a classic heavy rock single, succeeds without the cheap sensationalism.

Gary Glitter: *Do You Wanna Touch Me (Oh Yeah)* (1973)

First eleven singles hit the Top Ten, which shows what an overflowing chest, a ridiculous barnet and silver suits can do.

Todd Rundgren: *I Saw The Light* (1973)

A major figure in American rock revealing his latent talent for insidious melody.

Elton John: *Candle In The Wind* (1974)

One of the seventies' best-selling rock performers with a surprisingly sensitive treatment of a much-abused subject.

The Eagles: *Lyin' Eyes* (1975)

Classic AOR country rock, a wistful tale of domestic subversion aimed right at the American housewife's heart.

John Lennon: *Imagine* (1975)

Years after the seminal album of the same name: the only Beatle with musical credibility intact.

David Bowie: *Space Oddity* (1975)

A phenomenally successful re-issue by the decade's single most influential figure.

Abba: *S O S* (1975)

One year later they were to be the world's best-selling group. Perfectly crafted, soulless rock/pop.

Queen: *Bohemian Rhapsody* (1975)

The triumph of studio trickery, glitter-posturing, androgyny, neo-Wagnerian pomp and second division heavy metal; all the angles were covered.

Boz Scaggs: *Lowdown* (1976)

Exemplary laid-back white soul; an expert repackaging job.

Blondie: *Heart Of Glass* (1979)

Ubiquitous disco reaches the New York new wave. Result: multi-million sales and a picture of Debbie on everyone's bedroom wall.

Index

Entries in bold indicate an album commentary

Abba, 323
Abyssinian Baptist Gospel Choir, 71f.
Abyssinians, 257
Ace, Johnny, 11, 84, 89
Ace, Richard, 236
Action, 153
Acuff, Roy, 131
Adams, Faye, 65
Adams, Marie, and the Three Tons of Joy, 81
Adderley, Cannonball, 93
Adler, Lou, 179ff.
Ad Libs, 88
Adverts, 284
Afrika Corps, 285
Aitken, Laurel, 239
Albion Band, 43
Albion Country Band, 54
Alcapone, Dennis, 240, 258
Alexander, Dave, 277
Allen, Frank, 158
Allen, Johnnie, 79
Allen, Lee, 33, 66, 77f.
Allen, Tony, and the Champs, 81
Allison, Mose, 162, 225
Allman, Duane, 104
Alpert, Herb, 179
Alphonso, Roland, 236, 242
Amazing Rhythm Aces, 142
Amboy Jukes, 269
Amon Duul II, 295
Anderson, Bill, 127
Anderson, Jon, 173
Andrews, Harvey, 213
Andrews, Lee, and the Hearts, 70
Andrews, Sam, 203
Angelic Gospel Singers, 71
Angels, 15
Animals, 152, 162f., 176, 229
ar Bras, Dan, 61
Archibald, 77
Armatrading, Joan, 213f.
Arnold, Eddie, 143
Artwoods, 153
Asheton, Ron, 276
Ashley, Steve, 54
Ashton, Tony, 277
Asleep at the Wheel, 133
Association, 181, 207
Atkin, Pete, 213
Atkins, Chet, 143
Attack, 154
Avalon, Frankie, 33, 188
Avery, Jim, 277
Axton, Estelle, 95

Bacharach, Burt, 67
Baez, Joan, 39f., 42, 47, 51, 211, 218
Baker, Ginger, 155, 165
Baker, LaVern, 90
Baker, Mickey, 27
Balin, Marty, 198f.
Ball, Kenny, 171
Ballard, Hank, 80, 89, 93
Band, the, 296, 298, 301f., 305, 310
Banks, Darrell, 117
Banned, 288
Barbarians, 269
Barber, Chris, 171
Barclay James Harvest, 315
Bare, Bobby, 144
Barrett, Syd, 169, 308, 313
Barri, Steve, 180f., 189
Barry, Jerry, 87
Barry, Margaret, 53
Barthol, Bruce, 202
Bartholomew, Dave, 21, 66, 78
Battiste, Harold, 78
Beach Boys, 179f., 188, 189f., 206, 263
Beale Streeters, 84
Beatles, 7, 37, 42, 91, 151, 157, 158, 176, 178, 189, 192, 204, 209, 261f., 270, 272f., 291, 307, 321f.
Beau Brummels, 182, 206, 287
Beck, Jeff, 155, 161, 306
Becker, Walter, 318

Beckford, Theophilus, 236
Bee Gees, 319f.
Bell, Derek, 60
Bell, Thom, 112
Bell, William, 95
Belvin, Jesse, and Phillips, Marvin, 81
Bennett, Cliff, 154, 174
Bennett, Tony, 129
Bennett, Wayne, 85
Benson, George, 98
Berline, Byron, 193
Berns, Bert, 67, 84, 288
Berry, Chuck, 16f., 19, 69, 116, 151, 159
Berry, Dave, 172, 175
Berry, Mike, 171
Big Bopper, 134
Big Brother and the Holding Company, 182, 184, 203
Big Three, 172ff.
Big Youth, 240, 250, 258
Bilk, Acker, 171
Birds, 172f.
Bishops, 287
Black Sabbath, 168, 307
Blaine, Hal, 180
Blake, Norman, 138
Bland, Bobby, 65, 84f., 94
Blondie, 266, 288, 320, 323
Bloomfield, Mike, 200
Blue Cheer, 203
Blues By Five, 175
Blues Magoos, 269f.
Blues Project, 269
Bob B. Soxx and the Blue Jeans, 86
Bolan, Marc, 266, 288
Bond, Graham, 152, 165, 172
Bond, Ronnie, 167
Bonzo Dog Band, 291
Booker T and the MGs, 95, 117, 162
Boone, Pat, 12
Boone, Steve, 190
Boothe, Ken, 238
Bootsy's Rubber Band, 100
Boston, 307
Bothy Band, 62
Bowie, David, 40, 141, 172f., 265, 276f., 297, 300, 305, 313, 317, 320, 322f.
Bown, Alan, 153
Bradford, Alex, 81
Branson, Richard, 298
Bread, 180
Brierley, Marc, 53
Briggs, Anne, 51f.
Brinsley Schwarz, 266
Britton, Chris, 167
Brooks, Baba, 242, 256
Brooks, Ernie, 278
Brown, Arthur, 154, 169, 178
Brown, Charles, 15, 101
Brown, Dennis, 257
Brown, James, 67, 94, 97, 99f., 108, 113, 125, 162
Brown, Jim Ed, 144
Brown, Joe, 149, 171f.
Brown, Johonny C. (Glen), 259
Brown, J. T., 75
Brown, Pete, 165
Brown, Roy, 34, 65, 67, 77
Brown, Ruth, 65
Browne, Jackson, 186, 212
Browns, 144
Bruce, Jack, 155, 165, 294
Bruce, Vin, 79
Bryant, Boudleaux and Felice, 25
Buckingham, Lindsey, 316
Buckley, Tim, 186, 211, 231
Buffalo Springfield, 185, 194f., 244
Burdon, Eric, 162f.
Burgess, Sonny, 32
Burke, Solomon, 96, 104, 117, 121, 245
Burlisson, Paul, 29
Burnette, Dorsey, 29
Burnette, Johnny, 29, 32
Burning Red Ivanhoe, 295
Burning Spear, 239, 245f., 247
Burton, James, 28, 139
Bush, Kate, 213f.
Busters, 33
Butler, Jerry, 107, 112
Butler, Joe, 190
Buttrey, Kenny, 138
Buzzcocks, 267, 280, 284, 289
Byrd, Donald, 98
Byrds, 126, 138, 180, 185, 189, 191f., 193, 207, 209, 264
Byrne, Jerry, 36, 81

Cadets, 33
Cale, John, 265, 278, 281
Cameron, John, 226
Campbell, Archie, 144
Campbell, Cornell, 257
Campbell, Glen, 180
Campbell, Ian, 53
Can, 286, 296
Canned Heat, 16
Cannon, Freddy, 14
Capaldi, Jim, 169
Captain Beefheart, 311
Captain Sensible, 282
Caravelles, 171
Carlton and the Shoes, 256
Carrabello, Mike, 205
Cars, 278
Carson, Martha, 144
Carter Family, 41, 47, 51, 123, 144; Carter, June, 130; Carter, Mother Maybelle, 131; Carter, A. P., 131
Carthy, Martin, 42f., 53f. 59
Casady, Jack, 199
Casey, Howie, and the Seniors, 173
Cash, Johnny, 20, 47, 125, 130, 135, 139
Castaways, 269
Celebrated Working Men's Band, 51f.
Chandler, Gene, 91, 108
Channel, Bruce, 36
Channels, 70
Chantays, 188
Chantels, 70
Chapin, Harry, 233
Chapman, Roger, 170
Charlatans, 182
Charles, Ray, 8, 65, 67, 94, 97, 100f., 114, 125
Charts, 70

Checkmates Ltd, 86
Chepito, Jose, 205
Chieftains, 53, 60
Chiffons, 91
Chi-lites, 119
Chimes, 70
Chimes, Terry, 282
Chin, Clive, 254
Chin-Loy, Herman, 240, **251**
Chocolate Watch Band, 269, 288
Chords, 66
Chosen Gospel Singers, 81
Christian, Roger, 180, 189
Chung, Geoffrey, 259
Cippolina, John, 201
Clannad, 43
Clanton, Jimmy, 79
Clapton, Eric, 153, 155, **161**, **164f.**, 292, 294
Clark, Dave, 176
Clark, Gene, 191f.
Clark, Petula, 171
Clarke, Gussie, 250
Clarke, John Cooper, **267**
Clarke, Johnnie, 241
Clarke, Michael, 191ff.
Clash, 267, 277, 280, **282f.**, 299
Cline, Patsy, 146
Clinton, George, 100
Clovers, 33, 90
Clue J and the Blues Blasters, 242
Coasters, 27, 80, 87
Coates, Dorothy Love, 71
Cobb, Ed, 271
Cobham, Billy, 295
Cochran, Eddie, 23, 27, 32, **151**, 279
Cocker, Joe, 172
Cohen, David, 202
Cohen, Leonard, 211, 219, 222
Cole, Nat 'King', 101
Collins, Bernard, 257
Collins, Judy, 211, **218f.**, 225
Collins, Shirley, 53f., 55
Colosseum, 156
Coltrane, John, 295
Commander Cody and His Lost Planet Airmen, 141f., 296
Commodores, 113
Cooder, Ry, 187, 296, **311**
Cook, Paul, 283
Cooke, Curley, 204
Cooke, Sam, 67, 81f., 94, 97, **101f.**, 238
Cooper, Alice, 322
Copper Family, 52, 53
Costello, Elvis, 266, **318f.**
Count Five, 269, 288
Count Machuki, 239
Country Gentlemen, 174
Country Joe and the Fish, **202**
Cousins, Roy, 257
Covay, Don, 119
Cramer, Floyd, 36
Crazy Cavan and the Rhythm Rockers, 32
Cream, 155, 165, 291, 294ff.
Creation, 177
Creedence Clearwater Revival, 16, 31, 182, 184
Crescendos, 33
Cresters, 174
Crests, 70
Crewe, Bob, 67
Croce, Jim, 233
Cropper, Steve, 104, 200
Crosby, David, 191f.
Crosby, Stills, Nash (and Young), 185, **192**, 195, 200
Crowns, 83
Crows, 11
Cryan Shames, 269
Crystals, 86
Curtis, Chris, 157
Curtis, King, 27
Curtis, Lee and the All Stars, 173
Curtiss, Dave, and the Tremors, **174f.**

Dale, Dick, and the Del-Tones, 188
Daley, Matador, 240
Daltrey, Roger, 303
Damned, 267, **281f.**, 284
Daniels, Charlie, 138
Danleers, 70
Danny and the Juniors, 13, 34
Darin, Bobby, 14
Daugherty, Jay Dee, 281
Davenport, Bob, 51f.
Davies, Cyril, 172
Davies, Idris, 50
Davies, Ray, 167
Davis, Carl, 108
Davis, Clive, 309
Davis, Mike, 274
Davis, Miles, 98, **294f.**, 309
Davis, Skeeter, 144, 147
Davis, Spencer, 155, 169, **177**
Davis, Tim, 204
Davison, Brian, 154
Dee, Mercy, 81
Deep Purple, 307
Delfonics, 112
Delmore Brothers, 145
Dennisons, 173
Denny, Sandy, 58f., 213
Densmore, John, 197
Denver, John, 212f., 233
Denver, Karl, 171
Derringer, Rick, 288
Devo, 268, 320
Devoto, Howard, 289
Diamond, Neil, 212f., 232
Diamonds (reggae), 241, 253
Diamonds (rock & roll), 35
Dickson, Jim, 191
Diddley, Bo, 16, 24, 72, 159, 201, 273
Dillard and Clarke's Expedition, 185
Dillon, Phyllis, and Hopeton, 243
Dion, 14
Dixie Cups, 87
Dixie Hummingbirds, **71f.**
Dixon, Luther, 91
Dixon, Willie, 74, 159, 197
Dobson, Dobby, 243, 248
Dodd, C. S. 'Coxsone', 235–9, 245f., 250, **251f.**, 252–7, 259
Dodd, Dickie, 270
Dodd, Ken, 153
Doe, Ernie K., 15, 78

Domino, Fats, 12, 15, 20, 33, 66, 77, 79, 237
Dominoes, 67, 82
Donahue, Tom, 182
Don and Dewey, 81
Donegan, Lonnie, 151, 171
Donovan, 42, 209ff., 213, 226
Doors, 180, 195, 196f., 276, 293
Dorsey, Lee, 15, 78
Dorsey, Thomas A., 72
Douglas, Craig, 171
Downliners Sect, 152, 175
Drake, Pete, 138
Dr Alimantado, 258
Dranes, Arizona, 71f.
Dreja, Chris, 161
Drifters, 67, 83f., 89, 93, 151
Drummond, Don, 236f., 242
Dubliners, 43, 53
Dubs, 70
Dudley, Dave, 147
Dunbar, Ainsley, 155
Dunbar, Sly, 241, 248
Duncan, Gary, 201
Dupree, Cornell, 98
Dury, Ian, 266
Dylan, Bob, 19, 40, 42ff., 48, 50, 52, 104, 126, 137f., 180, 184, 191f., 209–14, 215ff., 218, 226, 229, 231, 263, 301f., 306, 314, 317
Dynamites, 239

Eager, Vince, 149
Eagles, 185f., 299, 322
Easybeats, 177
Eater, 284
Ebonys, 112
Eccles, Clancy, 257
Echols, John, 196
Eddie and the Hot Rods, 267, 287
Eddy, Duane, 33, 188
Edmunds, Dave, 31
Edwards, Bobby, 146
Electric Prunes, 269, 288
Elliman, Yvonne, 319
Elliott, Bern, and the Fenmen, 174f.
Elliott, Jack, 53
Ellis, Alton, and the Flames, 243f.
Ellis, Steve, 291
Ellison, Lorraine, 119
Ellmore, Greg, 201
ELP, 315
Ely, Joe, 127, 142, 143
Emerson, Keith, 154
Emotions, 119
Enid, 315
Eno, Brian, 296, 308, 312f., 321
Erikson, Roky, 272
Escorts, 173f.
Estrada, Roy, 310
Eternals, 252, 257
Ethridge, Chris, 193
Evans, Gil, 295
Everly Brothers, 24f., 30, 125, 220

Fabian, 14, 26
Faces, 306
Fagen, Donald, 318
Fairport Convention, 53f., 58, 155, 230
Faith, Adam, 171f.
Falcons, 104
Fall, 267
Fame, Georgie, 149, 153, 161f.
Family, 170f.
Family Dog, 182
Fantastic Baggys, 181, 188
Farinas, 175
Farlowe, Chris, 154, 161, 177
Faron's Flamingos, 173f.
Farr, Gary, 154
Fatback Band, 113
Feathers, Charlie, 32
Felder, Don, 194
Fender, Freddy, 133
Fenton, P. T., 286
Ferry, Bryan, 312, 321
Finn, Mickey, and the Blue Men, 175
Firefall, 185f.
Fisher, Archie and Ray, 52f.
Five Satins, 33, 70
Flamingos, 70
Flatt, Lester, 132, 143
Fleetwood Mac, 75, 155, 186, 299, 316
Fleetwoods, 33
Flint, Hughie, 164
Flip City, 266
Flying Burrito Brothers, 185
Fogerty, John, 31, 140f., 185
Fontana, Wayne, and the Mindbenders, 174f.
Foote, Micky, 282
Ford, Emile, and the Checkmates, 171
Ford, Frankie, 79
Four Flames, 81
Four Just Men, 175
Four Pennies, 175
Four Seasons, 67
Four Tops, 118
Fowley, Kim, 278
Frank, Jackson C., 53
Franklin, Aretha, 109
Freberg, Stan, 14
Free, 155
Freed, Alan, 9f., 33
Frey, Glenn, 193
Frieberg, Dave, 201
Fripp, Robert, 296
Frogmen, 188
Funicello, Annette, 188
Funkadelic, 100, 119
Furay, Ritchie, 194
Fury, Billy, 149f., 171f.

Gabriel, Peter, 315
Gale, Eric, 98
Gallucci, Don, 277
Gallup, Cliff, 26
Gamble, Kenny, and Huff, Leon, 104, 112
Gant, Cecil, 65
Gacia, Jerry, 200
Gates, David, 180
Gates, Rev. J. M., 71
Gaye, Marvin, 97, 105, 106f.
Generation X, 284
Genesis, 155, 315
Gentle, Johnny, 149
George, Barbara, 78

George, Lowell, 310
Gerry and the Pacemakers, 152
Gibbs, Joe, 252
Gibson, Don, 144, 146
Gibson, Joel, 257
Gilmour, Dave, 169, 308
Gizmos, 285
Gladiolas, 90
Glaser, Tompall, 135
Glitter, Gary, 322
Goffin, Gerry, and King, Carole, 67, 84, 87, 91
Golden Gate Jubilee Quartet, 71
Goldner, George, 87
Golliwogs, 182
Gomelsky, Giorgio, 161
Good, Jack, 26, 149, 153
Goodman, Steve, 224f., 232
Gordon, Jim, 180
Gordon, Roscoe, 235
Gordy, Berry, 94, 105
Gottehrer, Richard, 288
Graham, Bill, 182, 205
Graham Central Station, 113
Graham, Davey, 42f., 53f., 55f., 57
Grant, Marshall, 130
Grant, Peter, 307
Grateful Dead, 182, 184f., 199f., 295
Great Society, 182
Grech, Rick, 170
Green, Al, 110f.
Green, Mick, 29
Green, Peter, 155, 164, 205, 316
Greenwich, Ellie, 87
Groundhogs, 155
Gruberger, Jay and Solomon, 285
Gryphon, 53
Guitar Slim, 81f.
Gurley, James, 203
Guthrie, Arlo, 48, 213, 232
Guthrie, Woody, 40f., 48, 49f., 215, 223f., 226
Guy, Buddy, 294

Haggard, Merle, 127, 136, 141
Haley, Bill, 11, 13, 25
Hall, Rick, 95
Hall, Tommy, 272
Hamilton, George, 144
Hamilton, Russ, 171
Hancock, Herbie, 98, 295
Hardin, Glen D., 139
Hardin, Tim, 211, 231, 306
Harper, Roy, 42, 53, 213
Harpers Bizarre, 181, 208
Harpo, Slim, 92
Harptones, 70
Harriott, Derek, 256
Harris, Emmylou, 139, 186, 225
Harris, Jet, and Meehan, Tony, 171
Harris, Ray, 32
Harris, Rolf, 291
Harris, Thurston, 33
Harrison, George, 91, 158
Harrison, Jerry, 278
Harrison, Wilbert, 66, 90
Harvey, Alex, 152
Hathaway, Donny, 118, 135
Hawkins, Dale, 35
Hawkins, Ronnie, 37, 201, 301
Hawkins, Screamin' Jay, 34
Hayes, Isaac, 98, 110
Headon, Nicky 'Topper', 282
Heartbreakers, 266, 289
Hedgehog Pie, 43, 53
Hell, Richard, 266, 289
Helms, Chet, 182
Hendrix, Jimi, 115, 155, 178, 293, 321
Henley, Don, 193
Henry, Clarence 'Frogman', 78
Heptones, 245, 250
Heron, Mike, 57
Hester, Carolyn, 47, 211
Hicks, Dan, and His Hot Licks, 296
Highland, Ken 'Gizmo', 285
Hill, Jessie, 78
Hillman, Chris, 191ff.
Hippy Boys, 240
Hirsch, Chicken, 202
Hoagan, Carl, 69
Holland–Dozier–Holland, 95, 115, 118; Holland, Eddie, 95
Hollies, 177
Holly, Buddy, 13, 15, 17, 23, 135, 143, 151, 172, 273
Holt, John, 244, 249, 252, 256
Honeybus, 172f.
Hooker, John Lee, 72, 76f., 81
Hookim, Joe Joe, 247f., 252f.
Hopkins, Lightnin', 74f.
Hopkins, Nicky, 201
Horslips, 43
House, Son, 65
Howard, Brian, and the Silhouettes, 175
Howard, Camille, 81
Howlin' Wolf, 65, 72f.
Hudson, Garth, 59
Humblebums, 53
Hunter, Ivory Joe, 65
Hutchings, Ashley, 55, 58

I Roy, 240, 249f., 258
Ian and the Zodiacs, 173
Ian, Janis, 88, 211, 233
Ifield, Frank, 171
Iggy Pop, 264, 276f., 285, 313
Impressions, 97
Incredible String Band, 42, 57
Inkspots, 66, 70
Innocence, 181
International Submarine Band, 193
Interns, 175
Intruders, 112
Irvine, Andy, 62
Isaacs, Gregory, 248, 250
Isley Brothers, 115, 238

Jackson Five, 118
Jackson, Mahalia, 71
Jackson, Millie, 114f., 118
Jackson, Tony, 157f.
Jackson, Wanda, 36
Jack the Lad, 43, 54
Jagger, Mick, 159f., 262, 304f.
Jagneaux, Rufus, 79
Jah Jerry, 242

Index

Jam, 267
Jamaicans, 243
James, Brian, 282
James, Elmore, 65, 75
James, Etta, 80
James Gang, 194
James, Homesick, 75
James, Jimmy, and the Vagabonds, 153
James, Skip, 41, 46, 60
James, Sonny, 144f.
James, Tommy, and the Shondells, 268
Jan (Berry) and Dean (Torrence), 179ff., 188f., 206
Jansch, Bert, 53f., 56f.
Jaynetts, 70
Jefferson Airplane, 182, 184f., 190, 195, 198f., 207, 274, 295; Jefferson Starship, 184, 186, 199
Jelly Beans, 88
Jennings, Waylon, 135
Jesters, 70
Jethro Tull, 155
Jilted John, 267
Jive Five, 70
Joe and Ann, 79
JoHansen, David, 279
John, Elton, 297, 305, 322
John, Little Willie, 80, 89, 94
Johnnie and Jack, 144
Johnny and the Hurricanes, 33, 188
John's Children, 288
Johnson, Blind Willie, 71
Johnson, Buddy, 65
Johnson, Robert, 45, 46, 65, 75
Johnson, Syl, 111
Johnston, Bob, 138
Johnstone, Bruce, 180, 288
Jones, Brian, 160, 304
Jones, George, 133f.
Jones, Grandpa, 144
Jones, Linda, 119
Jones, Little Johnny, 75
Jones, Mick, 282
Jones, Quincey, 98, 109
Jones, Ronnie, 161
Jones, Steve, 283
Joplin, Janis, 182, 203f., 225, 293
Jordan, Louis, 65, 69
Justis, Bill, 33

Kaiser, Kenny, 285
Kaiser's Kittens, 285
Kane, Arthur, 279
Kane, Eden, 171
Kansas, 307
Kantner, Paul, 198f.
Katz, Gary, 318
Kaufman, Matthew, 278
Kaukonen, Jorma, 199
Kaye, Lenny, 281
K. C. and the Sunshine Band, 319f.
Keith and Tex, 256
Kelly, Pat, 238, 244
Kendricks, Eddie, 106
Kenner, Chris, 78
Kershaw, Doug, 147
Keyes, Bobby, 277
Khourys, Richard, 236
Kidd, Johnny, and the Pirates, 171
Kilburn and the Highroads, 266
Killen, Louis, 51f.
King, B. B., 65, 84, 85
King, Ben E., 83, 91
King, Carole, 181, 185, 212, 221f., 223
King, Claude, 147
King Crimson, 291
King, Jim, 170
King, Pee Wee, 143
King Stitt, 239, 257
King Tubbys, 239, 253
Kingsmen, 271, 287
Kingston Trio, 51
Kinks, 166f., 168, 262, 273, 285, 287
Kiss, 265
Knetchel, Larry, 180
Knickerbockers, 269f.
Knight, Gladys, and the Pips, 117
Knight, Peter, 59
Knox, Buddy, 35
Kool and the Gang, 113, 319
Kooper, Al, 200, 216
Kootch, Danny, 186, 223
Korner, Alexis, 152, 159, 172
Kraftwerke, 296, 320
Kral, Ivan, 281
Kramer, Billy J., 152
Kramer, Wayne, 264, 274
Krieger, Robbie, 197
Kristofferson, Kris, 121, 139
Kunkel, Russ, 186

Lambert, Kit, 166
Lance, Major, 108, 117
Lane, Gary, 270
Larson, Nicolette, 186
Leadbelly, 42, 49, 51, 53, 128, 303
Leadon, Bernie, 193f.
Leaves, 180, 269
Led Zeppelin, 155, 307
Lee, Arthur, 196
Lee, Brenda, 36
Lee, Bunnie, 241
Lee, Curtis, 87
Lee, Laura, 118
Leeman, Mark, 154
Leiber (Jerry) and Stoller (Mike), 27, 67, 87
Lennon, John, 158, 322
Lesh, Phil, 200
Levene, Gerry, and the Avengers, 174
Lewis, Jerry Lee, 21, 32, 125, 137
Lewis, Peter, 200
Lewis, Rudy, 84
Lewis, Smiley, 77, 235
Liggings, Joe, 81
Liggins, Jimmy, 81
Lightfoot, Gordon, 223
Lindisfarne, 54
Lindley, David, 186
Little Feat, 185, 226, 296, 298, 310
Little Milton, 72f.
Little Richard, 12f., 22, 66, 81f., 93, 151
Little Roy, 240
Little Walter, 72ff.
Livingstone, Bunny, 247, 259

Lloyd, A. L., 51ff.
Locklin, Hank, 144
Lofgren, Nils, 267
Loggins (Kenny) and Messina (Jimmy), 185
Lomax, Alan, 49, 53, 73
London, Laurie, 171
Lonzo and Oscar, 143
Look, 285
Loudermilk, John D., 270
Love, 180, 196
Love Affair, 291
Love, Darlene, 86
Lovin' Spoonful, 181, 190
Lowe, Nick, 266, 282
Lurkers, 280
Lymon, Frankie, and the Teenagers, 34

MacColl, Ewan, and Seeger, Peggy, 52
MacGregor, Freddie, 259
Mack, Lonnie, 33
Maclaine, Pete, and the Clan, 174
Maclean, Don, 213, 232
Macon, Uncle Dave, 143f.
Magazine, 267, 289
Magic Mushrooms, 269f.
Magicians, 269
Magma, 295
Mamas and Papas, 181, 207
Man, 156
Manfred Mann, 152, 177
Mann (Barny) and Weil (Cynthia), 67, 84, 87
Mannassas, 185
Manzarek, Ray, 197
Marauders, 174f.
Marchan, Bobby, 79
Marco, 286
Mardin, Arif, 134
Marketts, 188
Mar-Keys, 95
Marley, Bob, and the Wailers, 237, 239, 246f., 259
Marriott, Steve, 172f.
Marsden, Beryl, 173
Martha and the Vandellas, 95
Marti, 50
Martindale, Wink, 145
Martin, Grady, 29
Martin, Jimmy, 131
Martyn, John, 53, 59f.; and Beverley, 59
Marvelettes, 151
Mason, Dave, 169f.
Matassa, Cosimo, 78
Matlock, Glen, 283
Mattacks, Dave, 58
Mayall, John, 152f., 155, 164, 172, 304
Mayfield, Curtis, 97, 109, 111, 238, 244; and the Impressions, 107f.
Mayfield, Percy, 65, 81f.
Maytals, 238
MC5, 264, 267, 274
McAuliffe, Leon, 133
McCartney, Paul, 158, 204, 321
McCarty, Jim, 161
McClean, Brian, 196
McClinton, Delbert, 37
McCook, Tommy, 236, 242
McCoy, Charlie, 138
McCoys, 288
McCracklin, Jimmy, 66
McCrae, George, 320
McDevitt, Chas, 171
McDonald, Country Joe, 202, 224
McDonald, Ralph, 319
McDowell, Fred, 41, 225
McGarrigle, Kate and Anna, 227
McGinn, Matt, 51f.
McGuinn, Roger, 180, 191
McGuire, Barry, 206, 231
McKay, Freddie, 251
McKay, John, 286
McKenzie, Scott, 181, 207
McLain, Tommy, 79
McLaren, Malcolm, 266f.
McLaughlin, John, 295
McNally, John, 157f.
McPhatter, Clyde, 67, 82f., 93
McTell, Ralph, 53, 213, 228f.
McVie, John, 164
Meaux, Huey, 273
Meisner, Randy, 193f.
Melcher, Terry, 179f., 189, 264, 288
Mello-Kings, 33
Melodians, 243
Melton, Barry, 202
Melvin, Harold, and the Blue Notes, 112
Memphis Horns, 135
Merseybeats, 173, 175
Meyer, Augie, 273
MFSB, 112, 319
Michael and the Messengers, 269
Mighty Avengers, 172
Mighty Diamonds, 247f.
Milburn, Amos, 33, 235
Miller, Jacob, 253
Miller, Jerry, 200
Miller, Ned, 147
Miller, Steve, 184, 203f.
Mills, Gary, 171
Milton, Roy, 81
Mingus, Charlie, 93, 314
Mitchell, Joni, 131, 185ff., 211f., 214, 219, 221, 223, 225, 292, 298, 302, 314
Mitchell's Christian Singers, 71
Mittoo, Jackie, 242, 253, 254f.
Mizell, Hank, 32
Moby Grape, 184, 200f.
Modern Lovers, 278,
Mojo Men, 269
Mojos, 172f., 175
Moloney, Paddy, 60
Money, Zoot, 153f., 161, 172
Monotones, 70
Monroe, Bill, 132, 143
Moody Blues, 156, 315
Moonglows, 70
Moore, Merrill, 21
Moore, Scotty, 26
Moped, Johnny, 284
Morris, Kenny, 286
Morris On Band, 53
Morrison, Jim, 197, 276, 293
Morrison, Van, 163, 296, 298, 302f.
Morton, George 'Shadow', 88, 279
Moses, Pablo, 259

Mosley, Bob, 200
Most, Mickie, 226
Mother Earth, 204
Mothers of Invention, **197f.**
Mott the Hoople, 322
Mouse, 269
Mousketeers, 270
Move, 154
Mr Fox, 54
Muldaur, Maria, 186, **225**, 311
Murcia, Billy, 279
Murphy, Walter, 319

Nashville Teens, 172f.
Nazz, 269
Nelson, Rick(y), 14, **28**, 139, 232
Nelson, Sandy, 33
Nelson, Willie, 127, 133, **134f.**
Nesmith, Michael, 232
Neville, Aaron, 78
Neville, Art, 81
New York Dolls, 265f., **279**, 289
Newman, Randy, 186, **227f.**, 231, 311
New Riders of the Purple Sage, 185
Nicholls, Roy, 136
Nice, 154f.
Nicks, Stevie, 316
Nico, 275
Nilsson and Cher, 86
Niney the Observer, 239, 258
Nitty Gritty Dirt Band, 131
Nitzsche, Jack, 188, 195
Nolan, Jerry, 279
Nucleus, 156
Nugent, Ted, 307

O Rex, 285
Ochs, Phil, 42, 210, **217f.**
O'Flynn, Liam, 62
Ohio Players, 113
O'Jays, 112
O'Keefe, Danny, 233
Oldfield, Mike, 298
Oldham, Andrew Loog, 172
O'List, David, 154
Olympics, 33
101-ers, 267
Orbison, Roy, **29f.**
Orioles, 66
Osborne, Joe, 180
Otis, Johnny, 11, 65, **80f.**
Otis, Shuggie, 81
Owens, Buck, 127, 136
Owens, Shirley, 91

Pablo, Augustus, 240, **253f.**
Page, Jimmy, 307
Palmer, Earl, 66
Paragons (doo-wop), 70
Paragons (reggae), 243f., 249, 256
Paramounts, 174
Paris Sisters, 33, 87
Parker, Bobby, 91
Parker, Charlie, 295
Parker, Colonel Tom, 18
Parker, Graham, 303
Parker, Junior, 65, 84
Parks, Dean, 318
Parks, Lloyd, 249
Parks, Van Dyke, 180, 186, 189
Parliament, 100
Parnes, Larry, 149, 172
Parsons, Gram, **138f.**, 192f.
Parton, Dolly, 127, 129, **140**, 144
Pastorious, Jaco, 314
Pate, Johnny, 108
Paul, Billy, 112
Paxton, Tom, 42, 210
Payne, Odie, 75
Pearl, Minnie, 143
Peebles, Ann, 111
Pegg, Bob and Carole, 54
Pender, Mike, 157f.
Penguins, 89
Pentangle, 53f.
Perkins, Al, 193
Perkins, Carl, 13, 15, **20**, 32, 125
Perkins, Luther, 130
Perry, Lee, 239, 246
Peterman, Jim, 204
Peters, Mark, and the Silhouettes, 173
Phillips, Little Esther, 80
Phillips, Phil, 245
Phillips, Sam, 142
Pickett, Wilson, 95, **103f.**
Pierce, Webb, 146
Pink Floyd, 154, 156, **168f.**, 295, 298, **308**
Pirates, 174f.
Pitre, Austin, 79
Planxty, 43, **61f.**
Platters, 34
Poco, 185, 193f.
Poets, 172
Porter, David, 110
Pottinger, Sonia, 244
Powell, Jimmy, and the Five Dimensions, 175
Powell, Keith, and the Valets, 175
Power, Duffy, 149
Premiers, 269
Presley, Elvis, 10, 12f., 17, **18**, 20, 22f., 29, 34, 125, 132, 139, 149, 197, 261
Presley, Reg, 167f., 263
Preston, Earl, and the TTs, 173, 175
Pretty Things, 152
Previn, Dory, 232
Price, Alan, 162f., 228, **229f.**, 231
Price, Jim, 277
Price, Lloyd, 66, 81f., 89
Prince Buster, 236ff., **243**, 244
Prince Jazzbo, 258
Prince Lincoln, 259
Prior, Maddy, 59, 213
Procol Harum, 178
Professor Longhair, 79
Pruett, Jeanne, 144
Public Image, 289

? and the Mysterians, 273, 288
Queen, 323
Quicksilver Messenger Service, 15, 184, **201**

Radiants, 118
Rafferty, Gerry, 233

Rainbows, 70
Raitt, Bonnie, 186, 225f.
Ram Jam, 49
Ramones, 265f., 280, 285, 289
Ray, Johnny, 12
Rays, 70
Redcaps, 175
Redding, Otis, 95, 102f.
Reed, Jerry, 148
Reed, Jimmy, 66, 76, 77, 159
Reed, Lou, 265, 275, 313
Reeves, Jim, 144, 146, 305
Reid, Duke, 235–9, 243, 249f., 252, 255f., 258
Relf, Keith, 161
Remains, 269
Renbourn, John, 53f., 56f.
Reparata and the Delrons, 33
Revere, Paul, and the Raiders, 268, 288
Reynolds, Jody, 33, 36
Rich, Charlie, 142, 147f.
Richard, Belton, 79
Richard, Cliff, 149, 152, 171f.
Richard, Keith, 160, 304
Richman, Jonathan, 278
Righteous Brothers, 86
Riley, Billy Lee, 32
Riley, Martin, 244
Riley, Terry, 308
Rivers, Tony, and the Castaways, 174
Rivieras, 206
Rivingtons, 33
Robbins, Marty, 146
Roberts, Rick, 193
Robertson, Robbie, 301
Robins, 27, 80
Robinson, Alvin, 87
Robinson, David, 278
Robinson, Smokey, 95, 102, 106f.; and the Miracles, 104f.
Rochell and the Candles, 70
Rockin' Vickers, 172
Rodgers, Jimmie, 47, 123ff., 128, 141, 274
Rodway, Jimmy, 258
Rogers, Jimmy, 74
Rogers, Kenny, 272
Rogers, Lelan, 272
Rolling Stones, 74, 92, 152, 159f., 161, 166, 261f., 270f., 273, 279, 281, 296, 299, 304, 311, 320f.
Ronettes, 86
Ronstadt, Linda, 186, 225, 299
Rosie and the Originals, 70
Ross, Annie, 314
Ross, Diana, 107
Rotten, Johnny, 267f., 283, 289
Roulettes, 175
Routers, 188
Roxy Music, 276, 312, 313, 321
Royals, 257
Royce, Earl, and the Olympics, 175
Ruby, Jack, 247
Ruffin, David, 106, 306
Rundgren, Todd, 279, 322
Rupe, Art, 82
Rush, Otis, 164
Russell, Leon, 141, 180
Rydell, Bobby, 26
Sagittarius, 269
Sahm, Doug, 127, 135, 273
Saint-Marie, Buffy, 232
Saints, 289
Sam and Dave, 95, 110, 117
Sam the Sham, 273, 287
Samwell-Smith, Paul, 161
Sandon, Johnny, and the Remo Four, 173
Santana, 184, 204f.
Savoy Brown, 155
Saxon, Sky, 208, 271f.
Scabies, Rat, 282
Scaggs, Boz, 204, 323
Schmit, Timothy B., 194
Scott, Jack, 30
Scott, Joe, 85
Scott, Tom, 314
Scotty, 256
Scruggs, Earl, 131f.
Scruggs, Randy, 131
Searchers, 152, 157f., 173, 175
Sebastian, John, 190
Sedaka, Neil, 14
Seeds, 180, 208, 264, 269, 271f.
Seeger, Pete, 42, 50, 51, 213
Seekers, 153
Self, Mack, 32
Sensations, 243
Severin (Havoc), Steve, 286
Sex Pistols, 261, 266ff., 277, 279–82, 283f., 286, 289
Seyton, Danny, and the Sabres, 173
Shadows, 151, 171f.
Shadows of Knight, 264, 269
Shakers, 173
Shangri-Las, 87f.
Shannon, Del, 14
Shannon, Ronnie, 109
Shapiro, Helen, 171
Sharp, Cecil, 39, 41
Sharp, Martin, 165
Sheffields, 174
Sheridan, Mike, and the Nightriders, 174f.
Sherrill, Billy, 126
Shire, David, 319
Shirelles, 15, 91, 151
Shirley, Roy, 238, 252
Shirley and Lee, 66
Shondell, Troy, 36
Shorter, Wayne, 309
Showmen, 78
Sibbles, Leroy, 245
Sigler, Bunny, 112
Silhouettes, 70
Silver, Horace, 93
Silvertones, 243
Simon, Carly, 212, 232
Simon, Paul, 43, 208, 211f., 220; and Garfunkel, Art, 212, 219f., 231
Simone, Nina, 214
Simonon, Paul, 282
Sims, Frankie Lee, 81
Sinclair, John, 274
Siouxsie and the Banshees, 276, 286
Sir Douglas Quintet, 204, 265, 273f.
Sir Lord Comic, 239
Skatalites, 237, 242, 254

Sklar, Lee, 186
Sky, Patrick, 210
Slaughter and the Dogs, 284
Sledge, Percy, 7, 96, 118, 121
Slick, Grace, 182, 198f., 202
Slickee Boys, 285
Sloan, P. F., 180f., 189
Sly and the Family Stone; *see* Stone, Sly
Small Faces, 172, 177
Smilin' Joe, 77
Smith, Connie, 144
Smith, Fred 'Sonic', 274
Smith, Huey, 22, 78f.
Smith, Patti, 266, 276, 280f., 317
Smith, Russell, 142
Smith, Slim, 238, 244
Smith, Warren, 32
Sneaky Pete, 193
Snow, Hank, 143, 145
Soft Machine, 154, 169, 295, 308
Sohl, Richard D. N. V., 281
Sonny and Cher, 207, 209
Sopwith Camel, 181
Soul Agents, 174
Soul Brothers, 242
Soul Children, 114
Soul Stirrers, 81, 102
Spaniels, 70
Spanky and Our Gang, 181, 208
Spann, Otis, 74
Spector, Phil, 15, 67, 86f., 88, 189, 207, 317, 321
Spellman, Benny, 78
Spence, Skip, 200
Spencer, Jeremy, 75, 316
Spinners, 112
Spooky Tooth, 155
Springfields, 171
Springsteen, Bruce, 267, 299, 316f.
Stafford, Jo, 129
Stamp, Chris, 166
Stamp, Terry, 277
Standells, 180, 208, 264, 269, 270f.
Staple Singers, 71, 111
Staples, Pete, 167
Starr, Freddie, and the Midnighters, 173
Steampacket, 153
Steele, Tommy, 149, 171
Steeleye Span, 53f., 58f.
Steely Dan, 185, 299, 317f.
Stein, Andy, 141
Stevens, Cat, 172
Stewart, Al, 53, 213
Stewart, Jim, 95
Stewart, Rod, 155, 172f., 231, 306, 320f.
Stills, Steve, 194f.
Stivell, Alan, 61
Stone (Stewart), Sly, 97, 113, 182, 206; and the Family Stone, 108f., 184
Stooges, 264, 267, 276f.
Storm, Rory, and the Hurricanes, 173
Strangeloves, 269, 287f.
Stranglers, 267
Strummer, Joe, 267, 282
Stylistics, 112
Styx, 307
Supremes, 95
Surfaris, 188
Sutherland, Stacy, 272
Swan, Billy, 37
Swan Silvertones, 81
Swarbrick, Dave, 54, 58
Swinging Blue Jeans, 176
Sylvain, Sylvain, 279
Syndicate of Sound, 288

Taj Mahal, 311
Talking Heads, 266, 278, 320
Tamblyn, Larry, 270
Taste, 155
Taupin, Bernie, 305
Tavares, 319
Taylor, Bobby, 112
Taylor, Chip, 168, 288
Taylor, Eddie, 76f.
Taylor, James, 185, 212, 222f., 265
Taylor, Johnnie, 119
Taylor, Kingsize, and the Dominos, 173
Taylor, Mick, 164, 304
Taylor, Vic, 243
Techniques, 243f., 258
Teddy Bears, 87
Teenage Boys, 285
Television, 266, 272, 289
Temptations, 105f., 111
Ten Years After, 156
Terrell, Tammi, 107
Tex, Joe, 96, 116, 238
Them, 152, 163, 172f., 287f., 302
Third Rail, 269
Third World War, 277f.
13th Floor Elevators, 204, 269, 272f.
Thomas, Carla, 103
Thomas, Irma, 78
Thomas, Rufus, 162
Thompson, Dennis, 274
Thompson, Hank, 145
Thompson, Richard, 54, 213; and Linda, 230
Thornton, Willie Mae, 80
Threadwell, George, 83
Three Degrees, 112
Three Tops, 243
Thunders, Johnny, 279
Til, Sonny, and the Orioles, 11
Timebox, 172
Timmons, Bobby, 93
Tomorrow, 154, 169
Tornadoes, 171f.
Tosh, Peter, 247, 257
Toussaint, Allen, 66, 78
Townshend, Pete, 166, 303
Townshend, Rob, 170
Tradewinds, 88, 181, 188f.
Traffic, 54, 155, 169f., 291
Tramps, 319
Trashmen, 188f.
Travis, Merle, 131
T. Rex, 321
Troggs, 167f., 263, 288
Tucker, Ira, 71f.
Tucker, Mo, 265
Tucker, Tommy, 91
Turbans, 33
Turner, Ike, 66, 86; and Tina, 86f., 92
Turner, Joe, 65

Turner, Lonnie, 204
Turtles, 181, 207
Twitty, Conway, 125

U Brown, 240
U Roy, 239f., 249, 258
Undertakers, 173
Uniques, 244
Unit 4+2, 176
Unwanted, 284
Upchurch, Phil, 91
Upsetters, 239
Uriah Heep, 307
Usher, Gary, 180, 189

V Rocket, 235f.
Vagrants, 269
Valance, Ricky, 171
Valens, Ritchie, 35
Valenti, Dino, 201
Valentine, Hilton, 163
Valentino, Tony, 270
Van Dyke, Leroy, 146
Van Eaton, James, 22
Vanian, Dave, 282
Vanilla Fudge, 88
Vee, Bobby, 15, 33, 263
Velvet Underground, 265, 267, 275f., 278, 281, 285f.
Ventures, 33, 188
Verlaine, Tom, 272
Vibrators, 267
Vicious, Sid, 283, 286
Vincent, Gene, 13, 26, 29, 125
Vincent, Johnny, 79
Voidoids, 266

Wadsworth, Derek, 229
Wagoner, Porter, 140, 144
Waits, Tom, 187
Walker, Gary, 79
Walker, Jerry Jeff, 127
Walsh, Joe, 194
Warhol, Andy, 265, 275
Warlocks, 182
Warriors, 172
Washboard Sam, 72f.
Washington, Geno, 153
Waters, Muddy, 19, 45, 65, 72, 73f., 85
Waters, Roger, 169, 308
Waterson, Mike and Lal, 54
Watson, Doc, 131
Watson, Johnny 'Guitar', 68, 204
Watson, Kim, 107
Wayne, James, 77
Wayne, Pat, with the Beachcombers, 174
Weather Report, 295, 309
Webb, Sonny, and the Cascades, 173
Welch, Bob, 316
Wells, Kitty, 144
Wells, Mary, 105, 107
West, Clint, 79
West, Dottie, 144
Wexler, Jerry, 109, 134
Whirlwinds, 175
White, Barry, 98, 110
White, Bukka, 85
White, Clarence, 192
Whitfield, Norman, 106f., 111
Whitney, Charlie, 170
Who, 165f., 303, 307, 317
Wilde, Marty, 149, 171f.
Williams, Hank, 22, 124f., 129
Williams, Johnny, 112
Williams, Larry, 33, 35, 66
Williams, Marion, 71
Williams, Maurice, and the Zodiacs, 90
Williamson, James, 277
Williamson, Robin, 57
Williamson, Sonny, Boy, 72f.
Willis, Chuck, 66, 90
Wills, Bob, 132f.
Wilson, Bob, 138
Wilson, Brian, 188f.
Wilson, Jackie, 67, 80, 90
Winter, Johnny, 74
Winwood, Steve, 155, 169, 177
Wire, 284
Withers, Bill, 98, 118
Womack, Bobby, 98
Wonder, Stevie, 98, 113f.
Wood, Chris, 169f.
Wood, Del, 144
Wood, Ron, 173, 306
Work, John, 73
Wray, Link, 24, 26, 35
Wright, Betty, 119
Wynette, Tammy, 126, 147

X Ray Spex, 284

Yanovsky, Zal, 190
Yardbirds, 152, 160f., 164, 177, 285
Yes, 155, 315
Yester, Jerry, 190
Young, Desmond, 258
Young, Neil, 186f., 194f., 233, 302
Young Tradition, 54
Youngbloods, 184, 207
Yule, Doug, 265
Yule, Tommy, 265

Zappa, Frank, 197f.
Zawinul, Josef, 309
Zephyrs, 174f.
Zevon, Warren, 186
Zombies, 172, 176